Critical Geographies of Youth

GENDER, FEMINISM, AND GEOGRAPHY

Jennifer L. Fluri, Series Editor
Amy Trauger, Series Editor

TITLES IN THE SERIES

Feminist Geography Unbound: Discomfort, Bodies, and Prefigured Futures
Edited by Banu Gökarıksel, Michael Hawkins, Christopher Neubert, and Sara Smith

CRITICAL GEOGRAPHIES OF YOUTH

LAW, POLICY, AND POWER

Edited by
Gloria Howerton
and Leanne Purdum

WEST VIRGINIA UNIVERSITY PRESS / MORGANTOWN

Copyright © 2023 by West Virginia University Press
All rights reserved
First edition published 2023 by West Virginia University Press
Printed in the United States of America

ISBN 978-1-952271-94-6 (paperback) / 978-1-952271-95-3 (ebook)

Library of Congress Control Number: 2023010642

Book and cover design by Than Saffel / WVU Press

We dedicate this book to young people who feel the weight of decisions made for them, and for those who have fought back against injustices in whatever ways they could.

CONTENTS

Acknowledgments — ix
Introduction — 1
    Gloria Howerton and Leanne Purdum

PART 1: ATTEMPTS TO CATEGORIZE AND MANAGE YOUTH — **17**

1. Working and Schooling: A Critical Geography of Child Labor and Compulsory Education Laws in the Early Twentieth-Century United States — 21
    Meghan Cope

2. Protecting Youth: The Dismantling of Youth as a "Particular Social Group" in Contemporary Asylum Law — 47
    Kristina M. Campbell

3. "Met with the Full Prosecutorial Powers": Zero-Tolerance Family Separations, Advocacy, and the Exceptionalism of the Child Asylum Seeker — 63
    Leanne Purdum

4. Understanding New York's Opt-Out Movement: How School Segregation Shaped the Nation's Largest Resistance to Standardized Testing — 87
    Olivia Ildefonso

PART 2: YOUTH RESISTANCE AND RESILIENCE — **105**

5. The Coming of the Superpredators: Race, Policing, and Resistance to the Criminalization of Youth — 109
    Marsha Weissman, Glenn Rodriguez, and Evan Weissman

6	BreakOUT!: Queer and Trans of Color Activism in New Orleans	126
	Krista L. Benson	
7	Black Youth Resistance to Policies, Practices, and Dominant Narratives of the St. Louis Voluntary Desegregation Plan	142
	Jerome E. Morris and Wanda F. McGowan	
8	The Tribunal of the Future: Youth, Responsibility, and Temporal Justice in US Climate Change Litigation	160
	Mark Ortiz	
	Contributors	177
	Index	183

ACKNOWLEDGMENTS

We would like to thank the team at West Virginia University Press, particularly Derek Krissoff and Charlotte Velloso, both of whom helped us navigate the new world of putting together an edited volume; the series editors and advisory board of WVU Press's Gender, Feminism, and Geography series, with special thanks to Amy Trauger for getting us started on this path; and Jonathan Rylander, director of the Center for Writing Excellence at the University of Wisconsin–Eau Claire. Without him, our introduction would be twice as long and half as clear.

INTRODUCTION

Gloria Howerton and Leanne Purdum

Entanglements with political and legal arenas and institutions engender complex situations that young people must navigate. Youth are governed, but with minimal official voice in government. They are blocked from many of the "approved" legal and political channels of power, yet still produce and lead movements that create change at various scales, often with a creative energy that shifts public understanding of complex issues. Categories associated with youth such as "child," "teenager," "minor," or "student" do more than simply mark age. They bear multiple and contextual meanings that are taken up by legal and political institutions in ways that directly impact lived experiences. Geographical and temporal context and intersecting identities further complicate these life stage–based categorical frameworks. Differently categorized young people have always been understood and treated differently from one another in political and socio-legal realms based on myriad intersecting identities such as race, ethnicity, sexuality, gender, and class.

This volume takes up undertheorized categorizations placed upon young people and considers their relationships to socio-legal and political landscapes in the United States. Landscapes of power are (re)produced by laws and policies that differently structure the daily lives of those within their jurisdiction, impacting their presents and their futures. Young people are denied access to many legally sanctioned paths to contest and shape law and policy, despite being directly impacted by them. Yet youth find ways to work within and reshape these social, political, and legal spheres, even as they are blocked from key political and legal decision-making processes. The chapters in this volume can be divided into two main themes: (1) legal and political categorizations entangling young people and the attempted management of youth, and (2) youth resistance and resilience in the face of oppressive political and legal categorizations, institutions, and structures. We follow Skelton in understanding youth as political actors rather than mere subjects in waiting (2010) and take up this work as part of a response to the call for geographers to treat seriously the political involvements of young people (2013).

This volume contributes to the field of youth geographies with a collection of chapters focused on youth interactions with law and politics. Law structures the rights of variously categorized people to act, move, and exist in varying spaces. Here we focus on those categorized as being outside of adulthood, because, as we will discuss, youth and childhood are often marked not by what they *are*, but by what they *are not yet*. We argue that understanding the socio-legal positionings of youth (by adults) and the (re)positionings (by youth themselves) offer insights into other systems that create socio-spatial unevenness. Laws and policies are more than decrees recorded by legislatures: laws create and perpetuate social categories. They become the basis for policing and enforcement mechanisms. Laws do not only shape the discursive aspects of society. They quite literally produce physical landscapes via prisons, walls, schoolyards, or neighborhoods. As we consider the way that space is produced (see Lefebvre 1984), critical legal geographers pay special attention to the co-constitution of law and space and the materialization of "the legal" (Delaney 2010; Braverman et al. 2014). Critical legal geographies also attend to how legal systems create social categorizations, as well as how these categorizations maintain societal power structures (Goldberg 2002; Nyers 2006; Zolberg 2006; Alexander 2010; Welke 2010).

While many of the chapters in this volume consider the experiences of young persons, it is not the young people *themselves* that we seek to examine. As Qvortrup (2002) notes, there is considerable difference between analyzing "childhood" as an ever-present (though changing) form and analyzing children themselves. We articulate "youth" not only as a category but also as a critical modality for analyzing larger systems, political climates, and structures governing lives and constraining movements in particular ways. Further, understanding how youth and childhood are constructed in varying contexts provides insight into the institutions, self-perception, values, prejudices, desires, and perceived possibilities of a given group at a given time. Chapters in this volume may consider lived experiences of youth, but in a manner that details the functioning of power relations or how they are challenged.

Geography's methodological and theoretical pluralism allows for a variety of voices and audiences. With this volume we seek to illustrate how the categorizations of youth function in and through the legal and political systems, as evident from the bodies of research spanning critical race theory, legal geography, and feminist geopolitics, among others. As we later describe, we situate this book within the youth geographies subfield. Although not all of the writers featured in this volume are geographers by training, or even academics, all of the pieces included carry analytical frameworks that examine the spatial dynamics of legal systems, which deepen our understanding of the uneven spatialities shaping the lives of young people.

Gilmore (2002) writes that "a geographical imperative lies at the heart of every struggle for social justice; if justice is embodied, it is then therefore always spatial; which is to say, part of a process of making a place" (16). Rather than perpetually creating and defining borders that benefit colonizers and oppressors, geographers can examine the territoriality of power (Gilmore 2002), study the linkages between place and (in)justice, unravel the understandings of what is "natural" in space, and reveal the unfinished nature of place, leading to the freedom to imagine new spatial possibilities (McKittrick 2006). Geography gives us considerable insight into how power and its accompanying push-and-pull operates at different scales. Further, the consideration of space allows us to look deeply at relationships of power as not simply detached, floating things, but as (re)producers of the material world, and similarly gives consideration to how our material spaces (re)produce them. McKittrick (2006) argues that studying space's physicality and dimensionality—its constructions of borders that create inclusion and exclusion—allows us to expose how domination works on the terrain as a spatial project. It is this spatial project, she suggests, that "organizes, names, and sees social differences and determines *where* social order happens" (xiv, original emphasis). This normalizing tendency can be, and frequently is, challenged and remade by both dominant and marginalized peoples, as many of the chapters in this volume will show.

We begin with a discussion of youth and children's geographies, with a particular focus on how categorizations of young people have been conceived of within geography and the social sciences. Second, we address some contemporary issues of national significance that propelled us to bring together this collection. Third, we explore the temporal nature of categories of youth and childhood and how this temporality positions it as unique to other categories of identity. The remainder of this introduction provides a brief roadmap of this collection with brief chapter and theme introductions. The book can be read from cover to cover, but it is also meant to be accessible to those reading individual chapters.

CHILDREN'S GEOGRAPHIES AND GEOGRAPHIES OF YOUTH

We situate this work within the "fledgling" (Smith and Mills 2019) arena of youth geographies. There is no specific age range that defines "youth" or "child," making a spatial analysis of such categories complex. This category may be defined by an age, such as eighteen or twenty-one years, when a legal system draws a hard line. In other contexts "youth" and "childhood" have loosely drawn boundaries with myriad possible attached meanings. They are often predicated upon a multitude of intersecting identities that ascribe differing qualities to young persons based on varying perceptions of these identities. These differing perceptions have tangible consequences. One may think of Trayvon Martin and the media's propensity to "adultify" him and further consider how many BIPOC youth have been similarly denied the benefits of sympathy and leniency so often afforded to whites of the same age. See, for example, the conservative valorization of Kyle Rittenhouse after his arrest for multiple counts of homicide and reckless endangerment.

Mainstream research in geography is, to this day, primarily oriented around understanding the world of adults (Valentine 2019). Until the late 1960s, when William Bunge identified children as our largest minority and argued that they must be brought into geographical studies, the subjects of study in human geography were almost exclusively adults, and particularly white male adults (James 1990). Bunge countered what he perceived as the negative side of the quantitative revolution occurring within the discipline by focusing on spatial oppression. Children were especially important to his work. Aitken (2001) writes that for Bunge, "children were a barometer to measure the wellness of society and spatial statistics revealed the patterns of the sickness" (13).

A background in the development of children's geographies is necessary to understand the subsequent development of youth geographies. Youth geographies and children's geographies find considerable areas of overlap, often sharing space within the same journal. Yet there are key distinctions between the two. While still underrepresented within the field, children's geographies have grown significantly since Bunge's work on the spatial oppression of urban youth. There has been a long-running critical push to examine the roles that children and young people inhabit in society (James 1990). The understanding in the social sciences that childhood is socially constructed emerged in the mid-1970s due to the crisis of representation occurring in the social science disciplines at the time. The ability to genuinely describe the "other," including children, was brought into question (Aitken 2001). While the mid-1980s saw the emergence of a "new" sociology of childhood that began to take children's agency seriously in both making sense of and impacting the world around them (Matthews 2007), geographic research concerning children in this era began to focus on their everyday lived experiences rather than seeking out a universal structuring theory to explain childhood (Aitken 1994).

As Holloway noted in a keynote address to the 2014 *Children's Geographies* conference, the social constructivist approach to understanding childhood and its many facets has held a primary place in geographies of children and childhood since the 1990s. The social constructivist approach suggests that childhood as a concept and as an experience is discursively produced. It pushes back against the notion of the "universal child" and argues that child identity and childhoods are plural. Yet, although childhoods are variable "they are also intentional, predicated upon social, political, historical, geographical and moral contexts" (Aitken 2001, 57). Understanding children and childhood through this lens set the stage for early children's geographies to focus on the agency of children (Valentine 2019).

Recent decades have seen increasing youth-centered empirical research in the social sciences (Swauger, Castro, and Harger 2017). Still, as Blaisdell (2019) points out, overall acknowledgements of the voices and agency of very young children remain fairly limited. Youth are still often only considered in the context of their dependency upon adults (Evans 2008) or in terms of their behavior (McKendrick 2000). They have been positioned as "not-yet-adults," as "human becomings" (Holloway and Valentine 2000; Evans 2008), and as "not-yet-citizens" who are considered to be without full and serious claims to rights (Moosa-Mitha 2005). Indeed, the positioning of children as "less than adult" has also led to research on and with young people to be less valued than research centering the experiences of adults (Holloway and Valentine 2000).

Youth geographies diverge to a degree from children's geographies (Valentine 2019). The distinctions that arise are due in part to the scope of people represented within each category and a difference in analytical approaches. The journal *Children's Geographies* began in 2003, publishing geographical work centering on people aged twenty-five and under ("Coming of Age for Children's Geographies" 2003). Children's geographies as a whole has become more solidified as a subdiscipline, and some express concern that youth geographies could become, and indeed often is, simply subsumed within the former (Evans 2008; Smith and Mills 2019; Valentine 2019). "Children" and "young people" are often used interchangeably, leaving discussions of teenagers, for example, sidelined or marginalized (Weller 2006). Skelton (2007) notes that the global definitions of "child" taken from UNICEF and UNESCO can lead to the conclusion that it is a catch-all term that includes young people, arguing that this enveloping of one into the other is both problematic and predominant in youth discourses. UNESCO, for example, calls people between fifteen and twenty-four "young people," while the UN Convention on the Rights of the Child defines "children" as those under eighteen *unless* the law under which they live defines adulthood as being reached at an earlier age. Skelton leads us to ask what impact this has on young people who neither perceive themselves to be children nor are perceived within their societies as being children. Do they have different claims to rights? And if so, what are the implications of these rights delineations? What does it mean that these categorical life stage-based rights claims vary spatially?

In light of these questions, youth geographies create more space for the discussion of the experiences of teenagers and those in their early adulthood (Skelton 2019). Some of the work that is considered "youth geographies" found a home in *Children's Geographies*. However, youth geographies are currently more diffuse than children's geographies, not being centered within any particular journal. Instead, they are dispersed throughout multiple subdisciplines. Such work tends to be located in publications studying other issues that youth are experiencing or interacting with—for example, a study on migrant youth may be housed in a journal of migration. Important critical work on and with youth may receive more attention if housed within other subfields.

The lack of a solid disciplinary home can also be beneficial, leading to the understanding of "youth" as a framework not just for analyzing life stages, but for approaching the myriad institutions and systems structuring human interactions. While children's geographies have been critiqued for focusing too much on micro scales of children's day-to-day lives, youth geographies more readily push into larger scales and engage with wider debates. Indeed, "youth geographies highlighted the way space, place, scale and mobility were important for really understanding diverse youth cultures as both local and global sites of resistance" (van Blerk 2019, 33). As much as the lack of coalescence of youth geographies may be a concern, some of its most important work demonstrates the strength in its very flexibility. As Valentine, Skelton, and Chambers (1998) write in the introduction to *Cool Places*, "There is a danger that geographical work on young people's lives and experiences may be corralled into an enclosure marked 'youth geographies' rather than being an integral part of all areas of mainstream geographical research and debate [. . .] It is important to recognize the role which they play in all our geographies" (7).

Valentine (2019) argues that youth geographies make important contributions to geography as a whole "by shifting its focus from a preoccupation with boundaries, towards understanding contemporary structural problems as generational inequalities and giving a voice to the agency of young people" (30). We argue that studies of the ways in which young people interact with sociolegal and political structures and institutions gives us a fresh point of view for understanding the (re)production and maintenance of hierarchical and oppressive systems. It further provides creative ways for approaching these systems outside of the accepted venues primarily reserved for older people. As *Cool Places* demonstrated over two decades ago, youth subcultures harness significant creative energy—leading to not only hopeful new imaginings of potential futures but also new strategies to make them a reality. This volume responds to Skelton's (2019) "present absence challenge" based on the idea that "young people are everywhere and everyday present and yet are notable by their apparent absence within geographical knowledge production" (26).

Our case studies reveal how the state produces different categories of youth based around intersecting identities and in turn governs them differently. Focusing on a single country rather than taking a global approach gives us the opportunity to understand the finer details of the interactions young people have with a particular state and its accompanying techniques. The book considers the experiences of young people in the United States, a nation with the world's largest known prison system, an expanding immigrant detention regime, high rates of gun violence, immense social inequality, and conflicting constructions of history and national identity, and which is a major contributor to global climate change and environmental degradation. Each of these crises represents a strand within a larger interlocking web of legal systems that produce, and reproduce, their accompanying social categorizations, sets of discourses, and the physical spaces that people encounter as they move through the world. The gravity of these problems necessitates a set of questions: How are youth framed legally and politically in the US? What ideas about different youth categorizations are propagated to support or undermine policy and legislation? How have these framings and legal systems created the existing landscapes we might take for granted? What are the rights of future generations, and how do the ramifications of law and policy extend into the future? These questions guide this volume.

Critical youth geographies provide an underutilized lens for studying not simply youth themselves but also the systems and structures within which they experience the world. The possibilities for questions like those above to be answered by a critical youth geography approach are apparent in Katz's (2004) *Growing Up Global*, which provided insight into global capitalism and economic restructuring through a central focus on youth experiences. Thiem (2009) took a similar approach to understanding education as more than just its constituent institutions, systems, and practices; instead she discussed how it radiates outward, interacting with and impacting other arenas such as capital flows and migration. Understanding the positionings of youth by adults and the (re)positionings by youth themselves help us more fully understand other systems that create socio-spatial unevenness.

The worlds of youth are interconnected with larger social landscapes; their lives are intimately connected to produced structures and institutions, and they are often severely impacted directly by policy and legal systems. Katz (2004) notes that "the spaces of consequence in children's everyday lives tend to be extraordinarily local" (163), centered on the spaces of their homes, the homes of friends and family, school, and their neighborhoods. She argues that "given the intensely local nature of children's lives, the disintegration of public funding for housing, schools, and neighborhood open spaces hit them harder than other dwellers [. . .] and children have no right to even the veneer of public accountability that comes with citizenship" (163). It is no wonder, then, that Bunge and Bordessa, decades earlier, described children as being akin to canaries in a coal mine, able to "reflect the pressures of the environment more accurately" (1975, 1). There is much to learn about our systems and institutions from youth interactions with the spaces that encircle them.

CONTEMPORARY SITES OF YOUTH STRUGGLE

Geographers must more critically consider and theorize the lives of young people. To do this requires not just a study of lived experience, disconnected from the political realm so often ascribed to adulthood. We must also take seriously the idea that young people are political actors who resist, rework, and show resilience in the face of harmful political and legal decisions passed down to them from adults (Katz 2004). Contemporary social struggles display the inherent limitations to pursuing social change solely through the legal process. Youth are often aware of these limitations. Many young people are challenging the unsatisfactory legal frameworks that shape their lives in ways that can reframe the movements and strategies for the future, creating new pathways and realities. While young people may take inspiration and guidance from adults, they also have a nuanced evolution of thought about their own experiences. Further, youth may reframe and rework their approaches to resistance over time.

We are interested in the tensions found in the push and pull between young people's creation of alternate pathways to make their voices heard and the structural barriers that continue to mount before them. Ginwright and James (2003) contend that barriers to democratic participation represent the greatest challenge facing youth. For example, non-adults are "positioned outside most of the structures and ideals of modernist democratic theory, such as the public sphere and abstracted notions of communicative action or 'rational' speech" (Elwood and Mitchell 2012, 1). Still, youth respond to barriers with increased mobilization and demands for a voice in public policy that affects them (Ginwright and James 2003). Outside of geography, developmental scientists show that youth organizing leads to "individual youth development, improved schools and community institutions, and civic renewal in the broader society" (Kirshner and Ginwright 2012, 292). While youth-based research reveals challenges, it further reveals potential spaces of hope and opportunity.

Youth do not consistently face identical formulations of struggles, pressures, fears, aspirations, hopes, and futures across all generations. Aitken (2019) reflects on the twenty years since Skelton and Valentine's *Cool Places* (1998) created a new way forward for scholars interested in understanding the complex and contrasting spaces, experiences, and agency of youth and the cultures they create. He considers the different challenges and futures young people face today as compared to the late 1990s. He sees a world that is less politically and environmentally secure, a world in which economic power is more tightly consolidated within the hands of the elite, alongside the economic damage caused to younger generations during the Great Recession. He notes that perhaps "this generation has moved inward [. . .] to find itself through instant communications, social media, and digital technologies" (11). Contemporary studies of youth geographies must engage with "the implications of hazards and climate change; economic crises; protracted displacement, conflict and war among others and mainstream the outcomes of such issues for research with youth" (van Blerk 2019, 34). Only time will tell what scenarios will preoccupy future youth geographies.

Van Blerk (2019) challenges us to take seriously the uncertainty and the depth of the entrenched, multi-scalar struggles that young people will confront over the coming decades. A telling example of this situated uncertainty comes from a recent Pew Research Center (2018) report on teenager concerns about school shootings. Roughly 57 percent of respondents between the ages of thirteen and seventeen reported that they were either "somewhat" or "very" worried about the possibility of a shooting occurring at their school. Those rates increase to 60 percent for Black respondents, 64 percent for female respondents, and 73 percent for Hispanic respondents (Geiger 2018).

The entrenchment and magnitude of issues faced by today's young people looking toward their own future may seem overwhelming. However, Smith and Mills (2019) see other patterns: increases in youth mobilities, politicization, acknowledgment of youth as stakeholders, and more space being made for *and by* youth to become active participants in political struggles. Young people are mobilizing against issues such as gun violence and racialized policing, and for increased education access and mitigation of climate change—all realms of social life that impact youth now and throughout their lives. Further, social attitudes, particularly regarding LGBTQ+ matters, are changing rapidly, with young people often leading the push for the creation of safer and more welcoming landscapes for those marginalized by their sexual or gender identities. For example, roughly a third of Gen Zers know someone who uses gender-neutral pronouns (Parker, Graf, and Igielnik 2019), resulting in more open-minded approaches to gender on average from young people. The pushback they receive from adults who write off their concerns or describe them as puppets of other adults has done little to stop their movements. Even the recent proliferation of the phrase "okay, Boomer" demonstrates the feeling that older people are out of touch with the current lived experiences of the young, and that their critiques of how young people interact with the world largely formed for them by the "gerontocracy" are going largely unheeded.

THE (IM)PERMANENCE OF YOUTH

"Youth" is a complicated and, at times, contradictory category. Unraveling this complex nature is one of the main themes encapsulated in the chapters in this volume. While youth has much in common with other social categorizations such as race, class, or gender—all often treated as simple demographic facts belying their great complexity—age is a constantly changing marker. The youth of today will move out of this categorization as time passes, and younger people will take their place within this category. There is a temporality to it, a movement forward that necessitates looking toward the future. The marker of age shapes their day-to-day lives, the institutions and spaces they interact with, and their treatment within their social, political, and legal landscapes. Importantly, these alignments necessarily shift over time. Indeed, the adults in power who shape the political and legal institutions informing the lives of young people were, of course, once children themselves. Individuals can never become completely detached from their lived pasts. The effects of the particular socio-legal and political realities young people face often have consequences that follow across all life stages.

Youth have a different relationship with the future than any other social categorization. They are the future inhabitants of the social systems designed, entrenched, and perpetuated by adults. The decisions and consequences of categorization and law don't stop when the blurry parameters of "childhood" end. Lifelong consequences stem from interactions with socio-legal and political systems during childhood, shaping both individuals and generations. Race, gender, class, and other intersectional identities shape a person's relationship to the socio-legal system and the power relations that differently position each person within their milieu. However, perhaps only the categorization of "youth" can be designated as the one that all humans move through, and out of, over the course of an average human life span. During the "phase" of childhood, and arguably even before birth, we come into contact with social institutions that will impact the course of our lives. As the volume's chapters explore, youth interact with schools, policing, citizenship, and other socio-legal and political structures that impact every area of life, down to the quality of the very air they breathe.

We can then ask: What can we learn from "youth" as a category? How does age interact with other categories of identity to create different opportunities and challenges in the realms of law and policy? How can we think about a "temporal justice" that takes into consideration the future consequences of law and policy decisions for those with the fewest direct paths to legal and political decision-making? The ambiguous nature of the term "youth" is part of the difficulty in developing a fully formed subfield (Valentine 2019). Who counts within the category of "youth," and what does it mean to make this demarcation? These questions prompt consideration of what makes studying an apparent "life stage" worthwhile. There is tension in delineating between the relatively blurred lines of age-based life stages. Still, we argue that they are important objects of study because they illuminate the implications of the push-and-pull between those old enough to hold positions of power in law and politics and those falling into the categories of children, teenagers, and young adults, and the liminal transition stages between them (Skelton 2019). Those ranging from early childhood to early adulthood typically interact with those arenas of power as recipients of decisions, or alternately, reworkers or resisters (Katz 2004). While youth frequently push back through creative resistance or, for example, appearing in the courtroom as plaintiffs, they do so rather than acting as the judge or the policymaker. They are more often, due to their age, in a position to appeal to or convince older people to change how they will be treated and how the world will be left for them as they move into the future.

ROADMAP TO THE VOLUME

We divide this book into two parts. The chapters in the first part consider legal and political categorizations entangling young people and the attempted management of youth. The chapters in the second part revolve around themes of youth resistance and resilience in the face of oppressive categorizations, institutions, and structures. Each part begins with an introduction that considers the themes that tie the pieces together.

The chapters in part 1 bring together themes of categorization and management of youth, as well as the spaces that they inhabit. Taken together, they highlight the lack of a single, unified approach to youth "from above"—referring not simply to adults, but to complex systems of power. Following Aitken's recognition of the "strong connection between how we think about children, and how we legislate on their behalf" (2018, 7), the chapters presented in the first part of this volume analyze how adults "think about" young people, how this thinking creates forms of discourse that result in categorizations, how these categorizations are (re)produced, and their roles in creating and perpetuating both justice and injustice. These categorizations have immense gravity, legally sanctioning everyday lived realities such as detention, deportation, imprisonment, and other exclusions.

Part 1 begins with a chapter by Meghan Cope, wherein she presents a historical geographic reading of the evolution of child labor laws and compulsory schooling. Her work demonstrates the constructed nature of childhood and how its meanings vary according to intersecting identities as well as geographical and temporal context. The following two chapters consider the treatment and conceptualization of migrant youth within our legal system, exploring how interpretations of purported "law and order" result in demonstrations of power that target and exclude migrants from Central America. Kristina Campbell analyzes how "youth" as a category is mobilized in asylum law, revealing how the category is alternately constructed and dismantled for legal and political purposes. Campbell provides an important companion to the following chapter, in which Leanne Purdum explores the violence of "zero-tolerance" family separation policy. Purdum continues the interrogation of the violence inherent in law targeting migrant youth, adding in analysis of how the narratives of "helping" used by activists and critics of zero-tolerance separations can reinforce harm perpetuated within the legal system. In the part's final chapter, Olivia Ildefonso studies a parent-led anti–standardized testing movement. While the movement is framed as being in the best interest of students, she finds that the underlying goal is steeped in racial capitalism and the consolidation of wealth in the spaces of the school district and the neighborhood. Ildefonso's chapter, particularly taken alongside Purdum's work, highlights another key theme of this volume: law and policy that is superficially about young people is often utilizing that category to work toward surreptitious legal and political goals.

The pieces in this part reveal a constant rearranging and remaking of categories: Who gets to be considered a "child"? What protections and restrictions come with this category? We can consider, for example, how adolescents of color are often treated as older than they are in the criminal justice system in a way that their white peers are not, leading to harsher punishments. In that vein, we can consider how different identities intersect with age to create different social and legal expectations and investigate how categorizations play out differently across space. The power of the category of "youth" is not diminished by the lack of static, delineated boundaries or the absence of concrete meanings attached to categories. Instead, these chapters demonstrate how the flexibility of such categories is wielded by those with political and legal power. They show an ability to constantly negotiate ascribed messages about worth, deservingness, and protection to fit various narratives and needs, to make new inclusions and exclusions, and to make the consequences of legal and political framings of youth lasting and potent.

The second part brings together analysis of youth resistance and resilience to the categorizations explored in part 1. While both parts unpack the geographical processes that create difference and the landscapes of power these categorizations of youth produce, the four chapters in the second part add to this analysis, providing examples of youth activism and resistance informed by their lived experiences.

Marsha Weissman, Glenn Rodriguez, and Evan Weissman begin this part with a study of the school system as a node in the school-to-prison pipeline, detailing how students of color are ensnared in the criminal legal system. This chapter bridges the two parts by exploring the legal development of school policies that feed students into the prison system, and presenting interviews with directly impacted youth to highlight resistance to these processes. Formerly incarcerated young people, in the role of the "credible messenger," use their voices to become agents of change and offer expertise on the harm that "tough on crime" policies have in their communities. Krista Benson follows with a chapter that presents a case study of queer youth activists in New Orleans. It details how an LGBTQ+ youth of color organization deploys evolving strategies to build community and tackle complex issues with intersectional alliance. Benson analyzes how the BreakOUT! organization developed evolving collaborative practices with other organizations, to resist the over-policing of communities of color.

Themes around self-awareness and agency continue with Jerome Morris and Wanda McGowan's chapter centering the experiences of Black students taking part in a school desegregation plan in St. Louis. Although the policy was designed to counter structural racism in hyper-segregated cities, the chapter describes how the resulting program led to the attempted deculturalization of Black students and the systematic placement of Black students into inferior academic programs. Despite these struggles, students demonstrated resilience and resistance, advocating for themselves and for access to resources and inclusion needed to succeed in school. Finally, Mark Ortiz examines how young climate change litigants create what he calls "a tribunal of the future." The chapter details how young litigants challenge environmental destruction that will result in lasting impacts on future generations. They make a creative claim to rights for both themselves and for those to come. In doing so, they demonstrate the potential for youth to challenge powerful industries and institutions by harnessing the power of a legal system that otherwise routinely denies them a voice.

At a time of increased global inequality, continued racial capitalism, environmental degradation, struggles over citizenship, and state violence, youth resistance provides hope for possible better futures. These challenges reflect a struggle over the structures and channels of power created by previous generations and experienced by younger generations, as decisions are being made about and for them. However, the chapters in this part remind the reader that the categorizations and geographies of power shaping the realities of youth must also contend with their agency and dissent.

Taken as a whole, the collection attends to the tensions between oppression and resistance as analyzed through the lens of youth. There are myriad logics and strategies that those in power use to control and repress, yet we see many ways that young people are challenging these tactics. We are excited to see the futures that today's young people build as they find their power, both individually and collectively. We are hopeful as we consider those who will come after into these reimagined and reworked structures and spaces. We are also hopeful that readers of all ages will find reason for optimism as they struggle toward better futures.

Editors' Note: Some authors capitalize racial/ethnic categories to illustrate the socially constructed implications of groups, such as white or Black, while others do not. The editors left these decisions to each author.

REFERENCES

Aitken, Stuart. 1994. *Putting Children in Their Place*. Washington, DC: Association of American Geographers.

———. 2001. *Geographies of Young People: The Morally Contested Spaces of Identity*. New York: Routledge.

———. 2018. *Young People, Rights, and Place: Erasure, Neoliberal Politics, and Postchild Ethics.* New York: Routledge.

———. 2019. "What Happened to Adventurous Young People and Their Cool Places?" *Children's Geographies* 17 (1): 9–12.

Alexander, Michelle. 2010. *The New Jim Crow: Mass Incarceration in an Age of Colorblindness.* New York: New Press.

Blaisdell, Caralyn. 2019. "Participatory Work with Young Children: The Trouble and Transformation of Age-Based Hierarchies." *Children's Geographies* 17 (3): 278–90

Braverman, Irus, Nicholas K. Blomley, David Delaney, and Alexandre Kedar. 2014. *The Expanding Spaces of Law: A Timely Legal Geography.* Stanford, CA: Stanford University Press.

Bunge, William, and Ronald Bordessa. 1975. *The Canadian Alternative: Survival, Expeditions, and Urban Change.* Department of Geography, Atkinson College, York University.

"Coming of Age for Children's Geographies." 2003. *Children's Geographies* 1 (1): 3–5.

Delaney, David. 2010. *The Spatial, the Legal, and the Pragmatics of World-Making: Nomospheric Investigations.* New York: Routledge.

Elwood, Sarah, and Katharyne Mitchell. 2012. "Mapping Children's Politics: Spatial Stories, Dialogic Relations, and Political Formation." *Geografiska Annaler: Series B* 94 (1): 1–15.

Evans, Bethany. 2008. "Geographies of Youth/Young People." *Geography Compass* 2 (5): 1659–80.

Geiger, A. W. 2018. "18 Striking Findings from 2018." *Pew Research Center.* https://www.pewresearch.org/fact-tank/2018/12/13/18-striking-findings-from-2018.

Gilmore, Ruth W. 2002. "Fatal Couplings of Power and Difference: Notes on Racism and Geography." *Professional Geographer* 54 (1): 15–24.

Ginwright, Shawn, and Taj James. 2003. "From Assets to Agents of Change: Social Justice, Organizing, and Youth Development." *New Directions for Youth Development* 96: 27–46.

Goldberg, David Theo. 2002. *The Racial State.* London: Wiley-Blackwell.

Holloway, Sarah L. 2014. "Children's Geographies Annual Lecture 2013." *Children's Geographies* 12 (4): 377–92.

Holloway, Sarah L., and Gill Valentine. 2000. "Spatiality and the New Social Studies of Childhood." *Sociology* 34 (4): 763–83.

James, Sarah. 1990. "Is There a 'Place' for Children in Geography?" *Area* 22 (3): 278–83.

Katz, Cindi. 2004. *Growing Up Global: Economic Restructuring and Children's Everyday Lives.* Minneapolis: University of Minnesota Press.

Kirshner, Ben, and Shawn Ginwright. 2012. "Youth Organizing as a Developmental Context for African American and Latino Adolescents." *Child Development Perspectives* 6 (3): 288–94.

Lefebvre, Henri. 1984. *The Production of Space.* Translation by Donald Nicholson-Smith. Oxford: Blackwell Publishing.

Matthews, Sarah H. 2007. "A Window on the 'New' Sociology of Childhood." *Sociology Compass* 1 (1): 322–34.

McKendrick, John H. 2000. "The Geography of Children: An Annotated Bibliography." *Childhood* 7 (3): 359–87.

McKittrick, Katherine. 2006. *Demonic Grounds: Black Women and the Cartographies of Struggle.* University of Minnesota Press.

Moosa-Mitha, Mehmoona. 2005. "A Difference-Centred Alternative to Theorization of Children's Citizenship Rights." *Citizenship Studies* 9 (4): 369–88.

Nyers, Peter. 2006. *Rethinking Refugees: Beyond States of Emergency.* Global Horizons Series. New York: Routledge.

Parker, Kim, Nikki Graf, and Ruth Igielnik. 2019. "Generation Z Looks a Lot Like Millennials on Key Social and Political Issues." *Pew Research Center.* https://www.pewresearch.org

/social-trends/2019/01/17/generation-z-looks-a-lot-like-millennials-on-key-social-and-political-issues.

Pew Research Center. 2018. "2018 Pew Research Center's Teen Survey." https://www.pewresearch.org/wp-content/uploads/2018/05/PewResearchCenter_180418_Teens Guns_FT-Topline_FINALDATES.pdf.

Qvortrup, Jens. 2002. "Sociology of Childhood: Conceptual Liberation of Children." In *Childhood and Children's Culture*, ed. Flemming Mouritsen and Jens Qvortrup, 43–78. Esbjerg, Denmark: University Press of Southern Denmark.

Skelton, Tracey. 2007. "Children, Young People, UNICEF, and Participation." *Children's Geographies* 5 (1): 165–81.

———. 2010. "Taking Young People as Political Actors Seriously: Opening the Borders of Political Geography." *Area* 42 (2): 145–51.

———. 2013. "Young People, Children, Politics, and Space: A Decade of Youthful Political Geography Scholarship: 2003–13." *Space and Polity* 17 (1): 123–36.

———. 2019. "Youthful Geographies: From Cool Places to Hyper-Dynamic Asia." *Children's Geographies* 17 (1): 24–27.

Smith, Darren P., and Sarah Mills. 2019. "The 'Youth-fullness' of Youth Geographies: 'Coming of Age'?" *Children's Geographies* 17 (1): 1–8.

Swauger, Melissa, Ingrid E. Castro, and Brent Harger. 2017. "The Continued Importance of Research with Children and Youth: The 'New' Sociology of Childhood 40 Years Later." *Sociological Studies of Children and Youth* 22 (July): 1–7.

Thiem, C. H. 2009. "Thinking through Education: The Geographies of Contemporary Educational Restructuring." *Progress in Human Geography* 33 (2): 154–73.

Valentine, Gill. 2019. "Geographies of Youth—a Generational Perspective." *Children's Geographies* 17 (1): 28–31.

Valentine, Gill, Tracey Skelton, and Deborah Chambers. 1998. "Cool Places: An Introduction to Youth and Youth Cultures." In *Cool Places: Geographies of Youth Cultures*, eds. Tracey Skelton and Gill Valentine, 1–32. London: Routledge.

van Blerk, Lorraine. 2019. "Where in the World Are Youth Geographies Going? Reflections on the Journey and Directions for the Future." *Children's Geographies* 17(1): 32–35.

Welke, Barbara Young. 2010. *Law and the Borders of Belonging in the Long Nineteenth Century United States*. New Histories of American Law. New York: Cambridge University Press.

Weller, Susie. 2006. "Situating (Young) Teenagers in Geographies of Children and Youth." *Children's Geographies* 4 (1): 97–108.

Zolberg, Aristide R. 2006. *A Nation by Design: Immigration Policy in the Fashioning of America*. New York: Russell Sage Foundation; Cambridge, MA: Harvard University Press.

PART 1
ATTEMPTS TO CATEGORIZE AND MANAGE YOUTH

The discursive categories encircling youth are complex, changing, and inherently unstable. The four chapters included within this part engage this instability and problematize the meanings and concepts associated with "child" and "youth." They further highlight the power that the attached meanings hold in structuring not just the individual lives of youth but also the larger socio-spatial landscape.

The part begins with a chapter from Cope, who takes a historical geographic approach to understanding the construction of childhood in the United States, providing a detailed examination of the development of child labor laws and compulsory schooling. She considers the various roles that young people have been expected to take on over time and in different places: Should children be laborers and wage earners for their families? Should they be in schools, training to become educated citizens? Which children are expected to fulfill which roles? The chapter demonstrates that childhood is a construct that varies according to intersecting identities as well as geographical and temporal context. Cope considers not just *who*, but *where* specific framings of childhood become legally codified. She shows the conflicts and tensions present at different legislative scales, regional variations in attitudes toward children, the overall uneven geographies of child labor and schooling laws, and construction of childhood-in-place.

Cope's piece introduces threads that will continue to be sewn throughout the chapters in this part and the book as a whole. She documents particular ways in which race and ethnicity in particular act as major intersecting categories that differently define youth in the eyes of the law and society. Ildefonso's analysis of resistance to standardized testing, which closes this part, particularly draws out racial capitalism's role in differently positioning young people, informing which spaces they inhabit, what their spaces and experiences are like, and how they are valued. The various legal discourses running through these chapters not only develop our understanding of the perceptions of children and young people, but also show us the frame of mind, the desires, the fears, and the prejudices of those who shape law and policy.

Chapters by Campbell and Purdum pay special attention to how migrant youth are treated and conceptualized by our legal system. Just as "child" and "youth" are not static categories, law is similarly shifting. It is constantly renegotiated, reinterpreted, reformed, rebuilt. Yet, instead of undermining its potency, this flexibility provides a certain strength and longevity, as well as immense consequences for the groups targeted by policy. Campbell is directly concerned with how "youth" as a category is mobilized in asylum law, revealing both the construction and dismantling of this categorization. Key to asylum law is the idea that one must be a member of a "particular social group" to merit legal protection. Campbell details the legal arguments concerning whether or not "youth" should be considered a protected group under asylum law, and how temporality frames such a category. How does the law conceive of a category that people move through and out of over time? By shifting the legal constructions and meanings assigned to "youth," the legal system works to restrict safety and belonging to Central American families and others seeking asylum.

Campbell's chapter ties questions about categorical compositions to the ways in which the legal system provides paths for the politically powerful to restrict and restrain marginalized groups, such as migrant youth, through seemingly neutral arguments over categorical definitions. Campbell's discussion demonstrates how legal framings perform exclusions, restrict movements, and decree the right to physical presence and belonging. The chapter provides an important background to Purdum's chapter, in which she explores the violence that immigration and asylum law does to vulnerable populations. Through an analysis of zero-tolerance family separations, Purdum demonstrates that the policy was far from a neutral application of law and order. Rather, it was a discretionary demonstration of power. The concept of "the law" was used in this case to target and exclude migrants from Central America in a cultural moment that featured a narrative framing their arrival as a crisis. She further reveals how even "helping" narratives employed by immigration activists may actually reinforce some of the worst tendencies of the system, doing harm to migrant children and their families.

Both Campbell and Purdum explore the geographies of immigration law and policy that target young people. They are key to forming the barriers and gateways that produce the spaces of the nation-state through crafting the populations and possibilities of the territory. The decisions made in courtrooms and policy meetings expel young people from within state boundaries and rend apart differently positioned family members. Immigration discourses shape the law and policy that exist to design our national community.

Ildefonso's chapter closes the part, following threads established in Cope's introductory piece. Race and ethnicity in particular act as major intersecting categories that differently impact youth. Ildefonso analyzes a parent-led anti–standardized testing movement that is framed as being in the best interest of students. However, she finds that this resistance is steeped in racial capitalism and the consolidation of wealth in the spaces of the school district and the neighborhood. She further dives into a study of the production of a "local control" model of education. Local control acts as a form of economic and political power that privileges majority-white residential communities. This forms the backdrop of a racialized geography that is key to understanding the contemporary persistence of school segregation. Her case study of resistance to standardized testing in affluent white New York communities draws out racial capitalism's role in differently positioning young people, informing which spaces they inhabit, what their spaces and experiences are like, and how they are valued.

Taken together, the final chapters highlight another key theme that runs through both parts of this book: law and policy aimed at young people is often not about them alone, or even about them in particular. Both Campbell's work and Purdum's work lead us to consider how the category of the child is related to other key frames of categorization, such as "woman" and "family." What, we can ask, are the implications of positioning the "child" as the focal point of "family" while other categories, such as "father," are less securely bound to discourses of family, particularly in immigration and asylum law? Further, how is the category of "child" mobilized to control the movement of families and even larger populations and spaces? As Ildefonso shows, political fights centering young people and their commonly associated spaces (e.g., the school, the school district) may have little to do with the young people themselves. Her analysis reveals how little of the concern surrounding standardized testing in this instance is actually centered on children's experiences of schooling, but rather stems from the economic desires of adults. These chapters demonstrate how the flexibility written into youth-based categorizations is wielded by those with political and legal power to fit shifting and contextual agendas.

As the chapters in this part demonstrate, constructions of youth and childhood are not static. They are constantly (re)negotiated. They are geographically and temporally contextual. There are different meanings, expectations, exclusions, and enclosures placed around different identities that intersect with "child" or "youth." The harm caused by policies discussed in these chapters can be profound. And at times, these constructions are based on goals that go beyond individual young people themselves and further create, reshape, or reinforce larger systems.

CHAPTER 1

WORKING AND SCHOOLING: A CRITICAL GEOGRAPHY OF CHILD LABOR AND COMPULSORY EDUCATION LAWS IN THE EARLY TWENTIETH-CENTURY UNITED STATES

Meghan Cope

Should American children work or go to school? If they do work, what age is "too young" for textile mills or cotton fields or coal mines? Should rules about work and school depend on the child's gender? Race? Location? Family circumstances? And who counts as a "child" anyway? These are the types of questions that animated discussion in print media, government reports, and on the floors of statehouses across the US in the late nineteenth and early twentieth centuries, and their answers generated a patchwork of rules, opportunities, and disciplinary frameworks for children. Today's lengthy periods of "childhood" and "youth" in the Global North typically exclude full-time waged work, place high value on extended education, and accommodate economic dependency through the late teens, but these are fairly recent developments. One hundred years ago the cultural construct of the "ideal" American child was cast as white, male, sturdy, obedient, hardworking, and patriotic, and the ideal child*hood* was based on a nostalgic sense of the rural freedoms of privileged settler-colonial white Christian youth in an agrarian society. However, what is valorized as the *ideal* or "proper" childhood in popular media, advertisements, and toys is not always accessible—or even desirable—for everyone, even while the notion of an ideal has disciplinary power over families and children themselves (Bernstein 2011; Gagen 2004; Mills 2013; Wells 2011). Of course, who "counts" as a child has shifted over time and place, and, relatedly, legal and social constructions of the meanings and boundaries of *childhood* have always varied by gender, class, and race (Holloway and Valentine 2000). We see this in views that certain children are perceived as innocent angels in need of protection while others are seen as inherently suspect[1] and in need of discipline. We also see this in historical child labor and compulsory schooling laws and their uneven geographic implementation, which constitute the foundation of this chapter.

The industrial era in the US brought significant changes to both legal and de facto notions of childhood. These were unevenly applied across racial, ethnic, and gender lines such that some groups' status and opportunities as "children" were safeguarded while others' were contested. Children of color, in particular, have been viewed as no longer children at younger ages than whites, while simultaneously being perceived as never *truly* adults (Simmons 2015). Such multilayered and slippery concepts of childhood and youth are generated by and (re)produce geographies of power and oppression. In this chapter I complicate *geographically* the notion of childhood with a focus on the rapid changes of the early twentieth century to help reveal how legal frameworks were constructed based on notions of an "ideal" childhood, how laws varied across regions and scale, and how they produced contradictory spaces of legal status for young people.

While American children have always worked in some capacity (and, indeed, enslaved Black children had no choice), the processes of industrial wage labor starting in the late eighteenth century engaged children in a substantively different way than family farms and craft-based businesses did, by pulling them into different types of tasks, places, contact with non-family adults, and labor relations involving hourly wages and piece rates. With industrialization, child labor became more monetized than in agrarian settings, and families seeking to maximize their household income counted on children to contribute, part of a desperate cycle of poverty: "Need sets the child to work when it should have been at school and its labor breeds low wages, thus increasing the need" (Riis 1892, 92). Thus, nineteenth- and twentieth-century debates about whether and how children should work, for how many hours, and in what relationship to education were both based on *and* contributed to shifts in the construction of "childhood."

However, views of children as legitimate wage earners were tarnished by perceptions of industrial dangers and risk, judgment was harsh on "lazy" parents who forced their children to work, and the appeal of school expanded greatly. Zelizer notes an early twentieth-century pendulum swing from seeing children as financial assets who contribute their wages to the family toward viewing children as "economically worthless but emotionally priceless" (1985, 3), especially among white families of the growing middle class. She argues that the shift can be traced to turn-of-the-century forms of patriarchal capitalism and the "cult of true womanhood" in which the expert full-time wife and mother actually became an idealized symbol of white middle-class status (9). Many other factors contributed to this shift toward "priceless" children too, including lower rates of child mortality, smaller family sizes, longer life expectancies, class mobility (for whites), and maturing industries. These factors, of course, varied geographically, as explored below.

Different concepts of childhood are supported by legal frameworks that simultaneously reflect the sentiments of the time and place, but laws are differentiated at the national, state, and community level, and making changes to laws is highly contested and very slow. This means that cataloging laws on social issues at any moment in time is merely a snapshot of an uneven and lumbering process. Further, because laws are the product of their *context*— the cumulative social values and practices they restrict or encourage, generally designed by and for the benefit of those in power—they also have uneven impacts across social dimensions. Indeed, scholars have noted that "in many cases, social reform legislation, instead of *preceding* and precipitating social change, actually *followed* and was a response to social change" (Moehling 1999, 72, emphasis added). Child labor laws in the US were enacted on a state-by-state basis, often with exceptions for particular industries (such as agriculture, which used a lot of child labor, many of them immigrants and Black workers), until the passage of federal standards via the Fair Labor Standards Act in 1938, and its expansion in 1949, though it too had many caveats and loopholes. Compulsory schooling has a similarly fragmented history (and to this day is only codified in state law) and was deeply entwined with child labor laws: if children weren't working, attending school "kept them off the streets" and away from the temptations of "idleness," according to contemporary observers. Table 1.1 identifies key moments and policy changes in child labor politics, while the maps below demonstrate these uneven processes across both time and place.

There are many excellent histories of early twentieth-century changes regarding child labor and compulsory schooling (Ensign 1921; Fliter 2018; Hindman 2002; Lindenmeyer 1997; Mintz 2004; Trattner 1970); I lean

Table 1.1. US Child Labor Policies and Legislation: Change over Time

May 1813	Connecticut enacts first law requiring schooling of working children
February 16, 1832	New England Association of Farmers, Mechanics, and Other Working Men creates a committee to investigate child labor
July 22, 1836	Union members at the National Trades' Union Convention make first proposal recommending states establish minimum ages for factory work
March 27, 1848	Pennsylvania becomes first state to set a minimum age for factory workers at twelve; in effect, the law is the first statewide ban of child labor based on age
April 16, 1852	Massachusetts becomes first state to limit child labor by passing a comprehensive compulsory school attendance law
December 28, 1869	Knights of Labor founded; responsible for the introduction of labor legislation in the South in the 1880s
November 15, 1881	Federation of Organized Trades and Labor Unions founded and calls for abolition of child labor (later changed name to AFL)
April 25, 1904	Private, non-profit National Child Labor Committee formed with mandate "to combat the danger in which childhood is placed by greed"
January 23, 1907	Legislation passed to allow secretaries of commerce and labor to investigate and report on child labor
April 9, 1912	US Dept. of Labor establishes Children's Bureau with the mandate to investigate and report on the welfare of children
September 1, 1916	Congress passes the Keating-Owen Act, the first federal child labor law, restricting interstate commerce of goods made with child labor
June 3, 1918	Supreme Court overturns Keating-Owen Act as unconstitutional
February 24, 1919	Congress passes Child Labor Tax Law, takes effect April 25, 1919
May 15, 1922	Supreme Court strikes down Child Labor Tax Law as unconstitutional
April 26, 1924	House of Representatives Adopts Child Labor Amendment to the Constitution giving Congress the right to limit labor of those under eighteen; Senate adopts it June 2
June 28, 1924	Arkansas becomes first state to ratify Child Labor Amendment; after initial ratifications, several failures and setbacks stall the CLA for a decade
June 16, 1933	President Franklin Roosevelt signs the National Industrial Recovery Act with codes preventing persons under sixteen from working in various industries
May 27, 1935	The Supreme Court rules that the National Industrial Recovery Act is unconstitutional
June 30, 1936	Walsh-Healy Public Contracts Act requires those receiving government contracts to have a forty-hour week, fair pay, and minimum working age
April 12, 1937	Supreme Court upholds the National Labor Relations Act
June 25, 1938	Congress passes the Fair Labor Standards Act; President Franklin Roosevelt signs the law the same day
June 5, 1939	Supreme Court decides that the Child Labor Amendment is still alive: a state that previously rejected the amendment may reverse itself and vote for ratification
February 3, 1941	Supreme Court upholds Fair Labor Standards Act, preempting the Child Labor Amendment
October 19, 1949	Congress amends FLSA, broadening child labor provisions

Data compiled from Fliter 2018; Hindman 2002; NCLC 1938; and Trattner 1970.

heavily on these histories, but also on reports produced at the time by the US Department of Labor's Children's Bureau, which operated from 1912 to 1946, and the private, nonprofit National Child Labor Committee (NCLC), founded in 1904, as well as census data and related analyses. Most of the secondary materials are based on chronological accounts of conditions, political debates, laws proposed and either passed or defeated, and policies implemented. I take a geographic approach to the topic, looking at different scales of legislative action, state-level border conflicts in the passage and enforcement of relevant laws, and regional variations, specifically as derived from their underlying sociocultural, economic, and political differences. I finish the chapter with a reflection on the role of legal changes on the construction of childhood-in-place.

A HISTORICAL GEOGRAPHY OF CHILD LABOR AND COMPULSORY SCHOOLING

Just as underlying natural features (e.g., harbors, minerals) or local resources (e.g., investment capital, skilled labor) influenced the geography of industrialization in the US, that pattern of industrialization also influenced the adoption of child labor laws. The period of the early to mid-nineteenth century saw changes along these lines coming from two political directions: those concerned about the labor and education of children (often rooted in religious expectations for literacy and industriousness), and those concerned about protecting the position (and wages) of adult male breadwinners, including trade and craft organizations (see table 1.1). Thus, Connecticut passed the first law requiring that working children achieve a minimum level of schooling in 1813, Pennsylvania passed the first age-based law restricting labor among children under twelve in 1848, and Massachusetts passed a compulsory school attendance law in 1852 that would have effectively limited child labor if it had actually been enforced (E. Abbott 1908). Similarly, various trade organizations, which wanted to prevent working men from being undercut by low-wage children, investigated child labor as early as 1832, proposed minimum ages for factory work in 1836, introduced labor legislation in the South in the 1880s, and called for the abolition of child labor as early as 1881 (Fliter 2018). Overall, by 1880, seven states had a minimum age for employment[2] and twelve had maximum hours for young workers[3] (Johnson 1935). These trends continued through the rest of the nineteenth century, with distinct regional patterns: the most industrialized and urbanized states passed laws earlier, while states characterized by extractive industries (agriculture, mining, forestry) and those with mostly rural populations had few or no restrictions on child labor. By the same token, states with large populations of Black

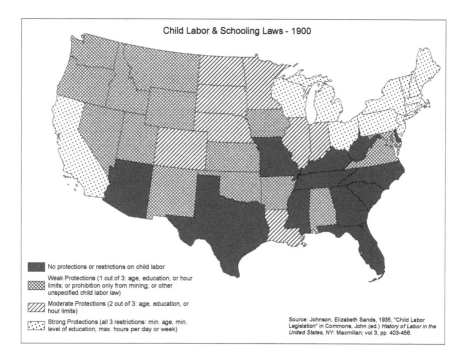

Fig. 1.1. Child labor and schooling laws—four levels of protections for children, 1900. Cartography by Gemayel Goxcon.

children, whose labor was taken for granted and for whom education was seen as risky to white supremacy, were generally the last to guarantee *any* children educational access, lest it elevate those who were formerly enslaved above even the poorest whites. Indeed, as Karen Wells (2011, 21) has brilliantly argued in her use of Foucauldian bio-political analyses on global constructions of childhood, "The narrative of children's lives as gradually improving after the advent of child-saving/child rights conceals how, in the same times and spaces, race functioned as a caesura in the population so that racialized others were excluded from the child-saving/child-rights project."

By the end of the nineteenth century, moral panics that were sparked from writings of international luminaries condemning the conditions of (white) child workers generated sufficient social and political will in some places to limit child workers' ages, hours, and levels of danger in industrial settings. Stories of children being maimed and killed in factories and mines helped accelerate the public outrage, albeit unevenly across regions in the US (Schuman

2017), with little attention spared for thousands of formerly enslaved Black children whose conditions of labor and chances for education had hardly changed since emancipation.

Progressives' disillusionment with the voracity of economic growth meant the *discourse* around child labor laws and compulsory school attendance was becoming increasingly national, though the laws were still highly fragmented at state and local levels. Indeed, Labaree traces the evolution of American educational rhetoric by Horace Mann and later education advocates, noting a pronounced shift from the nineteenth century's politically based goal of "making citizens for a republic" to the twentieth century's economically-based focus on "schooling for social mobility" (2011, 180–81). However, Labaree's meticulous historical account rests on broad national trends, rather than fine-grained geographic variations and the differentiations spurred by sexist and racial oppression that are my focus here. In fact, Johnson noted that "there was no single solution of the child labor problem" and that state-level strategies fell into four categories: "a minimum age below which they should not be allowed to work; a minimum of education which they should acquire before entering employment; a maximum number of hours for their employment; and some rules to protect them against especially hazardous or unhealthful occupations" (1935, 403–404; see also fig. 1.1). States took on different combinations of these, resulting in a dizzying patchwork of rules, exceptions, and internal geographic variations by rural and urban settings that changed over time. These twin policies—to regulate labor and require education—had common goals: "the need for children with foreign-born parents to be assimilated, the need for idle children to put their time to productive use, and the need for citizens to have some education" (Clay, Lingwall, and Stephens 2012, 9). The earliest and strongest child labor and compulsory schooling laws were seen in the Northeast and the Midwest of the US, while the Southern states, especially those invested in plantation economies, post–Civil War Black Codes, and violent racial oppression, were generally slower to regulate, as is explored below.

Those states that were early in passing child labor laws demonstrated a range of social, political, economic, and moral arguments in implementing such legislation, primarily centered around the risks of work and the benefits of education for children. For example, concerns were raised about children's physical and mental fitness, whereby work "dwarfs the body and stifles intellectual growth" (Lovejoy 1905, 52). There were significant (and legitimate) worries about exposing young workers to physical and "moral" hazards, ranging from operating saw blades to running errands for prostitutes. For instance,

Ohio required that "no child under sixteen years of age shall be engaged in any employment whereby its life or limb is endangered or its health is likely to be injured, or its morals may be depraved," and a 1903 Illinois law "prohibited absolutely the employment of children under sixteen years of age in a large number of enumerated occupations, as the cleaning and oiling of machinery, operating cutting and stamping machinery, and handling injurious chemicals" (both from Erickson 1905, 63). There was also a strong theme of training to create an educated (white, male) citizenry who could carry on the duties of the republic:

> [W]e are agitating and striving more and more, not only to save the children from the wrong kind of work at the wrong time and under wrong conditions, but at the same time to prepare them for the right kind of work at the right time and under right conditions *that the citizens of to-morrow may work for and be worthy of the highest ideals of the republic* (Lindsey 1905, 101, emphasis added)

Indeed, many of the first child labor laws in New England and adjacent states had begun as compulsory schooling laws based on the ideals of democratic citizenship combined with Christian concerns *for* reading religious texts and *against* idleness and "loafing" (Ensign 1921). In most places, it was more politically palatable to advocate for increased education for children than to restrict their waged labor, especially in seasonal harvest work, as seen in figure 1.2. As assistant secretary of the NCLC Owen Lovejoy wrote, "The aim is not just to keep the children from working, but to produce intelligent citizens. To this end we must legislate in harmony with the school laws" (Lovejoy 1905, 46).

Even in those contexts, however, proponents of universal education grappled with resistance based on perceptions of parents' rights to decide whether children should work or go to school. These conflicting views could even be seen within the actions of individual lawmakers. In one earlier example, Horace Mann, Massachusetts's first secretary of education, in 1837 "wanted all children to be in school, and carried their interests on his heart constantly, yet he was reluctant to sacrifice what he held . . . to be a principle of American democracy, the right of the parent to determine what his child should do" (Ensign 1921, 48). Sixty years later, when Southern states were confronted more sharply with the prospect of child labor restrictions and compulsory schooling, these same quandaries of parents' rights versus children's were still in play.

Fig. 1.2. Group of adolescent spinners in Washington Cotton Mills, Fries, Virginia. Lewis Hine, photographer. Courtesy of the Library of Congress, https://www.loc.gov/resource/nclc.02059.

In early twentieth-century documents and interpretations, the benefits of education were almost always for some party other than the individual child, whether employers, "democracy," some idealized national future, or specific states. For example, William Hand, writing from and about South Carolina (which had not yet passed a compulsory schooling law), argued:

> Since all classes of our heterogeneous society are active factors therein, the State [of South Carolina] maintains schools for all the children of all the people[4] in order to render its citizenship homogeneous in spirit and purpose. *The public schools exist primarily for the benefit of the State rather than for the benefit of the individual.* The State seeks to make every citizen intelligent and serviceable. The State compels the rich man to pay taxes to help support the schools, not because it owes the poor man's child an education, but because *the State needs the intelligent services of that child.* The schools are democratized by compelling the rich and poor alike to pay taxes according to their ability for something necessary to all. (Hand 1914, 105, emphasis added)

The same focus on the well-being of the country as a whole applied to child labor, with one reformer stating, "Just as in the commercial world the dollar is the unit of value, so in the body politic the child is the unit of value, and upon the soundness of the child depends the future of the state and nation" (McDowell 1909, 168). Period references to the state, nation, or republic were thus quite common, invoked both in terms of service by citizens and responsibilities of the government. Indeed, the child labor reformer Florence Kelley claimed: "The noblest duty of the Republic is that of self-preservation by so cherishing all its children that they, in turn, may become enlightened self-governing citizens . . . The children of today [1905] are potentially the Republic of 1930 . . . The care and nurture of childhood is thus a vital concern of the nation. For if children perish in infancy they are obviously lost to the Republic as citizens" (1905, 3). Notable in these quotes, however, is that the right to childhood—to the extent it was recognized at all—was predicated on children's *future* roles, rather than on any present rights *as children*. This is akin to what Holloway and Valentine have identified as a broad societal focus on "human becomings rather than human beings" (2000, 5). By framing concerns for children as rooted in concern for nation, republic, or state, these authors played part in a long-standing political discourse used across party lines. I argue, however, that this discourse not only tends to elide the *experience* of childhood by real children, but it also ignores deep racial and gender inequities through dependence on an assumed "ideal" (white, male) child. Thus we see the value of investigating the mutual construction of place, childhood, and social injustice as foundational to a critical historical geography of childhood.

By 1919 all forty-eight states and the District of Columbia had some age restrictions on labor and some form of compulsory schooling law in place (Hindman 2002). But how effective were they? Child labor critic Jacob Riis, in his visits to Lower East Side Manhattan tenements in the early 1890s, found that New York State's requirements merely promoted lying and a cottage industry of false documents: "That the law has had the effect of greatly diminishing the number of child-workers I do not believe. It has had another and worse effect. It has bred wholesale perjury among them and their parents . . . The child of eleven at home and at night-school is fifteen in the factory" (Riis 1892, 93). In her study of US Census data from 1880, 1900, and 1910, Moehling found that state-level "minimum age limits had relatively little effect on the occupation choices of children at the turn of the century . . . these restrictions contributed little to the long-run decline in child labor" (1999, 72), which is consistent with the observation that social policy tends to *follow* social change, rather than initiate it. Much of the eventual decline of child labor can be traced to broad demographic and economic shifts, such as high levels of international immigration, mechanization, increased family wages, and unionization. Further, an ideal of "proper" childhood as a period of education, play, and physical maturation rather than labor was expanding in some quarters, particularly among the growing white middle class.

At a finer level of resolution, rooted in the practicalities of daily life, another reason for the weak impacts of state-level legislation is that there were many exemptions for labor and schooling laws. In the same era (1910s–1920s) as several failed federal actions, various policies allowed children living more than two or three miles from school and those who were "physically or mentally incapacitated" to be exempted from compulsory education; similarly, many state laws allowed children to work instead of attend school if they needed to support a widowed mother and younger siblings, or in cases of such poverty that parents could not afford appropriate clothes and books (Lathrop 1919; see also fig. 1.3).

These exceptions took on larger cultural purchase. On the matter of reluctance to compel poor children to attend school, one reformer wrote the following in 1914:

> Objection is often made that compulsory attendance would work hardships in the homes of the poor. Is it not a fact that the poor child is the very one who most needs the aid of the State to bring him into possession of his own? He it is who must soon face the complexities of modern life and the insistent demands of citizenship with none of the advantages common to birth or wealth. The poor child is the very one whom the State ought to help, because he himself is helpless. The child of the poor must work, but is it either right or humane that he should be forever denied his share of his inheritance in order to be a breadwinner for a selfish, unfeeling father? If it be true that the American home cannot be supported by the adult members of the normal family, we are confronted with one of the gravest problems ever met in any country. *No State on a sound economic and social basis can afford to permit its children to be employed as breadwinners when they should be in school equipping themselves for productive citizenship.* (Hand 1914, 106, emphasis added)

Hand's feisty comments in defense of schooling, condemning "selfish" fathers, and his invocation of national standing and citizenship demonstrate the scale of the issue: when even parents were unwilling to support

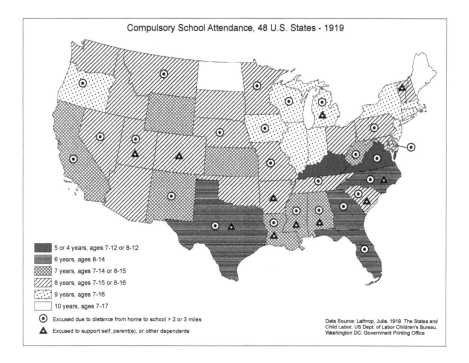

Fig. 1.3. State-level school attendance requirements (years and ages) and exemptions as of 1919. Cartography by Gemayel Goxcon.

compulsory schooling, what hope could advocates cling to? Perhaps this is the root of the shift Labaree (2011) observed in educational rhetoric away from lofty goals of democracy toward the seemingly crass appeal to the increased economic value of educated children with skills tuned to the emerging labor market. This shift Labaree identifies, toward seeing education as a "private good," rather than a public benefit of citizenship, was essential: if parents were to lose their children's earnings in the short term due to new laws, at least the content of their education was becoming more "vocational" and oriented toward work qualifications that would boost their long-term competitiveness in the market economy. Add to this the rampant falsification of children's ages, such as found by Riis (1892), and the near-total lack of enforcement mechanisms against truancy (Ensign 1921), and it is not surprising that actual school attendance levels were quite low and, of course, highly geographically varied.

A REGIONAL "CRAZY QUILT"

The geographic unevenness of child labor and schooling laws led to numerous contradictions, competitions, and conundrums involving at least three types of social-geographic contradictions: one regarding *scale* (state vs. federal), a second based on *borders* and the issues that arose when adjacent states had vastly different regulations, and a third relating to the substantial *regional divide* between the North and the South of the US. These are reviewed in turn, though the intertwined nature of their constitutive processes makes them difficult to separate.

The Children's Bureau and the National Child Labor Committee tried repeatedly to pass federal-level legislation, but their two major laws passed by Congress (the Keating-Owen Act in 1916 and the Child Labor Tax Law in 1919) were deemed unconstitutional by the Supreme Court only months after they took effect, generating tremendous frustration among activists and forcing them to continue to push for piecemeal state-level policies. Contemporary observers railed against the lack of federal-level progress, using geographic unevenness in their arguments:

> That national authority is essential to an effective campaign against child labor and in support of universal education has long been apparent. States with the most advanced standards share boundaries with those notoriously indifferent to the best interests of children. Entire sections of the country have been reluctant to remove young children from productive employment. The educational and higher industrial opportunities of a child have been determined far too completely by the locality in which he [sic] chanced to be born. To secure a degree of uniformity in opportunity and in standards, Federal interference has come to be regarded as a necessary and logical step. (Ensign 1921, 246)

And Florence Kelley, a long-time labor reformer, wrote in 1922:

> We have all failed . . . the state laws are a crazy quilt. No two of them are uniform. The children and the employers alike have a grievance because of the lack of uniformity. States' rights have meant, and do mean, the right to hand over the children as low-paid wage-earners to the exploiters. State child-labor laws will not do except as supplements to a federal law. Congress has now been told twice in four years by the Supreme Court that under the present Constitution it cannot act. Unless we are a nation of morons

we must recognize from forty years of failure in the states and these two decisions of the Court that *the Constitution must be changed*. (Quoted in Trattner 1970, 273 n., emphasis added)

Shortly after this letter, in 1924, both houses of the Congress passed the Child Labor Amendment, which would have amended the US Constitution to give Congress the "power to limit, regulate, and prohibit the labor of persons under 18 years old" (quoted in Fliter 2018, 141); after an initial flurry of five states[5] ratifying it within three years, all progress stalled until after the beginning of the Great Depression. Eventually, twenty-eight states ratified the amendment by the late 1930s, and it is technically still pending. But, as Fliter points out, "ultimately, the amendment was not necessary because in 1941, the Supreme Court upheld the fourth federal child labor law, the Fair Labor Standards Act [initially passed in 1938], thus achieving by legislation what could not be obtained by constitutional amendment" (Fliter 2018, 190).

The desire for federal uniformity by reformers was partly inspired by the dilemmas posed by regional variation, such as when the geographic footprint of an industry spanned sections of more than one state. For example, Lovejoy advocated for *industry*-wide standards, noting the contradictions of the "Pittsburgh District," made up of glass manufacturers in western Pennsylvania, eastern Ohio, and the northern panhandle of West Virginia. He observed:

Ohio has a fourteen year age limit for the employment of children, Pennsylvania a thirteen year limit, West Virginia a twelve year limit. Ohio prohibits the employment of children under sixteen at night, Pennsylvania permits the employment at night of children of thirteen, while West Virginia permits children twelve years old to work at night. The effect of such a situation is that the manufacturer in Western Pennsylvania, when approached on the subject of restriction of night labor for children, replies with a threat to move over into West Virginia if such a law is enacted, thus frightening legislators into inactivity, while in Eastern Ohio, along the boundary line, which is thickly dotted with glass factories, children are confessedly employed at twelve and thirteen years of age at night upon the plea that the industry cannot compete with West Virginia and Pennsylvania if the law were rigidly enforced. (Lovejoy 1905, 47–48)

Contradictions such as these undermined the state-based campaigns, adding justification for a federal approach, but they also fed into a capitalist-driven discourse about "progress" being based on industrialization and urbanization, and distinctly not on the protection of children.

This discourse of progress equating with industrialization and urbanization in the Northern US did not sit comfortably with the South. A strong regional tension is evident in arguments of the time whereby the policies and financial capital of the North were seen as exploitative and insensitive to the cultural values of the South. Efforts of Northern activists to pass child labor laws were taken as an affront by some in the South who claimed that limiting child labor would stunt the industrialization of Southern states: while the Northern states were receiving high numbers of immigrants, the South was more dependent on its regional labor forces to achieve "progress" (Anderson 1905). The assistant secretary of the National Child Labor Committee, A. J. McKelway, stated tartly,

> I would appeal to the people of the North to sweep before their own doors more carefully as the best means of helping us of the South. When Southern visitors to New York City see the size of the little newsboys and are aware of the newsboy law, they are not much impressed with the adequacy of law to protect children. When our Carolina manufacturers visit the Rhode Island cotton mills and find conditions there as bad if not worse than those in their own factories, it is hard for the advocates of the children's cause in the South to plead the better example of the North. (McKelway 1905, 22)

Further, because early twentieth-century state-level child labor laws were mostly focused on industrial, mining, and commercial employment with virtually no attention given to child agricultural work, places that had primarily agricultural economies—mostly Southern states—were later in passing child labor laws. Importantly, the discourse of progress as associated with urban industrialization simultaneously valorized a nostalgic agrarian past that was assumed to be healthy for children *and* contributed to Southern "producer ideology," which "placed a premium on the physical production of the world's goods and asserted that those who made them comprised the true citizenry of a republic" (Schmidt 2010, 3). However, rosy imaginaries of child farmwork were rarely the reality in the context of large-scale industrial agriculture, much of it mere steps from plantation models of labor and production (Dart and Matthews 1924).

This agricultural blind spot was widespread: children working on family farms were perceived as wholesome, healthy, and engaged in important citizenship training. Hunter wrote, "children received practically their entire education either in the home or in the adjoining fields . . . the home was the center of the moral, educational, industrial, and social life" (Hunter 1904, 201–202). Children working on farms were assumed to be under their parents' benevolent supervision and thus insulated from the exploitation and dangers encountered by children working in factories. Even the reformer James McDowell from Mississippi assumed that a place with little industrialization or urbanization must be relatively free of child labor. He stated to the National Child Labor Committee in 1909:

> The necessity for such a [child labor] statute in Mississippi is not so great as in many of her sister states, principally because there are *so few children employed at work which is injurious to them*. There are no mines; no glass factories; no sweat shops; less than twenty cotton and woolen mills, and not more than half a dozen canning factories in which child labor is employed. There are *no large cities* in the state and consequently few paupers. Thus the evil is reduced to a minimum, and this condition is no doubt responsible for the long delay in the enactment of suitable statutes for the protection of helpless childhood. (McDowell 1909, 166, emphasis added).

In fact, although data are not available for the period in which McDowell was writing, we know that a decade later, in 1920, in Mississippi 25 percent of ten-to-fifteen-year-olds were working, representing over seventy thousand children (National Child Labor Committee 1928). In 1930, a startling 19 percent of all Mississippi ten-to-thirteen-year-olds, 33 percent of all fourteen-to-fifteen-year-olds, and almost 40 percent of all sixteen-to-seventeen-year-olds were "gainfully employed" in agriculture, representing a total of over one hundred thousand children working on farms in the state (Abbott 1933; see also fig. 1.3). To take this further, consider that the main cash crop in Mississippi was cotton: how "injurious" was such work for children? Two intrepid researchers from the Children's Bureau did a study of child workers in two cotton-producing Texas counties in 1920. They found that "the average day's work for 153 children ranging in age from 3 to 15 years was slightly under 100 pounds of cotton each," and "working 12 hours, a 6-year-old girl, who had begun field work at the age of 4, picked 80 pounds a day, and 4-year-old twins in the same family working beside their mother in the field put into her bag on an average 12 or 15 pounds a day" (Dart and Matthews 1924, 13). The authors go on to caution that "many children, both white and negro [sic] in sections of the country where cotton is grown are working long hours at tasks which appear to be *too heavy for them to perform without injury* to their health

Fig. 1.4. Original caption: "Cleo Campbell, 9 years old, picks 70–100 lbs of cotton a day. Expects to start school soon. 'I'd ruther go to school and then I wouldn't have ter work.' Father said she and her sister begin about 6am and work until 6 or 7pm with 1½ hours off at noon." Pottawatomie, Oklahoma. October 1916. Lewis Hine, photographer. Courtesy of the Library of Congress, https://www.loc.gov/resource/nclc.00627/.

and physique, and, in addition, they are *losing a large part of their schooling* on account of the work which they do in the cotton fields" (70, emphasis added; see also fig. 1.4). This did not match the nostalgic agrarian image of a child gathering eggs before school or shucking corn amid a jolly circle of aunts and grandmas, but it was very useful for maintaining boundaries of race, gender, and class.

Thus, when we consider that child farm labor was highest in the large industrial agricultural operations of the South *and* that Southern states were reluctant to regulate labor in general, it is clear that the largest group of child workers in the country had few protections. Even as late as 1930, the top eight states for child labor in agriculture were all in the South and, combined, employed over six hundred thousand children (fig. 1.5). The NCLC finally started investigating the issue in the 1930s, acknowledging in their 1938 report, "Agriculture in some respects presents one of the most serious of all child labor problems. It involves more than twice as many child workers as all other

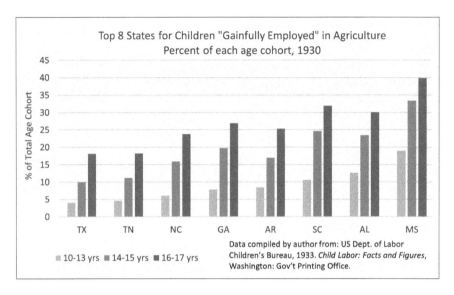

Fig. 1.5. Top eight states employing child agricultural workers, 1930. Note that the census is notorious for undercounting rural and Black populations, which suggests even higher numbers in reality.

occupations together; it includes a large number of very young workers; it employs thousands of children as migratory workers; it presents difficult problems of control" (National Child Labor Committee 1938, 25). Interestingly, despite the earlier documentation provided by Lewis Hine, the NCLC's staff investigator and photographer in the 1910s, which showed children like Cleo Campbell (fig. 1.4) in major cotton-producing areas of the central South, the photos in the 1938 report strategically show young white boys employed picking vegetables, and the discussion focuses on Colorado and California, with no mention of the high rates of child farm workers in the South or the fact that most of them were Black.

In fact, this was not just an *agricultural* oversight in attention to child labor; it was also a *racial* one. The plantation legacies of sharecropping, share tenancies (Hart 1977), and large-scale violent oppression and exploitation of Black workers of all ages kept African American families poor and nearly immobilized in an era of repeated turn-of-the-century recessions and violent Jim Crow laws, notwithstanding those who joined the Great Migration (Wilkerson 2010). Here, we see another reason why the South was slow to regulate child labor: difficult, low-wage, economically precarious physical labor was culturally assumed by whites to be "normal" or even "desirable" work for Black people (along with domestic service, which was also largely unregulated). Southern textile mills were notable in their racial make-up: "Blacks did not work inside the cotton mills" (Hindman 2002, 181), meaning that any concerns about Southern industrial child labor were attached to white children (Sallee 2004; Alphonso 2014). Sallee's meticulous analysis of the racial politics of Southern child labor laws identifies Southern Progressive reformers' willingness to sacrifice race progress for Black people in order to build a white, cross-class coalition opposed to child labor. To do so, they employed white supremacist discursive tactics, including eugenicist narratives of "our pure Anglo-Saxon stock" (Sallee 2004, 4). Taking this a step further, Sallee demonstrates how this coalition was needed for the Progressive movement's desire to "jump scale" to the national level:

> As a variety of Progressives analyzed and addressed the southern child labor problem and mobilized an interregional coalition of child welfare experts to campaign for reform, race defined the terms of the debate, putting manufacturers, who already claimed to value the whiteness of their workforce, on the defensive. The child labor reform campaign provoked posturing among employers, who, regardless of their actual treatment of workers, had a growing investment in exaggerating their concern for unfortunate whites. Moreover *the focus on whites defined the terms of the national debate, making it possible for northerners and southerners to work together without southern suspicion that "outsiders" were intervening out of an interest in African Americans' rights.* (Sallee, 2004, 6, emphasis added)

Similar patterns can be seen regarding schooling. In much of the South, under "separate but equal" provisions (*Plessy v. Ferguson* 1896), Black children were less likely to attend school than whites, whether due to the distance from home to the nearest "Negro school," family dependence on children's earnings, or intimidation on the journey to school (Wilkerson 2010). When Black children did make it to school, they faced additional obstacles, including poorly paid teachers, short school terms, dilapidated buildings, few to no books or instructional materials, and overcrowding. As the Texas-based report on child cotton pickers from the Children's Bureau in the early 1920s noted:

> Most schools for negro [sic] children were either poorly built one-room structures, many of them unceiled, or church buildings used as schools during the week . . . [they] were lacking in even the most essential equipment . . . Five of the 11 negro schools visited had no toilets at all . . . Only 4

of the 11 visited had a commercial type of blackboard ... Individual desks were found in none of the schools for negro children ... Teachers in negro schools invariably reported lower monthly and yearly salaries than white teachers. (Dart and Matthews 1924, 33–35)

Indeed, there was little political appetite in the Jim Crow South for compulsory schooling laws *because* they would apply to Black children, which sparked fear among all whites, especially those less educated (Hindman 2002). Demonstrating Sallee's findings of the racist tactics of child labor advocates in the South, Alfred Seddon, an NCLC investigator, played on Southern whites' fears of being surpassed by educated Black residents of Mississippi (which was the last state to pass a compulsory schooling law, in 1917 [Lathrop 1919]):

It seems as tho some people would allow the white children to degenerate thro ignorance rather than afford a chance to the negro [sic] to get an education. ... The Southerner, ardent upholder as he rightly is of perpetual white domination in the South, should be the most urgent in his demands that white children in the South should have at least an equal chance with the black children in developing the best that is in them. (Seddon 1908, quoted in Hindman 2002, 182, original spellings)

In another angle, reformer William Hand of South Carolina represented a rare view when he stated:

The negro [sic] child needs no compulsory law to put him into school. He is already there wherever and whenever possible. No matter what a man's views on negro education, his admiration is challenged by the zeal and eagerness of the negro child to go to school. His thirst for knowledge would be commendable in any race. Not only is the negro in school, but he is learning. (Hand 1914, 108–109)

Thus, reformers advocating for compulsory schooling across the South adopted different discursive tactics, with varying degrees of racist allusions. Sallee suggests that ultimately, "closing the mill door and opening the school door became synonymous with salvaging white southern manhood" (2004, 6), a rhetorical necessity for uneducated white men to hold and inflate race privilege. The geographic variation in state attendance laws was therefore important as a backdrop, but it is also clear that those states in the Jim Crow

Fig. 1.6. Original caption: "Pleasant Green School—one room colored [sic] school near Marlinton, WV." October 1921. Lewis Hine, photographer. Courtesy of the Library of Congress, https://www.loc.gov/resource/nclc.04341.

South that ostensibly required six or seven years of schooling (figs. 1.3 and 1.6) did so in a deeply racialized context in which the location, availability, and quality of Black children's schools stymied their education and encouraged their continuation in low-wage labor.[6]

A final striking difference between Northern and Southern states, which harkens back to Horace Mann's qualms in the 1830s, was the question of whether parents' rights or individual children's rights prevailed. While Northern states passed laws allowing states to intervene in family life for child protection, in the South the family was sacrosanct. Indeed, Alphonso notes the regional cultural differences as lying at the heart of the South's reluctance to regulate child labor:

> [S]outhern child labor laws evidenced a *relational* conception of a child as someone embedded within a family and within the purview of a parent's moral and legal authority. Child work was considered a family affair . . . [t]his southern ideal was in contrast to a contractual model of

domestic-relations laws ... [of] northern legal codes, which were centered on *individuals* rather than on interdependent domestic relations. (2014, 68, emphasis added)

In primary documents of the early twentieth century, this relational view comes through strongly, often identified in terms of the "rights" of the family to a child's labor and to parents' full discretion over their children's employment or education, free from "government intervention" (Anderson 1905). And, writing again on Mississippi, McDowell stated "we were met with the proposition that the state should not interfere with a parent's right to control his own child ... [but] it is the duty of the state to save the child, not only from corporate greed, but from its own parent, if necessary" (1909, 168). Meanwhile, to contrast this view with a Northern state, Oregon law laid out a very different relationship, identifying children "as wards of the state and subject to its control. As to them, the state stands in the position of *parens patriae*, and may exercise unlimited supervision and control over their contracts, occupations, and conduct, and the liberty and right of those who assume to deal with them. This is a power which inheres in the government for its own preservation" (cited in Fliter 2018, 2). Perhaps these state-level differences represent, in a snapshot, the shift from the power of the sovereign (father, in this case) toward the power of government to control and manage the bodies of the populace (bio-power), as Wells (2011) discusses in her extension of Foucault's analysis into global conceptualizations of childhood.

These tensions were echoed with regard to compulsory schooling as well:

[O]ne hears much about the sacred rights and personal privileges of the parent who neglects or refuses to send his child to school. Has the helpless child no sacred rights? Has the State not some privileges? ... When the State compels the parent to send his child to school, it is simply compelling the parent to put the child in possession of his own rightful inheritance. In a narrow sense that inheritance is his right to the benefit of what [funds] the State has collected and set apart for him; in a wider and truer sense it means his opportunity to make of himself all that his God-given abilities will permit him to become; in the broadest sense it is his becoming fitted to take his place in the State to perform the sacred duties of an intelligent and patriotic citizen. (Hand 1914, 105–106)

Although reformers may have overstated the North/South divide of these views about rights, we still see evidence of such schisms in our national politics, and the legacies of segregation, unequal opportunity, and deep-seated racial oppression are clearly still shaping today's children and our assumptions about an ideal childhood. Regional variations in child labor laws and compulsory schooling generated significant consternation but also demonstrated to observers diverse possible futures if more (or less) protective state laws were adopted.

CONCLUSION

The geographic perspective taken here enables a move away from linear historical narratives by linking regional variations, the scale of political discourse and action, border contradictions, and the production of place to their underlying cultural, economic, and political contexts. It also demands attention to the processes inherent in the construction of *childhood-in-place* as context-dependent, contingent, lived, embodied, and resisted. Broad social injustices and the oppressive practices of everyday life mean that some children were subject to labor exploitation, physical harm, and educational ignorance while others were not. Conceptualizations of childhood, race, class, and gender were mutually constitutive such that the production of *place* was simultaneously the production of a particular racialized, gendered, classed *childhood*. In this way, laws attempted to concretize specific ideals of childhood but the constructions of childhood-in-place meant the lived experience of child labor restrictions or compulsory schooling were mediated through these powerful contextual frames. In reconsidering the question of who "counts" as a child, it is clear that child labor and schooling reforms were ultimately a compromise between cultural ideals of what a "proper" childhood should look like and the affronts presented to that ideal by new forms of economic exploitation, racial oppression, and poverty.

Adopting a critical geographic perspective here enables us to understand these legal shifts not only as about ideals of childhood but also as ideals of the body, citizenship, democracy, and the Republic. Thus, not only were reformers' aspirations about children with sturdy bodies and informed minds, but they were about an ideal citizenry, an ideal nation, and an ideal future.

NOTES

1. One need only look at the current violence against Black boys by police and other agents of power to see these perceptions made fatally real. See also Agyepong (2018).
2. Massachusetts, New Hampshire, New Jersey, Pennsylvania, Rhode Island, South Dakota, Vermont, Wisconsin.
3. Connecticut, Indiana, Maine, Maryland, Massachusetts, Minnesota, Ohio, Pennsylvania, Rhode Island, South Dakota, Vermont, Wisconsin.

4. One cannot help but question how all-inclusive Hand's statement really was, considering how violently Blacks were excluded from "homogenous citizenship" in South Carolina.
5. Arizona, Arkansas, California, Montana, Wisconsin. See Fliter (2018) for the history of the role of the Catholic Church in preventing ratification in such otherwise protective states as Massachusetts and New York.
6. Of course, mere passage of a law does not ensure equality; as we see to the present day, race continues to serve as a major political force in education, with de facto segregation and unequal access to quality schools on the rise, even in supposedly liberal New York City (Shapiro 2019).

REFERENCES

Abbott, Edith. 1908. "A Study of the Early History of Child Labor in America." *American Journal of Sociology* 4 (17): 15–37.

Abbott, Grace. 1933. *Child Labor: Facts and Figures*. United States Children's Bureau. Publication 197. Washington: Government Printing Office. Accessed via Hathi Trust, https://www.hathitrust.org.

Agyepong, Tera E. 2018. *The Criminalization of Black Children: Race, Gender, and Delinquency in Chicago's Juvenile Justice System, 1899–1945*. Chapel Hill, NC: University of North Carolina Press.

Alphonso, Gwendoline. 2014. "Of Families or Individuals? Southern Child Workers and the Progressive Crusade for Child Labor Regulation, 1899–1920." In J. Marten (ed.), *Children and Youth during the Gilded Age and Progressive Era*. New York: NYU Press, pp. 59–80.

Anderson, N. L. 1905. "Child Labor Legislation and the Methods of its Enforcement: The Southern States." *Addresses at the First Annual Meeting of the NCLC, NYC*. New York: National Child Labor Committee, pp. 77–93. Accessed via Hathi Trust, https://www.hathitrust.org.

Bernstein, Robin. 2011. *Racial Innocence: Performing American Childhood from Slavery to Civil Rights*. New York: NYU Press.

Clay, Karen, Jeff Lingwall, and Melvin Stephens. 2012. *Do Schooling Laws Matter? Evidence from the Introduction of Compulsory Attendance Laws in the United States*. Cambridge, MA: National Bureau of Economic Research, https://www.nber.org/papers/w18477.

Dart, Helen, and Ellen Matthews. 1924. *The Welfare of Children in Cotton-Growing Areas of Texas*. United States. Children's Bureau. Washington: Government Printing Office. Accessed via Hathi Trust, https://www.hathitrust.org.

Ensign, Forest C. 1921. *Compulsory School Attendance and Child Labor*. Iowa City, IA: Athens Press. Reprinted in *American Education: Its Men, Ideas, and Institutions* (New York: Arno Press and New York Times, 1969).

Erickson, Halford. 1905. "Child Labor Legislation and the Methods of Its Enforcement: The Northern Central States." *Addresses at the First Annual Meeting of the NCLC, NYC*. New York: National Child Labor Committee, pp. 53–65. Accessed via Hathi Trust, https://www.hathitrust.org.

Fliter, John. 2018. *Child Labor in America: The Epic Legal Struggle to Protect Children*. Lawrence: University Press of Kansas.

Gagen, Elizabeth. 2004. "Making America Flesh: Physicality and Nationhood in Early Twentieth-Century Physical Education Reform." *cultural geographies* 11 (4): 417–42.

Hand, William H. 1914. "The Need of Compulsory Education in the South." *Compulsory School Attendance*. US Bureau of Education Bulletin No. 2. Washington: Government Printing Office.

Hart, John F. 1977. "The Demise of King Cotton." *Annals of the Association of American Geographers* 67 (3): 307–22. https://doi.org/10.1111/j.1467-8306.1977.tb01144.x.

Hindman, Hugh. D. 2002. *Child Labor: An American History*. Armonk, NY: M. E. Sharpe.
Holloway, Sarah L., and Gill Valentine, eds. 2000. *Children's Geographies: Playing, Living, Learning*. London: Routledge.
Hunter, Robert. 1904. *Poverty*. New York: Macmillan.
Johnson, E. S. 1935. "Child Labor Legislation." In E. Brandeis and J. R. Commons (eds.), *History of Labor in the United States, 1896–1932*. New York: Macmillan.
Kelley, Florence. 1905. *Some Ethical Gains through Legislation*. New York: Macmillan.
Labaree, David. 2011. "Citizens and Consumers: Changing Visions of Virtue and Opportunity in US Education, 1841–1954." in D. Trohler et al. (eds.), *Schooling and the Making of Citizens in the Long Nineteenth Century: Comparative Visions*. New York: Routledge.
Lathrop, Julia. 1919. "The States and Child Labor, United States." Children's Bureau. Publication 58. Washington: Government Printing Office. Accessed via Hathi Trust, https://www.hathitrust.org.
Lindenmeyer, Kriste. 1997. *"A Right to Childhood": The US Children's Bureau and Child Welfare, 1912–1946*. Urbana: University of Illinois Press.
Lindsey, B. B. 1905. "Child Labor Legislation and the Methods of its Enforcement: The Western States." *Addresses at the First Annual Meeting of the NCLC, NYC*. New York: National Child Labor Committee, pp. 94–101. Accessed via Hathi Trust, https://www.hathitrust.org.
Lovejoy, Owen R. 1905. "The Test of Effective Child Labor Legislation." *Addresses at the First Annual Meeting of the NCLC, NYC*. New York: National Child Labor Committee, pp. 45–52. Accessed via Hathi Trust, https://www.hathitrust.org.
McDowell, J. R. 1909. "The Difficulties of Child-Labor Legislation in a Southern State." *The Child Workers of the Nation: Proceedings of the Fifth Annual Conference, Chicago, IL*. New York: National Child Labor Committee, pp. 166–71. Accessed via Hathi Trust, https://www.hathitrust.org.
McKelway, A. J. 1905. "Child Labor in Southern Industry." *Addresses at the First Annual Meeting of the NCLC, NYC*. New York: National Child Labor Committee, pp. 16–22. Accessed via Hathi Trust, https://www.hathitrust.org.
Mills, Sarah. 2013. " 'An Instruction in Good Citizenship': Scouting and the Historical Geographies of Citizenship Education." *Transactions of the Institute of British Geographers* 38: 120–34.
Mintz, Steven. 2004. *Huck's Raft: A History of American Childhood*. Cambridge, MA: Belknap Press.
Moehling, Carolyn. 1999. State Child Labor Laws and the Decline of Child Labor. *Explorations in Economic History*, 35: 72–106.
National Child Labor Committee. 1928. *Child Labor Facts*. Publication 343. New York: National Child Labor Committee. Accessed via Hathi Trust, https://www.hathitrust.org.
National Child Labor Committee. 1938. *Child Labor Facts*. Publication 372. New York: National Child Labor Committee. Accessed via Hathi Trust, https://www.hathitrust.org.
Plessy v. Ferguson. 1896. Text available at https://www.loc.gov/item/usrep163537.
Riis, Jacob A. 1892. *The Children of the Poor*. New York: Charles Scribner's Sons.
Sallee, Shelley. 2004. *The Whiteness of Child Labor Reform in the New South*. Athens: University of Georgia Press.
Schmidt, James D. 2010. *Industrial Violence and the Legal Origins of Child Labor*. Cambridge: Cambridge University Press.
Schuman, M. 2017. "History of Child Labor in the United States—Part 2: The Reform Movement." *Monthly Labor Review*, January. Bureau of Labor Statistics. https://www.bls.gov/opub/mlr/2017/article/history-of-child-labor-in-the-united-states-part-2-the-reform-movement.htm.
Shapiro, Eliza. 2019. "Desegregation Plan: Eliminate all Gifted Programs in NY." *New York*

Times, August 27. https://www.nytimes.com/2019/08/26/nyregion/gifted-programs-nyc-desegregation.html.
Simmons, LaKisha. 2015. *Crescent City Girls: The Lives of Young Black Women in Segregated New Orleans.* Chapel Hill: University of North Carolina Press.
Trattner, Walter I. 1970. *Crusade for the Children: A History of the National Child Labor Committee and Child Labor Reform in America.* Chicago: Quadrangle Books.
Wells, Karen. 2011. "The Politics of Life: Governing Childhood." *Global Studies of Childhood* 1 (1): 15–25. http://dx.doi.org/10.2304/gsch.2011.1.1.15.
Wilkerson, Isabel. 2010. *The Warmth of Other Suns: The Epic Story of America's Great Migration.* New York: Random House.
Zelizer, Viviana. 1985. *Pricing the Priceless Child: The Changing Social Value of Children.* Princeton, NJ: Princeton University Press.

CHAPTER 2

PROTECTING YOUTH: THE DISMANTLING OF YOUTH AS A "PARTICULAR SOCIAL GROUP" IN CONTEMPORARY ASYLUM LAW

Kristina M. Campbell

In its 1985 precedent decision *Matter of Acosta*, the Board of Immigration Appeals (BIA) defined "membership in a particular social group" for purposes of receiving protection under US asylum law (*Matter of Acosta* 1985). The right to asylum is codified in the Refugee Act of 1980, which is based on the 1951 Convention Relating to the Status of Refugees, provides protection to persons who have a well-founded fear of persecution on account of their race, religion, ethnicity, political opinion, or membership in a particular social group.[1] In *Acosta*, the BIA defined "membership in a particular social group" as an individual having a well-founded fear of persecution on account of his or her membership in "a group of persons, all of whom share a common, immutable characteristic. i.e., a characteristic that either is beyond the power of the individual members of the group to change or is so fundamental to their identities or consciences that it ought not be required to be changed."[2] Although it has long been argued by advocates that age can be considered a "common, immutable characteristic" sufficient to satisfy the *Acosta* test for establishing membership in a particular social group (Foster 2007; Ben-Arieh n.d.),[3] subsequent revisions of the requirements for a cognizable particular social group by the BIA in the last dozen years have brought into question what, exactly, is required to sufficiently articulate "membership in a particular social group" for youth who are fleeing persecution in their homelands.

The construct developed by the BIA in recent years requires that an individual seeking asylum on account of their membership in a particular social group needs to prove not only that they are a member of a group that is immutable, but also that the group is also "particular" and "socially distinct."[4] Because many—if not most—of the youth currently seeking protection from persecution in the United States are fleeing gang violence and recruitment, as well as sexual violence and involuntary servitude, it has become increasingly difficult for young asylum seekers to prove that their persecution has occurred on account of a protected ground. In this chapter, I will discuss the consequences—both intended and unintended—of the deconstruction of the term "youth," and how it is used as a qualifying or disqualifying element in the definition of what constitutes membership in a "particular social group" in light of contemporary BIA case law. I will also discuss how advocates can develop novel legal arguments and strategies going forward to develop precedents that protect vulnerable youth fleeing persecution from private actors in the future.

INTRODUCTION: PERSECUTION "ON ACCOUNT OF" A PROTECTED GROUND IN ASYLUM AND REFUGEE LAW

The 1980 Refugee Act, which is based on the 1951 Convention Relating to the Status of Refugees, requires individuals seeking asylum in the United States to prove that they have a well-founded fear of persecution on account of an enumerated protected ground—race, religion, ethnicity, political opinion, or membership in a particular social group. The most difficult part of proving grounds for an asylum claim is often showing nexus between the feared persecution and the protected ground asserted. Recently, however, the legal sufficiency of the protected ground itself has become hotly contested, particularly in US asylum law. This is due to the changing and inconsistent definitions—in both domestic and international law—of what exactly a "particular social group" is, and what is necessary for one to have membership in such a group in order to be entitled to protection from persecution in asylum and refugee law.

In July 2018, when former United States attorney general Jefferson Sessions III issued a precedent decision in the BIA case *Matter of A-B-*, he stated that "generally, claims by aliens pertaining to domestic violence perpetrated by non-governmental actors will not qualify for asylum" (*Matter of A-B-* 2018, 320). Even more troubling, in July 2019, Attorney General William Barr issued a precedent decision in *Matter of L-E-A-*, which purports to hold—contrary to decades of precedent—that "most nuclear families are not inherently socially distinct and therefore do not qualify as 'particular social groups'" (*Matter of L-E-A-* 2019, 589).

The attorney general's decision in *Matter of L-E-A-* is not only an attack on what the United States Court of Appeals for the Ninth Circuit has called "the quintessential particular social group" (*Flores-Rios v. Lynch* 2015); it is an attack on the ability of young people to avail themselves of protection on account of a protected ground. For example, the respondent in *Matter of L-E-A-* claimed that he had been persecuted on account of his membership in the particular social group of his father's immediate family. More specifically, the respondent had been kidnapped by members of a Mexican drug cartel, *La Familia Michoacana*, as retaliation against his father for refusing to sell their drugs in his store (*Matter of L-E-A-* 2019, 583). The attorney general rejected the respondent's claim of persecution on the grounds that his purported social group was not a "particular social group" within the meaning of the Immigration and Nationality Act (INA) (ibid., 586).

Because many of the people worldwide who are currently seeking asylum on the basis of persecution by private actors are fleeing gang violence and domestic violence from nongovernment persecutors,[5] the relevance of the definition of "membership in a particular social group" has become especially important when evaluating the merits of these asylum claims under United States law. The attorney general's recent decisions interpreting the definition of "membership in a particular social group" to exclude from protection the family members of individuals persecuted by private actors is in direct conflict with guidance issued by the UNHCR Asylum Lawyers Project to protect youth fleeing persecution by private actors, especially Central American youth fleeing gang violence (UNHCR Asylum Lawyers Project 2016).[6]

THE MEANING OF "MEMBERSHIP IN A PARTICULAR SOCIAL GROUP" IN US ASYLUM LAW: THE *ACOSTA* STANDARD

The meaning of "membership in a particular social group" has been debated internationally since the inception of the 1951 convention, and likewise, its meaning has evolved considerably in the United States over the years. As previously noted, the BIA first clarified the meaning of "membership in a particular social group" in its precedent decision, *Matter of Acosta*, in 1985. In explaining the origin of the right to seek asylum based on fear of persecution on account of membership in a particular social group, the BIA explained that the ground "comes directly from the Protocol and the U.N. Convention"

(*Matter of Acosta* 1985, 232). The BIA went on to state, however, that "Congress did not indicate what it understood this ground to mean, nor is its meaning clear in the Protocol," ultimately concluding that

> [W]e find the well-established doctrine of *ejusdem generis*, meaning literally, "of the same kind," to be the most helpful in construing the phrase "membership in a particular social group" . . . Applying the doctrine of *ejusdem generis*, we interpret the phrase "persecution on account of membership in a particular social group" to mean persecution that is directed toward an individual who is a member of a group of persons all of whom share a common, immutable characteristic. (ibid., 233)

Thus, beginning with the *Acosta* decision in 1985, immigration trial courts, administrative bodies, and federal courts of appeals in the United States began analyzing asylum claims based on persecution on account of "membership in a particular social group" by first asking whether members of the particular social group shared a "common, immutable characteristic" (ibid., 233). The BIA further clarified in *Acosta* that "whatever the common characteristic that defines the group, it must be one that the members of the group cannot change, or should not be required to change because it is fundamental to their individual identities or consciences" (ibid.). The BIA also clarified that in this analysis, "[t]he particular kind of group characteristic that will qualify under this construction remains to be determined on a case-by-case basis" (ibid.).

MATTER OF C-A-: THE ADDITION OF THE "SOCIAL VISIBILITY" REQUIREMENT FOR PARTICULAR SOCIAL GROUPS

The *Acosta* standard for the meaning of "membership in a particular group" remained controlling precedent until 2006, when the BIA issued its decision in *Matter of C-A-*. In this precedent decision, the BIA announced a new test for determining whether a particular social group is sufficiently cognizable to sustain a claim of membership in that group as grounds for protection from persecution. While reaffirming the "common, immutable characteristic" standard announced in *Acosta* (*Matter of C-A- 2006*, 955), the BIA also announced the application of a new standard for determining the "cognizability" of a particular social group: social visibility (ibid., 959).

The BIA stated that "[t]he recent *Guidelines* issued by the United Nations confirm that 'visibility' is an important element in identifying the existence of a particular social group. The *Guidelines* explain that the social group category was not meant to be a 'catch all' applicable to all persons fearing persecution"

(*Matter of C-A-* 2006, 960, emphasis in original). Thus, in order to determine whether or not a particular social group is sufficiently visible, the BIA concluded that because "the *Guidelines* state that 'a social group cannot be defined *exclusively* by the fact that it is targeted for persecution . . . persecutory action toward a group may be a relevant factor in determining the *visibility* of a group in a particular society'" (ibid., emphasis in original).

The addition of the "social visibility" requirement by the BIA in the particular social group analysis under US law caused confusion about how it should be applied almost immediately by adjudicators. In response, United States Citizenship and Immigration Services (USCIS) issued a policy memorandum on January 12, 2007, providing guidance on how to apply the new requirements for analyzing the legal sufficiency of a particular social group in light of the BIA's decision in *Matter of C-A-* (USCIS 2007). The policy memorandum explains that

> While either immutability or fundamentality is required of any particular social group, the fact that a characteristic is immutable or fundamental does not alone mean that those who share it are necessarily members of a particular social group . . . Under *Matter of C-A-*, a particular social group must also have "social visibility." . . . In other words, the group must be recognizable and distinct in the society; often, a distinctive trait shared among group members will be an indication that the group is perceived as socially visible or distinct. (ibid.)

USCIS also emphasized in its policy memorandum that "[t]he social 'visibility' or 'distinction' test is not an alternate test for establishing a social group, when an immutable or fundamental characteristic is not present" (USCIS 2007). This is because, as the USCIS memorandum notes, "[s]ome international guidance might be read as applying it as an alternate test" (ibid.). Therefore, although guidance was issued to assist in the interpretation and application of the new "social visibility" requirement for particular social groups, the new standard remained amorphous and difficult to apply consistently in practice.

MATTER OF S-E-G-: YOUTH AND THE DEVELOPMENT OF NEW REQUIREMENTS FOR PARTICULAR SOCIAL GROUPS

Shortly after the BIA's decision in *Matter of C-A-*, the BIA issued another precedent decision concerning what constitutes a particular social group (PSG) with its holding in *Matter of A-M-E- & J-G-U-* in 2007, holding that "[f]actors to be considered in determining whether a particular social group exists include whether the group's shared characteristic gives the members the requisite social visibility to make them readily identifiable in society and whether the group can be defined with sufficient particularity to delimit its membership" (*Matter of A-M-E- & J-G-U-* 2007). This time, the BIA held that in addition to immutability and social visibility, a PSG must also be "particular" (ibid.), which the BIA has interpreted to mean that a cognizable group "must also be discrete and have definable boundaries—it must not be amorphous, overbroad, diffuse, or subjective" (*Matter of M-E-V-G-* 2014). Finally, in 2008, the BIA issued its precedent decision in *Matter of S-E-G-*, in which the BIA applied all three new particular social group requirements to a specific group of persons: youth.

Matter of C-A- had concerned whether confidential police informants in Colombia were a particular social group within the meaning of the statute, and *Matter of A-M-E- & J-G-U-* rejected the respondents' argument that their status as "affluent Guatemalans gave them sufficient social visibility to be perceived as a group by society or that the group was defined with adequate particularity to constitute a particular social group" (*Matter of A-M-E- & J-G-U-* 2007). *Matter of S-E-G-* was the first in a line of cases that questioned whether groups of young people—specifically, groups of young men who are subject to gang recruitment in Central America—are the type of groups protected from persecution under domestic and international refugee law.

The Respondents in *Matter of S-E-G-* were Salvadoran youth, a female aged nineteen and her sixteen-year-old brothers, who fled El Salvador on account of persecution they suffered at the hands of the transnational criminal organization the Mara Salvatrucha, or MS-13 (*Matter of S-E-G-* 2008, 579). The brothers had been harassed, stolen from, and beaten by MS-13 members, and their older sister was threatened with rape, if they did not join the gang (ibid., 580). On one occasion, the brothers were told that "their bodies might end up in a dumpster or the street someday" if they did not acquiesce to the demands of the gang (ibid.).

After the siblings fled to the United States, they sought asylum on account of their membership in two particular social groups: (1) Salvadoran youth who have been subjected to recruitment efforts by MS-13 and who have rejected or resisted membership in the gang based on their own personal, moral, and religious opposition to the gang's values and activities, and (2) family members of such Salvadoran youth (*Matter of S-E-G-* 2008, 581). The immigration judge found that the respondents failed to prove that there was a nexus between their past persecution or their well-founded fear of future persecution on account of a protected ground and rejected their claims (ibid.).

On appeal, the BIA considered whether the respondents' first proposed particular social group—Salvadoran youths who have resisted gang recruitment, or family members of such Salvadoran youth—"constitutes a 'particular social group' cognizable under section 101(a)(42) of the Act" (*Matter of S-E-G-* 2008, 582). The BIA stated that "[i]n deciding this question, we are guided by our recent decisions holding that membership in a purported social group requires that the group have particular and well defined boundaries, and that it possess a recognized level of social visibility" (ibid.).

Most troubling in its decision in *Matter of S-E-G-* is the BIA's commentary on the very nature of "youth" and its relationship to gang recruitment for the purpose of seeking protection from persecution. Regarding "youth," the BIA stated that

> We agree with the Immigration Judge that "youth" is not an entirely immutable characteristic but is, instead, by its very nature, a temporary state that changes over time. The mutability of age is reflected in this case by the fact that the male respondents are now 18 years old, and the female respondent is 21. Therefore, the respondents are no longer considered "children," as that term is commonly understood. In saying this, however, we acknowledge that the mutability of age is not within one's control, and that if an individual has been persecuted in the past on account of an age-described particular social group, or faces such persecution at a time when that individual's age places him within the group, a claim for asylum may still be cognizable. (*Matter of S-E-G-* 2008, 583)

By holding that " 'youth' is not an entirely immutable characteristic" (ibid.) while at the same time acknowledging that "the mutability of age is not within one's control" and that it may still be possible for someone to be part of a cognizable "age-described particular social group," the BIA has put youth seeking protection from persecution on account of a protected ground in an untenable situation. In what cases will youth whose age has been "at least one central reason"[7] for their persecution be able to demonstrate that their age is a sufficiently immutable characteristic—to say nothing of the BIA's new particularity and social visibility requirements?

By instituting a "particularity" requirement for PSGs to be recognized as sufficient grounds for receiving protection from harm in addition to the *Acosta* standard and the already amorphous "social visibility" requirement, the BIA cleverly—and rather disingenuously—found a legal way to address the "floodgates" concern of Central American migration to the United States (see Cheng

2011). The BIA did this by cloaking it in ostensibly neutral language applicable to all asylum applicants seeking protection on account of their membership in a particular social group: "This generalisation feeds into the floodgates argument, the fear of letting in more immigrants when the general perception is that there are already too many. If fear of gangs is grounds for being granted asylum, a huge number of people would suddenly qualify, it is argued" (Cheng 2011, 51).

However, as the BIA precedent decisions concerning the interpretation and analysis of "membership in a particular social group" demonstrates, applying a "particularity" requirement for groups to be cognizable, *Matter of A-M-E- & J-G-U-* in addition to the existing requirements of immutability and social visibility, had the effect of foreclosing most—if not all—claims for asylum based on persecution by transnational criminal organizations.[8]

USING VULNERABLE YOUTH TO REDEFINE THE MEANING OF A PARTICULAR SOCIAL GROUP: *MATTER OF E-A-G-*, *MATTER OF W-G-R-*, AND *MATTER OF M-E-V-G-*

Following its precedent decision rejecting youth and gang recruitment as a cognizable particular social group for the purposes of seeking protection from persecution in *Matter of S-E-G-*, the BIA doubled down on its attempts to completely reshape the interpretation and analysis of the meaning of "membership in a particular social group" under the INA§ 208. In 2008, the BIA issued its precedent decision in *Matter of E-A-G-*, which held that the respondent, "a young Honduran male, failed to establish that he was a member of a particular social group of 'persons resistant to gang membership,' as the evidence failed to establish that members of Honduran society, or even gang members themselves, would perceive those opposed to gang membership as members of a social group" *(Matter of E-A-G-* 2008). The BIA further held that "[b]ecause membership in a criminal gang cannot constitute membership in a particular social group, the respondent could not establish that he was a member of a particular social group of 'young persons who are perceived to be affiliated with gangs' based on the incorrect perception by others that he is such a gang member" (ibid.).

The particular social group rejected by the BIA concerning youth in *Matter of E-A-G-* set the stage for the BIA's remarkable decisions on the interpretation of what is sufficient for establishing membership in a particular social group in the precedent decisions of *Matter of W-G-R-* and *Matter of M-E-V-G-* in 2014. First, in *Matter of W-G-R-*, the BIA made several holdings that attempted to clarify the meanings of their previous social group precedent decisions. First, the BIA held that "[i]n order to clarify that the 'social visibility' element required to establish a cognizable 'particular social group' does not mean literal or 'ocular' visibility, that element is renamed as 'social distinction' " (*Matter of W-G-R-* 2014). The BIA was required to rename the "social visibility" requirement due to the erroneous interpretation of the meaning of the phrase by many immigration judges, requiring the intervention of several federal circuit courts of appeals to clarify the meaning of the term.[9] Second, after once again confirming the necessity of demonstrating that a particular social group is immutable, particularly, and "socially distinct within the society in question" (ibid.), the BIA held that "[a]n applicant has the burden of demonstrating not only the existence of a cognizable particular social group and his membership in that particular social group, but also a risk of persecution 'on account of' his membership in that group" (ibid.).

Third, and finally, the BIA used the facts of the respondent's case in *Matter of W-G-R-* to once again stress its previous findings that "youth"—in particular, youth who have been persecuted by transnational criminal organizations—is not, in and of itself, a "particular social group" in which membership alone is sufficient to lead to eligibility to seek asylum on account of a protected group. The BIA held in *Matter of W-G-R-* that the respondent was ineligible for asylum because of a well-founded fear of persecution on account of his membership in a particular social group because the respondent had not proved that " 'former members of the *Mara 18* gang in El Salvador who have renounced their gang membership' constitute a 'particular social group' or that there is a nexus between the harm [the respondent] fears and his status as a former gang member" (ibid.).

In its analysis about why former gang membership is not a cognizable particular social group for purposes of asylum, the BIA relies heavily on its newly-created element of "particularity" to justify its interpretation of the requirements of a cognizable PSG.[10] This is very important because, as the BIA notes in a footnote, several circuit courts of appeals had already determined that former gang membership itself is an immutable characteristic (ibid., 215).[11] Thus, under the *Acosta* standard that was used to determine whether a particular social group is cognizable until 2006, youth who were former gang members would have been able to receive protection from persecution on account of their membership in that group if they could demonstrate a nexus between their group membership and their well-founded fear of persecution.

Similarly, in its most recent precedent decision in which the respondent was a vulnerable youth, *Matter of M-E-V-G-* 2014, the BIA rejected the particular social group "Honduran youth who have been actively recruited by gangs but who have refused to join because they oppose the gangs." In *Matter of M-E-V-G-*, the BIA reiterated two of its key holdings in *Matter of E-A-G-* about the renaming of the "social distinction" requirement, and the three-pronged test for proving membership in a cognizable particular social group (*Matter of M-E-V-G-* 2014). Relying on a case from the United States Court of Appeals for the Third Circuit,[12] the BIA stated that "an agency can change or adopt its policies . . . the Board may add new requirements to, or even change, its definition of a 'particular social group' " (ibid., 229).[13]

The precedent decision in *Matter of M-E-V-G-* is particularly notable because the BIA gives a rather lengthy explanation of why it has decided to abandon the *Acosta* interpretation of "membership in a particular social group" and add the new requirements of "social distinction" and "particularity." The BIA stated:

> *Matter of Acosta* was decided based on whether a common immutable characteristic existed . . . Because there was no common immutable characteristic in Matter of Acosta, we did not reach the question whether there should be additional requirements on group composition. At the time we issued *Matter of Acosta,* only 5 years after enactment of the Refugee Act of 1980, relatively few particular social group claims had been presented to the Board. Given the ambiguity and the potential breadth of the phrase "particular social group," we favored a case-by-case determination of the particular kind of group characteristics that would qualify under the Act . . . This flexible approach enabled courts to apply the particular social group definition within a wide array of fact-specific asylum claims. Now, close to three decades after Acosta, claims based on social group membership are numerous and varied. The generality permitted by the *Acosta* standard provided flexibility in the adjudication of asylum claims. *However, it also led to confusion and a lack of consistency as adjudicators struggled with various possible social groups, some of which appeared to be created exclusively for asylum purposes.* To provide clarification and address the evolving nature of the claims presented by asylum applicants, we refined the particular social group interpretation first discussed in *Matter of Acosta* to provide the additional analysis required once an applicant demonstrated membership based on a common immutable characteristic. (*Matter of M-E-V-G-* 2014, 231–32, emphasis added)

The BIA's claim that additional factors were necessary to "clarify" what constitutes a cognizable particular social group for the purposes of asylum is suspect, especially given the language in *Matter of M-E-V-G-* that "some [possible social groups] appeared to be created exclusively for asylum purposes" (ibid.).

It defies logic to claim that part of "simplifying" the interpretation of the meaning of a phrase requires that two additional, confusing, and amorphous standards be applied. Moreover, the fact that *all* of the precedent decisions issued by the BIA involving the interpretation of the phrase "particular social group" between 2006 and 2014 concerned claims by respondents who were fleeing persecution by transnational criminal organizations, along with the dicta in *Matter of M-E-V-G-* alleging that certain particular social groups were created only for the purposes of seeking asylum, gives support to the argument that the BIA's reinterpretation of the meaning of "particular social group" was done in order to foreclose legitimate asylum claims by individuals fleeing gang recruitment and persecution.[14] As most of these individuals are Central American youth, the result has been the opposite of what the BIA claimed it was trying to do—an increase in incredibly complicated, inconsistent, and confusing case law concerning who may receive asylum on account of their membership in a particular social group, and who may not.[15]

MATTER OF A-B- AND *MATTER OF L-E-A-:* THINLY VEILED ATTACKS AGAINST CENTRAL AMERICAN WOMEN AND YOUTH SEEKING ASYLUM

The ability of individuals to seek asylum on account of persecution by private actors, especially women and youth, came under direct attack by the BIA in 2018 and 2019. In June 2018, then attorney general Jefferson Sessions issued a BIA precedent decision in *Matter of A-B-* (2018). *Matter of A-B-* overruled the 2014 BIA precedent decision *Matter of A-R-C-G-*, which held that "married women in Guatemala who are unable to leave their relationship" is a cognizable particular social group (*Matter of A-R-C-G-* 2014). However, rather than just overruling the BIA decision in *Matter of A-R-C-G-*, Sessions used the decision to narrow the definition of "particular social group" in manner that excludes women and youth who are victims of gang violence and domestic violence:

> Social groups defined by their vulnerability to private criminal activity likely lack the particularity required under *M-E-V-G-*, given that broad

swaths of society may be susceptible to victimization. For example, groups comprising persons who are "resistant to gang violence" and susceptible to violence from gang members on that basis "are too diffuse to be recognized as a particular social group." ... Victims of gang violence often come from all segments of society, and they possess no distinguishing characteristic or concrete trait that would readily identify them as members of such a group. (*Matter of A-B-* 2018, 335)

Sessions's dicta in *Matter of A-B-* is an obvious attack on the ability of victims of domestic violence and gang persecution to receive asylum on account of their membership in a particular social group. He concludes the decision with the following rumination, which leaves no doubt *Matter of A-B-* was intended to foreclose the availability of asylum to women and youth seeking refuge in the United States on account of persecution by private actors:

In reaching these conclusions, I do not minimize the vile abuse that the respondent reported she suffered at the hands of her ex-husband or the harrowing experiences of many other victims of domestic violence around the world. I understand that many victims of domestic violence may seek to flee from their home countries to extricate themselves from a dire situation or to give themselves the opportunity for a better life. But the "asylum statute is not a general hardship statute." *Velasquez*, 866 F.3d at 199 (Wilkinson, J., concurring). As Judge Wilkinson correctly recognized, the Board's recent treatment of the term "particular social group" is "at risk of lacking rigor." ... Nothing in the text of the INA supports the suggestion that Congress intended "membership in a particular social group" to be "some omnibus catch-all" for solving every "heart-rending situation." (*Matter of A-B-* 2018, 346)

Sessions's decision in *Matter of A-B-* was meant to be a death blow to the asylum claims of women and youth seeking protection on account of their membership in a particular social group. However, in July 2019, new attorney general William Barr took the efforts to deconstruct the meaning of "particular social group" to exclude women and youth even further. Contrary to decades of precedent at both the BIA and in federal circuit courts of appeals, Barr overruled the 2017 BIA decision *Matter of L-E-A-*, which held that members of an immediate family may constitute a particular social group (*Matter of L-E-A-* 2017). In his 2019 decision overruling *Matter of L-E-A-*, Barr concluded that "most nuclear families are not socially distinct and therefore do not qualify as 'particular social groups.'" He stated that:

> All particular social groups must satisfy the criteria set forth in *Matter of M-E-V-G-* and *Matter of W-G-R-*, and a proposed family-based group is no different. An applicant must establish that his specific family group is defined with sufficient particularity and is socially distinct in his society. In the ordinary case, a family group will not meet that standard, because it will not have the kind of identifying characteristics that render the family socially distinct within the society in question. (*Matter of L-E-A-* 2019, 586)

Attorney General Barr's attack on family as a "particular social group" is an unabashed attempt to prevent Central American refugees—who are primarily women and youth—from availing themselves of protection from persecution. The respondent in the 2017 decision in *Matter of L-E-A-* was determined to have presented membership in the cognizable social group of his immediate family (*Matter of L-E-A-* 2017, 40, 42). The respondent in *Matter of L-E-A-* had been targeted by gang members in his native Mexico because his father would not allow them to sell drugs at his store (ibid., 41). Consistent with decades of precedent, the BIA relied on its own precedent to affirm that the respondent's claim of membership in a nuclear family was a cognizable particular social group (ibid., 42). However, Barr stated:

> I recognize that a number of courts of appeals have issued opinions that recognize a family-based social group as a "particular social group" under the asylum statute . . . These decisions do not purport to contradict the Board's "particular social group" framework and, in my view, they have relied upon outdated dicta from the Board's early cases . . . the reference to "kinship ties" in *Matter of Acosta* provides no justification for a broad assumption that an applicant's nuclear family will constitute a valid particular social group in his society. (*Matter of L-E-A-* 2019, 589–90)

This complete repudiation of the *Acosta* standard by Barr leaves no doubt that the deconstruction of the definition of "particular social group" has all but foreclosed the availability of asylum for persecuted youth in the United States. Although recent BIA precedents do not explicitly state that this is the intention, the results are clear in practice (see American Immigration Lawyers Association 2019). Without an act of Congress to clarify the meaning of "particular social group," the availability of asylum on account of this ground looks bleak for persecuted youth.

CONCLUSION: PROTECTING VULNERABLE YOUTH UNDER THE NEW LEGAL CONSTRUCTION OF "MEMBERSHIP IN A PARTICULAR SOCIAL GROUP"

The BIA's creation of these two additional prongs for demonstrating membership in a particular social group, and the fact that all of the precedent cases decided by the BIA between 2006 and 2014 involved individuals who feared persecution by transnational criminal organizations, strongly supports the argument that the BIA crafted this new, three-pronged test for determining whether a particular social group is cognizable for the purpose of seeking asylum on account of a protected ground. Even before these decisions, practitioners and scholars of asylum and refugee law had argued that the interpretation and analysis of the term "membership in a particular social group" was disproportionately affecting the ability of Central American youth fleeing persecution by transnational criminal organizations to apply for and receive protection (Uchimaya 2013, 109, 111).

In recent years, there has been a movement by experts in the field to return to the *Acosta* standard for determining whether an individual has a well-founded fear of persecution on account of his "membership in a particular social group"—whether that group shares a common, immutable characteristic that is fundamental to their identity and that cannot or should not be changed (*Matter of Acosta 1985*). Although the mutability of age is often debated, other scholars have argued convincingly that age may be considered an immutable characteristic in the context of both gang membership and gang recruitment.[16] Thus, if vulnerable youth will be able to avail themselves of the protection from persecution that they deserve under both domestic and international law, there needs to be a coordinated, sustained effort by advocates and scholars to reframe what is necessary to demonstrate "membership in a particular social group" under the framework currently in place in United States jurisprudence.

NOTES

1. *See* United Nations High Commissioner for Refugees (UNHCR), Convention and Protocol Relating to the Status of Refugees, text of 1951 Convention Relating to the Status of Refugees and text of 1967 Protocol Relating to the Status of Refugees. Available at https://www.unhcr.org/protect/PROTECTION/3b66c2aa10.pdf.
2. *See* 8 U.S.C. § 1158(b)(1)(B).
3. *See generally* Foster (arguing that age can be an immutable characteristic, since being

young and vulnerable often identifies one as a target for persecution); *see also* Ben-Arieh (n.d.; "In response to deportation orders, in the early 2000, lawyers began to argue that Salvadoran youth faced persecution as perceived or actual gang members.")
4. See infra.
5. See Ben-Arieh, supra note 3 ("In most gang-related claims, the persecution involves non-state actors"). Also see para. 65 of the *UNHCR Handbook on Procedures and Criteria for Determining Refugee States* (hereafter UNHCR Handbook), stating that persecution may "emanate from sections of the population that do not respect the standards established by the laws of the country concerned." The UNHCR Handbook further provides that "[w]here serious discriminatory or other offensive acts are committed by the local populace, they can be considered as persecution if they are knowingly tolerated by the authorities or if the authorities refuse, or prove unable, to offer effective protection."
6. See UNHCR Asylum Lawyers Project ("UNHCR has taken the view that the refugee definition, found in Article 1 of the 1951 Convention relating to the Status of Refugees and Article 1 of the 1967 Protocol relating to the Status of Refugees, 2 should be read to encompass claims from Central American children fleeing gang recruitment and/or gang related harms").
7. 8 U.S.C. § 1158(b)(1)(B).
8. *See generally* Ben-Arieh, note 3.
9. *See e.g. Temu v. Holder*, 740 F.3d 887 (4th Cir. 2014).
10. Explaining that "youth" as a particular social group is not sufficiently particular because it "falls outside the 'outer limit' of the particular social group definition."
11. "Other circuits disagree as to whether former gang membership is an immutable characteristic. Compare *Cantarero v. Holder*, 734 F.3d 82, 85–86 (1st Cir. 2013) (holding that former gang membership is not an immutable characteristic), with *Martinez v. Holder*, No. 12-2424, 2014 WL 243293 (4th Cir. Jan. 23, 2014) (holding that former gang membership is an immutable characteristic), *Urbina-Mejia v. Holder*, 597 F.3d 360, 366 (6th Cir. 2010) (same), and *Benitez Ramos v. Holder*, 589 F.3d 426, 430 (7th Cir. 2009) (same)."
12. *Johnson v. Ashcroft*, 286 F.3d 696 (3rd Cir. 2002).
13. Quoting *Johnson v. Ashcroft*, 286 F.3d 696 (3rd Cir. 2002), 700.
14. See Ben-Arieh, *supra* note 3: "American courts rejected asylum claims based on gang violence on the grounds that the state were [sic] trying to crack down on gang violence. They routinely held that, even though the claimant was credible, the violence was a 'personal problem' rather than 'police neglect' or something the government was 'unable or unwilling' to control."
15. See Ben-Arieh: "[I]n the United States asylum requests from those fleeing gang-related violence in Mexico reached a record 5,551 in 2010. On the other hand, only 165 were granted, meaning that for an individual fleeing gang-related violence, finding protection under the 1951 Refugee Convention is still very difficult."
16. *See e.g.* Foster, *supra* note 3.

REFERENCES

American Immigration Lawyers Association. 2019. "AILA: AG's Decision Ignores Precedent and Is the Latest Attempt to Restrict Asylum." July 29. AILA Doc. No. 19072905. https://www.aila.org/advo-media/press-releases/2019/ags-decision-ignores-precedent-restrict-asylum.

Ben-Arieh, Gayla. N.d. "Gang-Based Asylum Claims." Amera International. https://www.amerainternational.org/gang-based-asylum-claims.

Cheng, Gracye. 2011. "Gang Persecution as Grounds for Asylum in the USA." *Forced Migration Review* 37: 50–51.

Flores-Rios v. Lynch. 807 F.3d 1123, 1128 (9th Cir. 2015).
Foster, Michelle. 2007. *International Refugee Law and Socio-Economic Rights: Refuge from Deprivation.* Cambridge University Press.
Matter of A-B-. 2018. 27 I&N Dec. 316 (A.G. 2018). https://www.justice.gov/eoir/page/file/1070866/download.
Matter of Acosta. 19 I & N 211. (BIA 1985). https://www.justice.gov/sites/default/files/eoir/legacy/2012/08/14/2986.pdf.
Matter of A-M-E- & J-G-U-. 24 I&N Dec. 69 (BIA 2007).
Matter of A-R-C-G-. 26 I&N Dec. 388 (BIA 2014).
Matter of C-A-. 23 I&N Dec. 951 (BIA 2006).
Matter of E-A-G-. 24 I&N Dec. 591 (BIA 2008). https://www.justice.gov/sites/default/files/eoir/legacy/2014/07/25/3618.pdf.
Matter of L-E-A-. 27 I&N Dec. 40 (BIA 2017). https://www.justice.gov/eoir/page/file/969456/download.
Matter of L-E-A-. 27 I&N Dec. 581 (A.G. 2019). https://www.justice.gov/file/1187856/download.
Matter of M-E-V-G-. 26 I & N Dec. 227 (BIA 2014). https://www.justice.gov/sites/default/files/eoir/legacy/2014/07/25/3795.pdf.
Matter of S-E-G-. 24 I&N Dec. 579 (BIA 2008).
Matter of W-G-R-. 26 I & N Dec. 2018 (BIA 2014).
Refugee Act of 1980. PL 96–212, 94 Stat. 102. https://www.archivesfoundation.org/documents/refugee-act-1980.
Uchimaya, Diane. 2013. "Falling through the Cracks: Gang Victims as Casualties in Current Asylum Jurisprudence." *La Raza Law Journal* 23 (1): 109–62.
UNHCR Asylum Lawyers Project. 2016. "UNHCR's Views on Child Asylum Claims: Using International Law to Support Claims from Central American Children Seeking Protection in the US." http://www.unhcr.org/580a77b04.pdf.
USCIS. 2007. "Guidance on Matter of C-A-." https://www.refworld.org/pdfid/4ec3b1ad2.pdf.

CHAPTER 3

"MET WITH THE FULL PROSECUTORIAL POWERS": ZERO-TOLERANCE FAMILY SEPARATIONS, ADVOCACY, AND THE EXCEPTIONALISM OF THE CHILD ASYLUM SEEKER

Leanne Purdum

In June 2018, amid international outrage over the separation of migrant[1] children from the parents with whom they crossed the border, an audio recording was leaked to the public. In it, detained children cry out for their parents. The article accompanying the audio described the cruelty: "They scream 'Mami' and 'Papá' over and over again, as if those are the only words they know. The baritone voice of a Border Patrol agent booms above the crying. 'Well, we have an orchestra here,' he jokes. 'What's missing is a conductor'" (Thompson 2018).

During the summer of 2018, "family separations"[2] dominated national and international news. In response to arrivals of migrants at the US-Mexico border, including parents with children, the president of the United States issued an executive order directing the US attorney general to make the criminal prosecution of immigration offenses a "high priority" (Trump 2017). Unauthorized presence in the US is a civil violation (American Immigration Council 2020), and many immigration cases are treated as civil (non-criminal) matters. However, federal prosecutions, including prosecution of the laws related to illegal entry and illegal reentry,[3] have "accelerated greatly since the

1990s" reaching a two-decade high (Gramlich and Noe-Bustamante 2019). These prosecutions featured a sharp increase between 2017 and 2018, when the events in this chapter took place.[4]

Increasingly, the social construct of the "illegal immigrant" has embedded itself in the geographical imaginary of the nation. A "geographical imaginary" is a taken-for-granted spatial imaginary that is implicated in naturalizing hierarchies and social structures (Gregory 2009). Scholars demonstrate how the concept of the "the illegal immigrant" as a legally and socially defined figure has emerged, gaining attention and power over the last one hundred years (Ngai 2004; Chomsky 2014). Much research examines the results of this created concept becoming deeply embedded in socio-legal structures, depicting an immigration system that criminalizes, polices, detains, and deports migrants with increasing power and diminishing oversight (Stumpf 2006; De Genova and Peutz 2010; Coleman 2012). The US-Mexico border is increasingly policed and militarized (Nevins and Aizeki 2008; De León 2015). Immigration law has become so deeply intertwined with criminal law that scholars combine the two in the concept of "crimmigration" (Stumpf 2006). These concepts are reflected in Erica Meiners's suggestion that instead of "mass incarceration," scholars use the term "targeted criminalization" (2016, 2).

As a result of this increase in crimmigration, immigrant detention is a growing portion of the US carceral system, with over two hundred detention centers throughout the country (Detention Watch Network n.d.). A spate of statutes from the late twentieth century expanded detention and deportation practices (Immigrant Legal Resource Network 2019). Many people are detained for the misdemeanor violation of first time entry without inspection. And adding another layer of complexity to this created social system, corrections corporations boast of the profits earned from detention and deportation.[5]

This criminalization scheme drove policy despite historically low numbers of apprehensions at the US border. In 2018, the high levels of immigration-related prosecutions coincided with numbers of apprehensions at the border far lower than those recorded throughout most of the 1990s and early 2000s (Gramlich and Noe-Bustamante 2019).[6]

It is important to note that many, if not all, of the migrants targeted under the "zero-tolerance" policy described in this chapter are seeking asylum in the US. Later in this chapter I outline many limitations to the asylum system. However, this does not negate the fact that asylum law provides legal protection and safety for many fleeing violence in their home countries. The crimmigration system I introduced above includes increasing scrutiny, sorting, and limitations on persons claiming asylum. Increasingly, those attempting to stop migrants from seeking asylum, such as under the Trump administration's "zero-tolerance" policy, rely on tropes of asylum seekers as "bogus," illegitimate, and taking advantage of overgenerous international law (Mountz 2010). These discourses serve to undergird restrictions on asylum seekers.

Human rights organizations note that seeking asylum protections is legal even when it results in unauthorized entry. In their critiques of the zero-tolerance policy, they cite the fact that parties to the 1951 United Nations Convention Relating to the Status of Refugees, including the US, are prohibited from sanctioning, prosecuting, or otherwise imposing penalties on asylum seekers "on account of their illegal entry or presence" (Human Rights First 2018, 12).

It is under this context that Attorney General Jeff Sessions announced in April 2018: "[An] escalated effort to prosecute those who choose to illegally cross our border... To those who wish to challenge the Trump Administration's commitment to public safety, national security, and the rule of law, I warn you: illegally entering this country will not be rewarded, but will instead be met with the full prosecutorial powers of the Department of Justice" (US Department of Justice 2018). To pursue this "zero-tolerance" policy, Customs and Border Protection (CBP) officers were directed[7] to prioritize prosecutions of unauthorized migrants crossing the border. Persons charged with criminal immigration violations are in custody of the US Marshals Service (USMS) while awaiting trial. The fact that children cannot be held by USMS was used to legitimate the separation of children from parents. Official discourse often portrayed the family separations as a lamentable side effect of prosecution, a mere side effect of prosecuting adults. However, the discourses and actions of officers and policy makers, as well as public discourses about the policy, reveal other motivations that deserve attention.

At the height of public outcry against the systematic separations in summer 2018 2,814 children were identified in federal custody. Over the next year a series of investigations and a court-ordered recount indicated at least 1,556 more separated, with estimates from October 2019 totaling more than 5,400 children (American Civil Liberties Union 2019; Spagat 2019). Ultimately, litigation of *Ms. L. v. ICE* (2018),[8] a class action lawsuit against the family separation policy, led a federal judge to order a stop to the practice in June 2018 (Cheng 2018). However, the court order allowed for an exception: separations could take place if there is "a determination that the parent is unfit or presents a danger to the child," exceptions that advocates argue are exploited to continue separations (Murdza 2020; see also Associated Press 2019; Jordan 2019; Abdel-Motaleb, Lopez, and Udelsman 2020). As a result of these exceptions, while the mass separations may have slowed, they continue at the time of writing.

The analysis in this chapter stems from my volunteer work with detained families, where I saw the consequences of the zero-tolerance policy firsthand. Beginning in 2015, I volunteered as a legal assistant with the Dilley Pro Bono Project,[9] providing services to mothers detained with their children in the South Texas Family Residential Center in Dilley, Texas (hereafter, Dilley). As a volunteer in 2018 I took the declarations of women recently reunited with their children and detained together, often after months of separation. Sections of the declarations I transcribed and translated were included, along with others, in a report published by the American Immigration Council (AIC) and the American Immigration Lawyers Association (AILA) (2018). Other volunteers took declarations that were published by the Dilley Pro Bono Project (2018). The analysis presented in this chapter is based on these declarations, notes from my volunteer experience, and reports from other organizations working with separated parents.

This chapter examines the interplay and co-construction of social discourse and legal categorizations. In the first section of the chapter, I contextualize the zero-tolerance family separations within scholarship on legal categorizations and belonging. I argue that the zero-tolerance policy was far from a neutral application of law and order, and was instead a discretionary show of power against immigrants in a moment of intense struggle over belonging and inclusion in the US. In the second section, I examine the advocacy efforts against the separation policy to show that discourses can have harmful consequences, even from well-intentioned advocates. I analyze how the rhetoric of the exceptionalism of the child limits advocacy, and I look to criminal justice reform and abolitionist framings as pathways forward.

SOCIAL CONSTRUCTION OF LAW AND ZERO-TOLERANCE SEPARATIONS

Scholars examining the social construction of legal systems draw our attention to the categorizations that undergird laws and the power relations that uphold them. The zero-tolerance family separation policy I analyze in this chapter is one acute example in a long history of power struggle over the inclusion and exclusion of people seeking citizenship and other forms of legal inclusion in the US.

Though they have immense impact, the rules of citizenship are created, rather than neutral. Scholars show us that immigration laws do not neutrally filter "legal" from "illegal." Instead, they are products of power struggles over rights, belonging, and inclusion. The beginnings of a solidified conception of US national identity were founded on constructed differences (Welke 2010). Citizenship and full legal participation were reserved for the white, male, and able bodied (ibid.). Importantly, Welke argues that the policing of these categories was an act that defined the identity of the community, noting that "inclusion and privilege of some, in part, was defined by the exclusion and subordination of others." Through the act of determining who was "within" and who was "outside" of citizenship limits, the state produced citizens (8). Close inspection of immigration policy reveals complicated webs of law that facilitate citizenship and legality for some, while producing and perpetuating illegality for others (Ngai 2004). We can see these theories at work in the current struggles over immigration and legal inclusion in the US: the cruel treatment of children and their parents under the guise and of law and order can similarly be understood to legitimate legal systems and their respective constructed identities, such as the rightful citizen, the law abider, or the "illegal" immigrant. Considering this scholarship, then, the act of excluding migrants from legal belonging does the work of nation-building. The discursive and structural creation of rules reaffirms the belonging of members, while performing the exclusion of those unwanted by dominant groups.

During the public debate of the separations, I observed a range of sentiments in online commentary and personal conversations. Some were sympathetic to the plight of separated children but felt that the separations constituted a justifiable consequence of breaking "the law." These comments often did not acknowledge that asylum seeking is legal under international and federal law. Other online comments stated, "that's what you get for coming to my country." De León refers to this rationalization of separation, detention, and deportation as "historical amnesia," resulting in many citizens who "draw stark divisions between the 'noble' European immigrants of the past and Latino border crossers of today,' and erasing the violence that many immigrant groups experienced" (2015, 26). I argue that the term "historical indifference" is also appropriate, whereby citizens (especially ancestors of white Europeans) imagine their own citizenship to be "natural," when it was facilitated by a created legal system and promoted concurrently with the restriction of others based on race, gender, and mental and physical ability. This disconnect of logic results in a callous ability to "put nationality before humanity" (26).

Under the zero-tolerance policy officers often showed apparent disregard for the facts of the case and the legal position of the migrant crossing the border. For example, even though the policy was purportedly targeting those who "choose to illegally cross our border" (US Department of Justice 2018), in some cases children were separated from parents regardless of the legal status of the person crossing the border.[10] Some children were indeed taken from parents after they presented themselves to CBP officers at a legal port of entry as applicants for asylum. For example, a young mother from Guatemala legally presented herself at a port of entry and asked for asylum with her six-year-old daughter. CBP officers told her that she would be going to prison and that her daughter would be taken from her. The officer told her that she "didn't have a right to speak" and that she "had stepped into a country that was not [hers]" (AIC and AILA 2018, 18). The fact that the policy claimed to enforce law and order while separating children from even those who entered the country with no possible charges against them reveals that this policy was far from a neutral application of immigration law.

Another woman who crossed the border recounted that an officer said to her, "What are you doing here? You came to a country that is not yours, and now look at you" (AIC and AILA 2018, 26). Some parents were told they would never see their children again. One recounted an officer saying, "Did you know your children were going to be adopted by families that you don't know?" The officer followed this by stating that forced separation and adoption was "the law right now," even though this was false (author's research journal 2018). The law itself was unchanged, even as officers were urged to prioritize prosecutions. These comments reflect that the concept of "the law" was used to target and exclude migrants from Central America in a cultural moment, framing them as part of a border crisis.

One mother told me she was apprehended by a CBP border officer who smelled of alcohol when she crossed the border. When the officer announced the news that their children would be taken from them, another woman with whom she crossed the border began to pray. The officer mocked them, yelling "Here, there is no God!" (author's research journal 2018). Others I met described the moments when their children were taken from them by officers, one telling of terrified children who "grabbed onto their [mothers'] shirts out of fear and would not let go" (AIC and AILA 2018, 18). Some older children were falsely told that their parents would meet them on a bus, while younger children were physically wrenched out of parents' arms, by officers who put them "in headlocks" (ibid.).

In several documented cases parents were brought to the brink of suicide by the imprisonment and lack of knowledge of their children. One of the women from whom I took a declaration described being so distraught by the separation from her daughter that she contemplated throwing herself from the third floor of the detention center.[11] She survived with the support of another separated mother who pleaded with her to persevere through the trauma and live to see her daughter again (AIC and AILA 2018, 9; author's research journal 2018). Another report, corroborated by a detained mother, told of a father who committed suicide after he was informed that his daughter would be taken from him, perhaps to never be seen again (author's research journal 2018; see also Miroff 2018).

The statements of parents separated from their children demonstrate how these actions, which terrorized migrants seeking to enter the US, were justified as "the law" even as they undercut notions of legality and due process. For example, detained parents navigated the asylum process under extreme duress. Separated mothers and fathers were forced to undergo the asylum screening process, referred to as a "credible fear interview,"[12] without knowledge of their children's whereabouts. One mother described being so distraught that her entire interview consisted of her repeating "I don't want anything, I just want my daughter. Please give me my daughter" (AIC and AILA 2018, 11). Others arrived at the phone kiosk in the detention center expecting their children to be on the other line, only to find an officer waiting to determine their legal opportunity for asylum.

In addition, I heard examples of officers coercing separated parents into waiving their rights to legal processes in exchange for reunification. After this questionable legal process, those whose interviews were denied by asylum officers were forced to sign deportation papers. In many examples, Immigration and Customs Enforcement (ICE) officers took advantage of the emotional distress of separation to force parents to sign deportation orders. One mother described how "[an officer] demanded that she sign deportation papers and yelled at her when she refused. [The officer] became so hostile that she was terrified he would strike her. He physically intimidated her, stood over her, and became red in the face as he demanded she sign the papers" (AIC and AILA 2018, 14). This officer earned the nickname "The Deporter." By attempting to deport this woman, the officer enforces a particular version of "law and order" in which neither the validity of the asylum claim nor the legality and fairness of the process nor the consent of the signee seem to have much importance.

The descriptions of the zero-tolerance separations that I present in this section upset the argument that the zero-tolerance policy was a neutral application of law and order. Moreover, mounting examples of officer actions show questionable legality and a lack of due process. After a temporary injunction halted the zero-tolerance separation policy, parents with final orders of removal were given a form, most of which was in English; only a portion was in Spanish.[13] The form offered two options: be deported without their children, or be reunified and deported with their children. Only after negotiations with the American Civil Liberties Union (ACLU) was the option added of speaking to an attorney before deportation (AIC and AILA 2018, 5). Immigration officers frequently coerced separated parents to abandon their asylum cases in exchange for being reunited with their children. These parents were not informed of the option to continue their legal case and be reunited with their children (Shepherd 2018). Speakers of indigenous languages described being forced to sign the form without any attempts by officers to explain what was happening to them and without any interpretation (AIC and AILA 2018). In another example, separated parents recounted that the forms given to them came pre-populated with a handwritten checkmark placed next to option 1: "I want to be deported with my children" (Arand 2018).

Upon close examination, the discourses, actions, and policies that made up the zero-tolerance policy were far more than neutral enactments of law and order. The zero-tolerance policy was enabled by the legal system, which targets and criminalizes many migrants, yet it was also a discretionary policy during a time of acute struggle over belonging and inclusion. The news reports of sobbing children drew attention the world over. In response to the violence of this policy, protest abounded, and immigration activists and many others concerned with child welfare moved to change the policy. I turn my attention now to these efforts and analyze the discourse, actions, and policies used by advocates of immigrant children.

"FAMILIES TOGETHER": LIMITATIONS OF DISCOURSE AND CONSEQUENCES OF ADVOCACY FOR CHILDREN

In late July 2018, as I drove down the interstate in San Antonio, Texas, I passed two white buses with license plates reading DEPARTMENT OF HOMELAND SECURITY. There were no other markings on the bus. I sped up, followed the buses, and looked in the side windows. Rows of young children were seated inside. I saw tiny ponytails, some small faces looking out the window, and no adults except for a woman wearing a guard's dress shirt sitting directly

Fig. 3.1. A speaker at a protest during the June 2018 Families Together protest in San Antonio, Texas. Signs on stage read "I am in a baby prison!," "We were just asking for asylum," and "Stop the militarization of indigenous lands." Photo credit: Debra Ponce, SA Stands.

behind the driver, solemnly facing the children. These, I was certain, were separated children being transported to facilities where they would be reunited with the parents with whom they crossed the border. While I did not know the exact destination of the buses I passed, this incident took place just days before the court-ordered deadline to reunify all children separated from their parents, and in a location central to both of the family detention centers where some were taken after reunification, including the South Texas Family Residential Center in Dilley.

Most children taken from their parents were eventually returned to them due to the activism and litigation brought by individuals and organizations. Litigation may have been effective at slowing the enactment of separations and requiring reunifications (see *Ms. L. v. ICE*), but the immense public reaction to the cruelty of the zero-tolerance separations likely helped build pressure on the policy. As many as 750 cities held protests against family separations (McCausland, Guadalupe, and Rosenblatt 2018). (See fig. 3.1 for an example of protest.) Crowds ranging from a few dozen to thirty thousand people marched, sang, held rallies, and demanded that children be returned to their parents. A viral fundraiser started by a concerned observer raised more than $20 million for RAICES Texas, a nonprofit (Yaffe-Bellany 2018). The American Academy of Pediatrics and the American College of Physicians spoke out against the harm caused by separations (Kraft 2018; Lopez 2018).

The public uproar against the zero-tolerance separation of children from their parent(s) was, arguably, successful in building pressure against this policy. It is also true, however, that advocates should be aware of the potentially harmful effects of the ways in which they advocate. In this section, I analyze the discourses that were used prominently by a range of advocates against family separations in summer 2018, critiquing some of the ways in which activists and concerned community members utilized framings of children and asylum seekers. Discourses have policy impacts. The language that advocates used to challenge family separations often led to suggested policy changes that circled around implied hierarchies of immigrants based on deservingness. Therefore, I believe it is important to examine and critique the methods that advocates use and the discourses commonly found in struggles for social change. As a long-term member of a pro bono volunteer group and an active member of the Athens Immigrant Rights Coalition, I consider myself to be critiquing *with* advocates rather than critiquing from outside of advocacy groups.

The limitations to advocacy that I describe in this section will elicit little surprise to many seasoned anti-detention and anti-prison organizers. Many organizers and activists orient their work around abolitionist, freedom of movement frameworks as they attempt to shrink or reform a complex prison industrial complex, of which immigrant detention is part. Loyd, Mitchelson, and Burridge, whose edited volume directly bridges anti-detention and anti-prison work, describe how "the shared vision of the abolitionist and no borders agenda fosters the understanding that freedom of movement and freedom to inhabit are necessarily connected" (2012, 10). These movements "challenge institutions of state violence and the apparently neutral ideologies of illegal immigration and criminality" (11).

Broadly speaking, proponents of abolition argue that prisons and detention centers are not places of rehabilitation. Instead, they act as sites of control and warehousing (Garland 2001; Gilmore 2007; Wacquant 2009). Anti-prison organizer Rose Braz explains abolition this way: "Abolition means a world where we do not use prisons, policing, and the larger system of the prison industrial complex as an 'answer' to what are social, political and economic problems" (Samuels and Stein 2008, 11). Therefore, an abolitionist framework considers the power relations that create criminal categories as well as who benefits from walls and cages, and who become targets of policing mechanisms in a highly stratified society. I return to these insights to examine the advocacy efforts against the zero-tolerance family separation policy.

When "Families Together" Means "Families in Detention"

Opposition to the zero-tolerance policy came from a wide range of political positions and vastly different viewpoints on immigration policy. Country-western singer Willie Nelson declared that "Christians everywhere should be up in arms" (Hudak 2018). Former first lady Laura Bush decried the policy, stating, "this zero-tolerance policy is cruel. It is immoral. And it breaks my heart" (Bush 2018). She advocated for a "kinder, more compassionate and more moral" response to migrants, whom she frames in terms of a "crisis" (ibid.). The US Conference of Catholic Bishops framed their opposition to the policy in terms of care for children, who "are not instruments of deterrence, but blessings of God" (2018). They advocated for the creation of immigration enforcement policies that place children in the least restrictive environment, emphasizing to "keep families together" (ibid.).

"Keep families together" was a prominent slogan in the campaigns to end family separations. However, the phrasing reveals a common issue in immigration activism: how to call attention to the suffering of the most vulnerable, in this case, children, without suggesting problematic policy solutions or minimizing the suffering of others. In the case of the "keep families together" slogan, activists were faced with the reality that an end to family separations would not stop the broader practice of criminal prosecutions for unauthorized entry. Instead, upon reunification of the children to their parents, the family units[14] and those arriving after the enactment of zero-tolerance policies would likely be sent to one of the three existing family detention centers, euphemistically called "residential centers." Doctors writing as experts for the Department of Homeland Security Office of Civil Rights and Civil Liberties seemed to understand this risk, referring to the detention of children with a parent as "the likely alternative" to separating parents from their children (Allen and McPherson 2018). In another statement, the American Academy of Pediatrics (AAP) spoke against zero-tolerance separations and noted the limitations to "togetherness": "The [AAP] agrees with ending this abhorrent practice, which drew widespread outcry among pediatricians, advocates, and the American public. Families should remain together . . . Sadly, however, continuing to maintain the 'zero-tolerance' policy will put more children in detention facilities, an environment the AAP states is no place for a child, *even if they are accompanied by their families*" (Kraft 2018, emphasis added).

The comparison of the trauma of family separation to the relative "togetherness" of family detention works to reframe the discourse, causing some to agree that family detention is relatively less violent and therefore a preferable solution to family separation (Purdum 2021).[15] In a striking example, Chuck Todd, host at NBC News, pressed Kellyanne Conway, then an adviser to the president, about the trauma of the zero-tolerance policy. At one point, the exasperated host cries out, "You can keep the families together! Why don't you create a family detention center?" Kellyanne responds, "We had those [family detention centers,] but the Democrats are holding up funding to expand those . . . expanding, really doubling the detention center capacity, we don't have the capacity" (Meet the Press 2018). The family detention centers he suggests could be constructed did (and do, at the time of this writing) already exist.

Here, Todd advocates for the expansion of the detention and deportation regime, through his concern for children. His solution to the violence of separation is merely to offer another, less overtly violent solution that is part of the very same effort to criminalize migration and its accompanying detention regime. By asking only for an end to the practice of family separation, while asking to "keep the families together," Todd proposes exactly the same solution that the Trump and Obama administrations have advocated and fought for over years of litigation: to build and expand family detention. This is a clear example of how the capitulation to the horrors of one policy can be used to expand, entrench, and empower those vested in immigrant detention.

One of the potential policy outcomes of this discourse becomes clear: advocating against family separation and proposing to "keep families together" perpetuates the idea (almost certainly unintentionally by many advocates) that once children are placed back with their parents, it does not matter where they go. Rather than asking, "Under which scenario is detention acceptable?," an abolitionist politics of detention would assert that no humans should be in detention and asks us to consider *why* and *how* people become *detainable*. By perpetuating the idea that detention of a child with their mother is "better," and therefore more acceptable, than family separation, "families together" can assert the notion that some kinds of detention practices are "better" than others, ultimately expanding the detention powers of the state. The knowledge of this pitfall to advocacy is likely what led many organizations to create materials declaring "Families together AND free!" (see fig. 3.2).

Fig. 3.2. A flyer advertises the "Families Belong Together and Free" Rally in El Paso, Texas, on June 30, 2018. Collected by author. Flier creator: Unknown to author

The Exceptionalism of the Child Asylum Seekers: Reifying Criminality of Others

Other predominant discourses emerged in the protests over the separations. Slogans such as "Children don't belong behind bars" and "Asylum is not a crime" were present at events across the country. These slogans intend, no doubt, to call attention to the plight of the most vulnerable in the detention system. Unfortunately, and perhaps as an unintended consequence, the rhetoric of the exceptionalism of some groups, such as the child and the asylum seeker, can have the effect of reifying positions of criminalization for others.

Anthropologist Liisa Malkki offers insight into the modern-day representations of children by humanitarians who offer aid (2015). The focus on the innocence and purity of children releases them from responsibility of their situations and ingratiates children to humanitarians who can envision this child as their own. However, she finds that these representations have consequences, including a "stripping of personhood of the child" that makes it possible for helpers to ignore the child's relationships to other people (101). These relationships would likely reveal ties to many facets of the social constructs of illegality described in this chapter: a separated child may have a detained mother categorized as an asylum seeker or a young brother living in the US and attempting to navigate the legal process, they may be hoping to live with a father long established in the US and subject to deportation because of "illegal presence," or any of many other scenarios that deserve attention from an expanded anti-detention, abolitionist perspective. I analyze two of these categories here as they relate to the advocacy that stemmed from zero-tolerance separation. First, I discuss the limits to the "asylum seeker" category, as it is being limited by the current administration, and the limits inherent to the definition of asylum seeker. Second, I analyze the narrative of criminality that was common through advocacy efforts to show that it has propensity to reinscribe innocence narratives and obscure the power relations and the intersections of the immigration detention system with the American prison system.

First, many advocates framed their opposition to family separations in terms of care for asylum seekers, a common argument being "asylum seekers should not be treated this way." It is true that many of the persons arriving at the US-Mexico border pass the asylum screening interview, called the credible fear interview. Their "positive" results from the interview are testament to the fact that many of the women and children, as well as family members not detained with them, have suffered immense trauma that made them flee to the US. The strength of their legal claims is coupled with the fact that lawyers and legal assistants regularly provide legal orientations and personal legal consultation to detained persons. While there are many dedicated volunteer lawyers, detained women and children receive special attention from pro bono lawyers and are often prepared in ways that single adults in detention may not be. This provides them the necessary knowledge and understanding of the interview, which gives an advantage over those who do not get legal attention.

The assertion that asylum seekers should not have their children forced from them comes with the potential result of naturalizing categories of deservingness of migrants. These categorizations, in which asylum seekers are upheld as more deserving of care than others, undergird the criminalization of migrants and uphold the detention and deportation of those who do *not* pass the asylum screening process. In other words, this framing can reinforce the idea that those not categorized as asylum seekers *do* deserve to have children taken, be detained, or be deported. This stance is problematic when viewed through critical scholarship on the categorization of criminality, which I presented in the previous section.

The Trump administration has drastically limited the legal protections of asylum seekers: the updated legal guidance and law that officers use to determine granting rates has resulted in a downward shift in acceptance rates since 2019. Between 2014, when the South Texas Family Residential Center opened, and 2019, roughly 98 percent of women detained there with their children passed their screening interview with an asylum officer. Recent changes have plummeted these granting rates to between 25 and 50 percent. Specifically, at the time of writing, changes made by the Trump administration include the elimination of client rights during the credible fear process. Detained persons no longer receive advance notice of interviews, have no ability to reschedule interviews, and no longer receive orientation to the credible fear process from US Citizenship and Immigration Services (USCIS). In other recent changes, interviews are now conducted by CBP officers instead of asylum officers from USCIS, many interviews are done by phone instead of in person, and the interviews are almost always conducted by men, which dramatically affects the screening interview process. This situation that can affect the woman's ability to share important details of her case, particularly those who have experienced sexual assault or domestic violence. In addition, the administration's "safe third country" transit ban requires many migrants[16] to pass higher standards during asylum screening than those associated with credible fear interviews. Beyond the detention center, the administration's Remain in Mexico program has effectively blocked migrants from crossing the border to pursue asylum, and the legal process continues from highly contested "tent courts," which some reports show grant 0.01 percent of asylum cases, compared to 20 percent grant rate for migrants not in the program (Solis 2019). Advocating against the separations of those whom the state characterizes as "asylum seekers" is fraught due to the severely limited nature of asylum law and the legal restrictions being put into place with the Trump administration (for more on limits to asylum, see Campbell in this volume).

Beyond the ways in which asylum processing is itself being dismantled, the exclusion of poverty and economic need from asylum law makes it imperative to consider the ways that illegality and criminalized migration undergird uneven economic systems. If only bona fide asylum seekers deserve to escape family separation, the policy outcome may be the taking of children from other categories of immigrants, such as those who cross the border looking for work or to reunite with their own families already residing in the US. Scholars show that legal systems that purposefully exclude workers and the poor from legal belonging are inextricably linked to the global economy. Geographer Joseph Nevins explains how "global apartheid" is maintained by prisons and detention centers aimed at managing mobility in a system upheld by the criminalization of movement (2012). To criminologist Katja Aas, the ability of states to make migration into a question of legality has obscured the condition of inequality by shifting discourse toward policing and away from issues of global economic disparity (2013, 34).

The second prominent argument against zero-tolerance separation was that asylum seekers should not have their children taken from them because they "are not criminals." As I have shown in examples throughout this section, the intersections of the immigration detention system with the US prison system require advocates to consider the conversations around criminal justice reform and examine the categories actively being dismantled by activists inside and outside of the immigration debates. Escobar critiques the "immigrants are not criminals, immigrants are hard workers" messaging that is predominant in immigrant rights advocacy (2008). She acknowledges that these "attempts to distance immigrants from criminality" are intended to protect immigrant communities from criminalization, but she finds that this language "turns into violent acts themselves when the innocence of some is secured at the expense of others" (57). Specifically, criminality in the United States is constructed primarily around Blackness and Black bodies, and messaging by immigrant rights groups seeking to distance themselves from notions of criminality is problematic in its propensity to normalize legal systems historically targeting Black people (68). Ultimately, Escobar urges advocates to move away from the slogan that "No One is Illegal" toward "No One is Criminal" (69), to effectively acknowledge the intersection of criminality with immigrant illegality. This intertwining of criminal and immigration law is well studied in legal scholarship. Stumpf finds the interconnectivity of criminality to illegality to be "perhaps not surprising" because both are "designed to create distinct categories of people" (2006, 380), resulting in what Loyd, Mitchelson, and Burridge call the "differentiated or second-class citizenship in a particular nation-state" (2012, 8).

Innocence narratives that center children often serve to obscure the power relations and mechanisms of criminality while reifying the detention and imprisonment of others. Erica Meiners explains that "child saving" logics are found both in the campaigns to open and perpetuate prisons and in those to close them down. She notes: "Even when communities challenge the criminalization of young people, particularly young folks of color, a focus on the child reinforces key carceral logics.... The harmed child (or its close proxies, youth or student) reinforces criminalization and the wider carceral regime. Child safety is demanded, yet these various forms of child protection—including increased punishment, surveillance, and/or policing—invariably function to harm many, often the very populations these strategies purport to protect" (Meiners 2016, 6, 77). Meiners's work is essential for thinking through logics of family separation and how the focus on safety for children can reinforce separations and imprisonment. For example, the family separation process continues, at a potentially smaller scale, under legal guidelines that include separating children from parents deemed to be "unfit." These separations are frequently against parents who have "criminal histories," which are subject to the same pitfalls described by advocates of broader criminal justice reform. These include separations based on unverified suspicions, crimes unrelated to a parent's ability to care for the child, and immigration offenses (Abaya 2019). Attention to this category would reveal that the "unfit" label is often applied to those with criminal records, which can include reentering the US after a previous deportation, working without permission, and arrests for driving without a license. Accepting the separation of children from parents deemed to be criminals (and therefore "unfit") may serve to legitimate the perpetuation of the entrenched legal system upholding immigrant "illegality." The suggestion that asylum seekers are "not criminals" also ignores the many ways in which the asylum-seeker label is produced through the legal system and through the court process, described above. Contrasting the most sympathetic migrants to the archetype of the "criminal" serves to reify these categorizations and works against more substantive change at the roots of the immigrant detention system.

CONCLUSION: ADVOCATING AGAINST THE CRIMINALIZATION OF MIGRATION

In this chapter I have presented evidence that the zero-tolerance policy was far from a neutral application of law and order and discussed the ways the discretionary show of power weaponized the US legal system to reinforce social categorizations that target migrant families. I have also shown that there are caveats to centering the exceptionalism of the child asylum seeker in immigration advocacy. Instead of an exceptional act by an anti-immigrant administration, the zero-tolerance policy is better understood as what Cook calls "an acutely and sharply articulated version of everyday repression and violence" (2019). While it is true that the Trump administration weaponized family separation in a systematic policy to a degree that had not been seen in recent immigration policy, the zero-tolerance separations are the result of a long line of building blocks made possible by previous administrations.

"Family separation" itself, when assigned only to the events of summer 2018, is a problematic term in that it obscures the long line of family control, detention, and separation taking place throughout US history, including Japanese internment, Native American off-reservation boarding schools, the children of slaves taken from their parents and sold into further slavery, and immigration detention and deportation.

Laura Briggs writes, in *Taking Children: A History of American Terror*:

> Taking children has been a strategy for terrorizing people for centuries. There is a reason why "forcibly transferring children of the group to another group" is part of international law's definition of genocide. It participates in the same sadistic political grammar as the torture and murder that separated French Jewish children from their parents under the Nazis and sought to keep enslaved people from rebelling or to keep Native people from retaliating against the Anglos who violated treaties to encroach on their land ... Like enslavement and the Indian wars, the current efforts by the Trump administration to terrorize asylum seekers is white nationalist in ideology. It is an attempt to secure a white or Anglo future for a nation, a community, a place. (2020, 7–8)

In addition, critics of the advocacy outpouring against separations in the summer of 2018 noted that husbands are often taken away from mothers and children, friends are taken out of communities by ICE raids, and loved ones are deported. All of these are family separations, and the prison system separates many families. Of course, the policy of zero tolerance was unique in that it removed all accompanying parents from the migrant child, leaving them alone, in foster care, and categorized as "unaccompanied." However, the context of this term can only be fully understood, and therefore combatted, with a historical understanding of the roots of the policy.

Discourses of the exceptionalism of the child asylum seeker can also minimize the violence that occurs against countless differently categorized migrants. González agrees that there is a "sobering indication of the callousness sweeping over much of the country" reflected in a report that more than 25 percent of the American public supported the family separation policy (2018, 3). He contextualizes the policy as an apex of a long history of anti-immigrant sentiment and political portrayal of Latinos as a national threat, declaring that the extent of the everyday harm of the immigration policing regime has been "overshadowed" by the spotlight put on child victims of the family separation zero-tolerance policy (4).

However, nuanced advocacy can be found in abolitionist and anti-illegality frameworks, which were present in the protests. Signs painted with "no human is illegal," "no one is illegal on stolen land," and "stop deportations" were frequent. These phrases, among others, question the very criminalization of migration and center the legal structures of detention and deportation, and in some cases extend to questions of settler colonialism. Instead of relying on the exceptionalism of children to make arguments against zero-tolerance separations, which I have problematized in this chapter, these slogans get closer to situation the zero-tolerance as a particularly harmful consequence of criminalized migration, instead of an exceptional act. Anti-detention organizations are well aware of the need to care for individuals while pursuing systemic change. As Santa Fe Dreamers Project attorney Charlie Flewelling explained during a campaign to protect transgender detained persons, "we will continue to simultaneously support those who are detained while pushing for abolition of immigrant detention and ICE" (Brockway, Flewelling, and Love 2020).

Many advocates and organizers see the historical connections and are using them as a warning while offering visions of a better future. Survivors of Japanese internment camps organized against the family separation policy. George Takei warned, "unless we act now, we will have failed to learn at all from our past mistakes. Once again, we are flinging ourselves into a world of camps and fences and racist imagery" (2018). Another activist noted, "The current administration is using the very same language that led to our mass incarceration—[During Japanese internment] they charged us with being a risk to national security, and there's similar rhetoric now to frighten people. It's connected to what took place over 70 years ago" (Wilson 2019).

Many of the women I spoke with in Dilley met and bonded with other women in detention centers for single adults. The women I spoke with were well aware that the national uproar and litigation against the zero-tolerance policy had resulted in their release and subsequent reunification with their children. However, they were also aware of the friends and acquaintances left behind in these detention centers who were not receiving attention and aid because they did not come with children. We must continue to critically examine the legal and social categorizations that determine who is categorized as either deserving or not deserving of care through labels such as "child," "criminal," "asylum seeker," "family," "mother," and so on. And further, we must consider the consequences of limiting care to only those deemed as members of these vulnerable groups. It is possible to care for children and at the same time assert the right to migration, criticize the detention regime, and question the role of prisons in our society.

NOTES

1. A note on terminology: Freedom for Immigrants has a glossary of terms with an important discussion about "migrant" and "immigrant." They prefer "migrant" as the "most neutral and accurate term we have to describe any person who migrates, including refugees." The glossary acknowledges that the term "undocumented immigrant" has become the preferable term in the US for individuals present in the country without authorization. However, "many advocates in Europe avoid the term 'immigrant' altogether, as it implies migration in to 'our here,' whereas migrant is more neutral as to point of view." In this chapter I use the term "migrant" to describe persons recently arrived, and those detained for their arrivals at the border. However, in the larger discussions of the history of US immigration patterns, as well as the impact of policing and the legal exclusion of entire communities, I prefer the term "immigrant" to indicate the inclusion and long-term presence of these communities. I avoid the term "detainee," preferring "detained person" or "person in detention." For more, see https://www.freedomforimmigrants.org/terminology.
2. In this chapter I use the term "family separation" to refer to an act where US immigration agents separate a child from all parents with whom they crossed the border. The term is also widely used to refer to separations resulting from ICE raids, from deportations, and when one family member is detained without the others, as well as separations due to migrations.
3. Illegal Entry" 8 USC. § 1325, "Illegal Re-Entry" 8 USC. § 1326. For a good primer of prosecution related to border crossing, see American Immigration Council (2020).
4. Using DHS fiscal year dates of October 1 through September 30.
5. See for example, *Grassroots Leadership Inc., et al. v. Texas Department of Family Protective Services, et al.*, D-1-GN-15-004336. District court of Travis County, Texas. Exhibit 10 "GEO SEC Filing 10-K (4/27/2016)," in which the vice president for GEO Corrections and Detention reports to a 2016 GEO group earnings conference call that the Karnes City Family Residential Center "began operating with the new fixed monthly payment under a new five-year contract which is effective on November 1 of last year, *resulting in approximately $57 million in annualized revenues*" (emphasis added).
6. At the time of writing border apprehensions have risen relative to the historic lows, to numbers rivaling 2006 yet still far below apprehension numbers of the 1990s (Gramlich and Noe-Bustamante 2019).
7. The exact guidance is difficult to know. I have not seen clearly if CBP was directed to prosecute certain groups over others, or if these general prioritization orders were left to the discretion of local sectors and offices of CBP. The fact that not all unauthorized migrants were charged and separated suggests that some level of discretion was present. See Transactional Records Access Clearinghouse (2018).
8. Ms. L. is a Congolese woman who was separated from her seven-year-old daughter in November 2017, and the original plaintiff in the now class-action lawsuit.
9. https://immigrationjustice.us/volunteeropportunities/dilley.
10. This is despite former secretary of Homeland Security Kirstjen Nielsen's initial emphatic denial of this fact ("DHS Sec. Kirstjen Nielsen..." 2018).
11. In Spanish this is said as "the second floor."
12. The Credible Fear Interview is a screening interview through which US asylum officers determine if a migrant meets the threshold to continue an asylum case and halt imminent deportation. The interview results in a decision issued by the Asylum Office, a "Positive" or "Negative," indicating either the continuation of asylum proceedings or imminent deportation.
13. "With the exception of biographical information, the form was written entirely in

English—although a later version of the form offered brief summaries of the options in Spanish" (AIC and AILA 2018, 5).
14. Here meaning one parent with their children.
15. See my dissertation for a full analysis of family detention policy.
16. Specifically, those who are not Mexican citizens who traveled through Mexico before arriving at the southern border.

REFERENCES

Aas, Katja Franko. 2013. "The Ordered and the Bordered Society: Migration Control, Citizenship, and the Northern Penal State." In *The Borders of Punishment: Migration, Citizenship, and Social Exclusion.*, edited by Katja Franko Aas and Mary Bosworth. Oxford: Oxford University Press.

Abaya, Miriam. 2019. "Statement to U.S. Commission on Civil Rights Regarding Family Separation." Young Center for Immigrant Children Rights. April 12.

Abdel-Motaleb, Sarah, Roberto Lopez, and Andy Udelsman. 2020. "Family Separations Continue in South Texas, Years after They Allegedly Ended." *Texas Civil Rights Project Magazine.* October 21. https://news.txcivilrights.org/2020/10/21/family-separations-continue-in-south-texas-years-after-they-allegedly-ended.

Allen, Scott, and Pamela McPherson. 2018. "Letter to Chairman Grassley and Vice Chairman Wyden, Senate Whistleblowing Caucus." July 17.

American Civil Liberties Union. 2019. "ACLU Calls New Trump Administration Family Separation Numbers Shocking." October 24.

American Immigration Council. 2020. "Prosecuting People for Coming to the United States." Fact Sheet. January.

American Immigration Council and American Immigration Lawyers Association (AIC and AILA). 2018. "The Use of Coercion by U.S. Department of Homeland Security (DHS) Officials against Parents Who Were Forcibly Separated from Their Children." August 23.

Arand, Laila. 2018. "Declaration of Laila Arand." Case No. 18-Cv-00428-DMS-MDD. *Ms. L v. ICE.* July 28. https://www.courtlistener.com/docket/6316323/163/1/ms-l-v-us-immigration-and-customs-enforcement.

Associated Press. 2019. "More Than 5,400 Children Split at border, according to New Count." NBC News. Oct 29. https://www.nbcnews.com/news/us-news/more-5-400-children-split-border-according-new-count-n1071791.

Briggs, Laura. 2020. *Taking Children: A History of American Terror.* Oakland: University of California Press.

Brockway, Wes, Charlie Flewelling, and Allegra Love. 2020. "Press Release: ICE Closes Cibola County Correctional Center for Trans Detention." Santa Fe Dreamers Project. July 27. https://static1.squarespace.com/static/55131b32e4b068878aeb8c07/t/5e2f730efe937c2ebe358613/1580167950651/Cibola+County+Trangender+Pod+Closes.pdf.

Bush, Laura. 2018. "Separating Children from Parents 'Breaks My Heart.'" *Washington Post.* June 19.

Cheng, Amrit. 2018. "Family Separation in Court: What You Need to Know." American Civil Liberties Union. July 10. https://www.aclu.org/blog/immigrants-rights/immigrants-rights-and-detention/family-separation-court-what-you-need-know.

Chomsky, Aviva. 2014. *Undocumented: How Immigration Became Illegal.* Boston: Beacon Press.

Coleman, Mathew. 2012. "Immigrant Il-Legality: Geopolitical and Legal Borders in the US, 1882–Present." *Geopolitics* 17 (2): 402–22.

Cook, Daniel Thomas. 2019. "The Mire of Its Own Construction? Childhood Studies and the 'Crisis' at the Mexico-U.S. Border." *Childhood* 26 (1): 3–7.
De Genova, Nicholas, and Nathalie Mae Peutz, eds. 2010. *The Deportation Regime: Sovereignty, Space, and the Freedom of Movement*. Durham, NC: Duke University Press.
De León, Jason. 2015. *The Land of Open Graves: Living and Dying on the Migrant Trail*. Oakland: University of California Press.
Detention Watch Network. N.d. "Immigration Detention 101." https://www.detention watchnetwork.org/issues/detention-101.
"DHS Sec. Kirstjen Nielsen Denies Family Separation Policy Exists, Blames Media." 2018. CBS News, June 18. https://www.cbsnews.com/news/dhs-sec-kirstjen-nielsen-denies -family-separation-policy-exists-blames-media.
Dilley Pro Bono Project. 2018. "Handwritten Letters from Previously Separated Moms Detained in Dilley." Immigration Justice Campaign. https://immigrationjustice.us /advocacy/advocacy-issues/prolonged-detention/dilley-letters.
Escobar, Martha. 2008. "No One Is Criminal." In *Abolition Now! 10 Years of Strategy and Struggle against the Prison Industrial Complex*. Edited by the CR10 Publications Collective. Oakland, CA: AK Press.
Garland, David. 2001. *The Culture of Control: Crime and Social Order in Contemporary Society*. Chicago: University of Chicago Press.
Gilmore, Ruth Wilson. 2007. *Golden Gulag: Prisons, Surplus, Crisis, and Opposition in Globalizing California*. Berkeley: University of California Press.
González, Roberto J. 2018. "Cruel and Unusual." *Anthropology Today* 34 (5): 3–4.
Gramlich, John, and Luis Noe-Bustamante. 2019. "What's Happening at the U.S.-Mexico Border in 5 Charts." Pew Research Center. November 1. https://www.pewresearch.org /fact-tank/2019/11/01/whats-happening-at-the-u-s-mexico-border-in-5-charts.
Gregory, Derek, ed. 2009. *The Dictionary of Human Geography*, 5th ed. Malden, MA: Blackwell.
Hudak, Joseph. 2018. "Willie Nelson Speaks Out on Immigrant Family Separations at Border." *Rolling Stone Magazine*. June 14. https://www.rollingstone.com/music /music-country/willie-nelson-speaks-out-on-immigrant-family-separations-at -border-628791.
Human Rights First. 2018. "Punishing Refugees and Migrants: The Trump Administration's Misuse of Criminal Prosecutions." January. https://humanrightsfirst.org/library /punishing-refugees-and-migrants-the-trump-administrations-misuse-of-criminal -prosecutions.
Immigrant Legal Resource Network. 2019. "A New Way Forward for Immigrant Justice." June https://www.ilrc.org/new-way-forward-immigrant-justice.
Jordan, Miriam. 2019. "No More Family Separations, Except These 900." *New York Times*, July 31. https://www.nytimes.com/2019/07/30/us/migrant-family-separations.html.
Kraft, Colleen. 2018. "AAP Statement on Executive Order on Family Separation." American Academy of Pediatrics. June 20.
Lopez, Ana Maria. 2018. "ACP Objects to the Separation of Children from Their Parents at the Border." American College of Physicians. May 31.
Loyd, Jenna M., Matt Mitchelson, and Andrew Burridge, eds. 2012. *Beyond Walls and Cages: Prisons, Borders, and Global Crisis*. Athens: University of Georgia Press.
Malkki, Liisa H. 2015. *The Need to Help: The Domestic Arts of International Humanitarianism*. Durham, NC: Duke University Press.
McCausland, Phil, Patricia Guadalupe, and Kalhan Rosenblatt. 2018. "Thousands across U.S. Join 'Keep Families Together' March to Protest Family Separation." *NBC News*, June 30. https://www.nbcnews.com/news/us-news/thousands-across-u-s-join-keep -families-together-march-protest-n888006.
Meet the Press. 2018. "Kellyanne: 'As a Mother, as a Catholic' Nobody Likes Family

Separation Policy." NBC News. June 17. https://www.nbcnews.com/meet-the-press
/video/kellyanne-as-a-mother-as-a-catholic-nobody-likes-family-separation-policy
-1257722435903.

Meiners, Erica. 2016. *For the Children? Protecting Innocence in a Carceral State*. Minneapolis, Minnesota: University of Minnesota Press.

Miroff, Nick. 2018. "A Family Was Separated at the Border, and This Distraught Father Took His Own Life." *Texas Tribune*. June 9. https://www.texastribune.org/2018/06/09 /father-suicide-family-separated-texas border.

Mountz, Alison. 2010. *Seeking Asylum: Human Smuggling and Bureaucracy at the Border*. Minneapolis: University of Minnesota Press.

Ms. L. vs. ICE. 2018. United States District Court Southern District of California.

Murdza, Katy. 2020. "Judge Allows Certain Family Separations at the Border to Continue." *Immigration Impact*. American Immigration Council. January 21.

Nevins, Joseph. 2012. "Policing Mobility: Maintaining Global Apartheid from South Africa to the United States." In *Beyond Walls and Cages: Prisons, Borders, and Global Crisis*. Athens: University of Georgia Press.

Nevins, Joseph, and Mizue Aizeki. 2008. *Dying to Live: A Story of U.S. Immigration in an Age of Global Apartheid*. Open Media Series. San Francisco: Open Media/City Lights Books.

Ngai, Mae M. 2004. *Impossible Subjects: Illegal Aliens and the Making of Modern America*. Politics and Society in Twentieth-Century America. Princeton, NJ: Princeton University Press.

Purdum, Leanne. 2021. "Humanitarianism and Violence in the South Texas Family Residential Center: An Analysis of Humanitarian Detention." PhD diss., University of Georgia. https://esploro.libs.uga.edu/esploro/outputs/doctoral/humanitarianism-and -violence-in-the-south/9949420828902959.

Samuels, Liz, and David Stein. 2008. "Perspectives on Critical Resistance." In *Abolition Now! 10 Years of Strategy and Struggle against the Prison Industrial Complex*, edited by the CR10 Publications Collective. Oakland, CA: AK Press.

Shepherd, Kathryn E. 2018. "Declaration of Kathryn E. Shepherd." Case No. 18-Cv428- DMS-MDD. *Ms. L. v. ICE* Litigation. In Plaintiffs' Reply in Support of Motion for Stay of Removal, July 25. https://www.courtlistener.com/docket/6316323/153/ms-l-v-us -immigration-and-customs-enforcement.

Solis, Gustavo. 2019. "Remain in Mexico Has a 0.1 Percent Asylum Grant Rate." *San Diego Union Tribune*. December 15. https://www.sandiegouniontribune.com/news/border -baja-california/story/2019-12-15/remain-in-mexico-has-a-0-01-percent-asylum-grant -rate.

Spagat, Elliot. 2019. "Tally of Children Split at Border Tops 5,400 in New Count." *Associated Press*. October 25. https://apnews.com/c654e652a4674cf19304a4a4ff599feb.

Stumpf, Juliet. 2006. "The Crimmigration Crisis: Immigrants, Crime, and Sovereign Power." *American University Law Review* 56 (2): 367–419.

Takei, George. 2018. " 'At Least During the Internment . . .' Are Words I Thought I'd Never Utter." *Foreign Policy*. June 19. https://foreignpolicy.com/2018/06/19/at-least-during -the-internment-are-words-i-thought-id-never-utter-family-separation-children -border.

Thompson, Ginger. 2018. "Listen to Children Who've Just Been Separated from Their Parents at the Border." *ProPublica*. June 18. https://www.propublica.org/article /children-separated-from-parents-border-patrol-cbp-trump-immigration-policy.

Transactional Records Access Clearinghouse. 2018. " 'Zero Tolerance' at the Border: Rhetoric vs. Reality." July 24. https://trac.syr.edu/immigration/reports/520.

Trump, Donald J. 2017. "Executive Order: Border Security and Immigration Enforcement Improvements." January 25. US White House.

US Conference of Catholic Bishops. 2018. "U.S. Bishops' Migration Chairman Urges

Administration to Keep Families Together." June 1. http://www.usccb.org/news/2018/18-090.cfm.

US Department of Justice. 2018. "Attorney General Announces Zero-Tolerance Policy for Criminal Illegal Entry." Office of Public Affairs. https://www.justice.gov/opa/pr/attorney-general-announces-zero-tolerance-policy-criminal-illegal-entry.

Wacquant, Loïc J. D. 2009. *Punishing the Poor: The Neoliberal Government of Social Insecurity*. Politics, History, and Culture. Durham, NC: Duke University Press.

Welke, Barbara Young. 2010. *Law and the Borders of Belonging in the Long Nineteenth Century United States*. New Histories of American Law. New York: Cambridge University Press.

Wilson, Emily. 2019. "Formerly Incarcerated Japanese Americans Organize a Protest against Family Separation at the Border." *Hyperallergic*, March 27. https://hyperallergic.com/491933/then-they-came-for-me-jonathan-logan-shizuko-ina-protest.

Yaffe-Bellany, David. 2018. "A Viral Facebook Fundraiser Has Generated More than $20 Million for Immigration Nonprofit RAICES." *Texas Tribune*, June 27. https://www.texastribune.org/2018/06/27/viral-facebook-fundraiser-has-generated-more-20-million-immigration-no.

CHAPTER 4

UNDERSTANDING NEW YORK'S OPT-OUT MOVEMENT: HOW SCHOOL SEGREGATION SHAPED THE NATION'S LARGEST RESISTANCE TO STANDARDIZED TESTING

Olivia Ildefonso

In April 2015, parents in New York launched the largest coordinated action against standardized testing to ever take place in the United States. That year, parents who formed New York's "opt-out movement" either kept their children out of school during the three-day exam period or requested that their school provide a separate activity for students who were not participating. The movement started with a handful of districts in 2013, the year that New York implemented a new set of academic standards called the Common Core. By 2015 it was making national headlines. That year, more than two hundred thousand, or 20 percent, of New York state's 1.1 million eligible students in grades 3 through 8 refused to take the state-mandated English and Math Common Core exams.

The massive resistance seemed to be in direct response to Governor Andrew Cuomo's State of the State address that was given in January of the same year. In the address he talked about the need for a "dramatic" reform of the education system, which, he claimed, had failed poor and minority students. He blamed the power of the teachers' union to protect incompetent teachers and made the case for a new, robust evaluation system. The proposal included using the Common Core exams to determine half of teachers' evaluations. The announcement was immediately met with criticism from teachers and parents who warned of the negative implications of these "high-stakes" exams. They argued that linking students' exams to teachers' evaluations in such a significant way would lead to high levels of stress for both students and teachers. They also criticized the exams for narrowing the school curriculum and forcing teachers to "teach to the test."

While the New York State Education Department and Cuomo faced much criticism for their actions related to the implementation of the Common Core academic standards, the initial mandate for the exams stemmed from the federal government. In 2012, the Obama administration launched a competitive grant program that rewarded states for enacting certain educational policies, including adopting the Common Core State Standards and using the results of the Common Core exams to measure teacher performance. New York was among the first states to adopt the standards. Within two years, the standards were adopted by forty-five states and the District of Columbia.

The role of the federal government in incentivizing standardized testing in public schools began during the Cold War in order to promote science and math in schools; however, the current testing regime that focuses on teacher accountability can be traced back to the Reagan administration's 1983 "A Nation at Risk" report, which asserted that "a rising tide" of mediocre education in the United States was causing the national economy to fall behind other superpowers on the world stage (National Commission on Excellence in Education 1983). It called for new standards and accountability measures in schools in order to improve the rigor of education. The narrative was so powerful that every federal administration since then has taken up the claim that there is a crisis in the quality of public education that needs to be resolved with more standardized testing. Based on this history, media coverage (E. Harris 2015; Strauss 2016; Hildebrand 2018) and emerging scholarship (Ravitch 2020) has largely framed the opt-out movement as a fight between government officials who want more standards and accountability, particularly for low-performing urban school districts, and teachers and parents who see the negative effects of more testing on children. Yet, this analysis fails to take into consideration the place-based dimensions of the movement. In New York, as in much of the nation where testing refusals have occurred, the boycotts have overwhelmingly taken place in affluent white suburban school districts. In fact, a 2016 national survey of opt-out parents and teachers reported that the vast majority of respondents (91.8 percent) were white (Pizmony-Levy and Saraisky 2016). Additionally, the median household income for respondents was $125,000, significantly higher than the median household income for the United States of $55,322.

This reality raises a number of important questions. If the actions were primarily aimed at resolving a crisis in the quality of education, particularly in poor communities of color that tend to be concentrated in urban areas, then why is it that majority-white, high-performing suburban school districts are the ones fighting back? And if it is true that resources for test preparation determine success on the exams, which many poor communities lack and many affluent communities can easily afford, why are affluent communities the ones who are opting out?

This chapter will explore the race and class dimensions of the opt-out movement and analyze why the movement began in majority-white suburban school districts. I focus on the opt-out movement in New York, which at the time of this writing is still the largest boycott in the country. Through placing the movement within the state's history of school segregation and local control, I argue that, rather than being a fight *against* testing, the opt-out movement began as a fight *for* local control over public education by communities that have historically had the most control over their school districts.

While states have constitutional power over public education, most states grant home-rule power to local school districts. The legal authority given to local districts to levy taxes and bonds and to make decisions regarding personal and curricula is commonly understood as local control (Doyle and Finn 1984). Rather than viewing local control as a legal right shared by all local school districts, I argue that it is more accurately a form of economic and political power, which is contingent on a community's ability to raise enough local funding to govern their district in ways that they see fit and on the community's ability to influence educational policies at larger scales (e.g., the state and federal governments). Put more simply, the power to control is determined by both how much local funding a school district can raise and how much political power can be wielded by the community to influence larger-scale educational policies. This chapter will primarily focus on the aspect of local control that is related to economic power and local funding, although several examples will be given to also show how this translates into more political power to influence the educational system at large.

Since the founding of a system of public education in the United States, most public schools have been funded primarily by local property taxes (Du Bois 1998; Neem 2017). Under a system of local taxation, every school district must decide both how much money is needed to fund the school and how much funding can realistically be raised given the total assessed property value with the school district boundary. If a district is property poor, it will be difficult for the residents in that school district to tax themselves enough to reach their desired level of funding. This is why wealthy neighborhoods, on average, have had more highly funded school districts than poorer neighborhoods. Since the 1970s, states have greatly increased their role in supplementing school district funding in order to help equalize resources between school districts. However, state funding is often earmarked for certain programs and needs, which limits a community's ability to make decisions over how the money should be spent. Given these constraints, an important aspect of understanding local control is considering a community's ability to raise enough *local funding* to sufficiently fund their school district, without supplemental funding from the state or the federal government.

Seen through this lens, one important way that a community can gain more local control is by gaining more funding at the local level. To accomplish this goal, community members work together to make their school district appear desirable so that homes in their neighborhood will sell for higher prices in the housing market. This puts school districts into direct competition with one another. However, as this chapter will show, this competition is unfairly rigged to ensure that majority-white suburban school districts are the ones that will consistently win. Local control, therefore, is not shared evenly across school districts. School segregation creates an uneven geography of local control through which white Americans can maintain their privilege and their power over the public education system.

Importantly, the ways that school districts affect one another through a system of economic competition that privileges whiteness is hidden from view. Instead, school districts are regarded, both in public discourse and by formal educational policies, as independent entities that are shaped solely by the capabilities of the residents and youth that live within that school district. Geographer Christine Drennon explains that by erasing the history through which school districts have been, and continue to be, produced in relation to one another, "[E]ach school district, whether property rich or property poor, is understood as the source of its own identity, its own problems, and its own solutions; they are absolute [not relative] spaces and as such exist separate from one another and apart from that which they contain" (2006, 568). Therefore, youth are defined by the stereotypes that are assigned to their school communities, placing limits on some while boosting opportunities for others long before they can even demonstrate their capabilities. High-performing schools are attributed to caring residents in the district who work hard to provide quality education for their children. Low-performing school districts, on the other hand, are regarded as a failure of the community to realize a quality education and instill the values necessary for educational success. Additionally, the framing of school districts as existing independent from one another leads to educational policies that ignore the unfair competition *between* school districts for local funding and instead seek to address racial disparities by focusing on the perceived failure and lack of motivation by teachers, parents, and students *within* struggling school districts (Mitchell 2010).

I argue that a radical reframing of local control is necessary to reveal the causes of educational disparities in the United States and to make sense of why the nation's largest testing boycott began in wealthy white suburban school districts. I begin this chapter by outlining the origins of local control over public education in the United States. The first section establishes racial capitalism as a powerful framework for analyzing why a system of locally funded and racially segregated schools was formed in the United States, and why it continues to be reproduced to the present day. I argue that school segregation is structured on actions taken by white communities to secure their economic advantage in housing and education. To help ground this assertion, I provide a brief history of the production of whiteness and racial segregation in the United States. I conclude the chapter by placing the opt-out movement within this long history race-based economic competition between school districts.

THE ORIGINS OF SCHOOL SEGREGATION IN THE UNITED STATES

The biggest movement against standardized testing in the nation emerged from the state with the most segregated school system, within school districts that are some of the wealthiest and whitest in the nation. In order to make sense of the relationship between these superlatives, we need to understand the terrain of school segregation in the United States. Although school segregation has largely been framed as the lingering effect of an overtly racist past—in the South, this past centers around schools segregated by law (de jure segregation), and in the North, it centers around the effects of overtly racist housing policies (de facto segregation)—school segregation has always been, and remains, a central part of the American educational landscape (G. Orfield and Frankenberg 2014; Ayscue and Orfield 2016). To better frame this reality, I pose the following questions: Why is school segregation produced? What purposes does it serve? This section begins with a brief history of the origins of school segregation in the United States. I use a racial capitalism framework to analyze why a system of locally funded and racially segregated schools came to define the nation's educational landscape.

In *Black Reconstruction*, W. E. B. Du Bois shows that former enslaved

Africans made the first serious push for a free system of education for *all* Americans. Having long been denied the right to read or write, they came to see education as a means of liberation. During Reconstruction, Black communities throughout the South organized and went to great lengths to try to establish a system of racially integrated public schools funded by the state (Du Bois 1998, 638). Their efforts were forcefully challenged by white property owners who refused to pay for education for the laboring class and by white laborers who did not want more competition among the working class. As a result of these obstacles, Black communities aligned themselves with Northern white philanthropists who were economically invested in the South and did not want Black laborers, who made up the bulk of the workforce, to flee the region. In order to help keep Black laborers in the South, they championed racially segregated vocational schools (Du Bois 1998; Rooks 2017).

In response to the pressures from the alliance between Black laborers and Northern industrialists, white Southerners caved to demands to let African Americans have their own public schools but made their schools "just as bad as they dared to in the face of national public opinion" (Du Bois 1998, 665). Through creating separate schools with separate local funding streams, white Americans could ensure that they would not have to pay for the education of African Americans. Importantly, this system of local control gave them a new and powerful way to reinforce their domination of the capitalist system and accumulate more wealth for generations to come. To this point, Du Bois argues that school segregation "was never mere race separation"; it was always about white domination (695). He explains that white officials had many forms of direct control over the schools attended by African Americans. White officials decided how much—or rather, how little—should be spent, what could be taught, and what teachers should be allowed to teach Black children (694–95). Not surprisingly, white control led to the extreme underfunding of the schools for Black people (Du Bois 1998; Rooks 2017).

The formation of racially segregated and locally funded school districts can be understood, in geographic terms, as the formation of an important scale of uneven development through which the schools for white children are continuously invested in and developed in contrast to the schools for Black children. In a system of local funding, money for the school district is raised by the local community. If a community wants more money for the school, the primary method is through attracting residents with higher incomes. This system of local funding sets communities into competition with each other in order to attract wealthy individuals. As this competition plays out over time, schools not only remain separate and unequal, but the inequality between them grows as wealth concentrates into majority-white communities (M. Orfield 2011).

The pattern of uneven development that has shaped school segregation in the United States is not unique to schools. Uneven development is one of the primary ways in which capitalism shapes space (Smith 2010). In order to produce goods and services, capitalism requires both competition and cooperation between groups of people. However, the ways in which people decide to group themselves and form alliances is not random. Rather, it has largely been informed by racialized social hierarches (Robinson 2000). Cedric Robinson shows that even before the emergence of capitalism, the social construction of race was used to justify divisions in the labor process, such as who would be the slaves or serfs and who would be the masters or lords. His critical point is that race has *always* been constructed for economic ends. Therefore, capitalism did not create race, but rather the capitalist system arose out of an already racialized society, and through its expansion into a world system, it both intensified preexisting racial divisions and created entirely new ones. Thus, as Black radical scholars working in the framework of racial capitalism, such as Robinson, have painstakingly worked to bring to our attention, there has never been a moment in the history of capitalism when capitalism has not been "racial capitalism."

The connection between the social construction of race and capitalism is exemplified by the production of whiteness in colonial America. Before the American Revolution, it was fairly common for European indentured servants, African slaves, and Native Americans to unite and stage rebellions and revolts against the European ruling class (Fields 1990; Roediger 1991; Robinson 2000; Buck 2001). In order to break up the solidarity between oppressed groups, the ruling class offered concessions to European indentured servants who were already granted important advantages, such as the right to bear arms (Fields 1990).[1] Over time the alliance between the European ruling class and the European working class was justified and naturalized with racial explanations, producing the concept of whiteness and white supremacy (Fields 1990; C. Harris 1992; Omi and Winant 2014).

By the time the issue of public education was raised during Reconstruction, white laborers already saw themselves as an entirely distinct group from Black laborers, despite the fact that in their day-to-day life they had much more in common with the struggles of their fellow wage laborers than white members of the capitalist class. Critical to these racial divisions was the creation of segregated spaces. Instead of understanding Black people's quest for freedom as an opportunity for class solidarity, white laborers considered the employment of Black people a threat to their ability to obtain employment and earn higher wages (Roediger 1991; Buck 2001). The intense resistance from white workers resulted in segregated spaces of every kind. After the Civil War, Black people were separated from white people in unions and workplaces, transportation, public accommodations, neighborhoods, recreational facilities, prisons, the armed forces, and schools in both Northern and Southern states (Du Bois 1998; Cox 1970). Thus, we see that segregated schools, like all spaces of racial segregation, were produced as an economic defense mechanism by white Americans to preserve their power, wealth, and dominance under racial capitalism (Omi and Winant 2014; Lipsitz 2011).

The construction of segregated schools helped to produce a racial ideology that both normalized and justified racial segregation. Since the policy of local control or "home rule" meant that communities were responsible for their own school districts, educational disparities between the schools attended by white children and the schools attended by Black children were legitimated with racial explanations. The success of white students helped to create the dangerous myth, which still exists today, that white parents and youth care about education, while students of color are often failing because people of color do not value education. With these racial ideologies in play, American education could be viewed as a great equalizer, despite the boundaries put in place to enforce white supremacy.

Importantly, it was not just the school district boundary that separated students by race; white parents mounted racial partitions at every scale of the educational system. Segregation within multiracial schools was accomplished through the creation of tracking systems in which students of color were offered different classes with different curricula than their white counterparts. The origins of race-based tracking can be traced back to 1850 to the federal court ruling in *Roberts v. The City of Boston*, and today it is a standard practice throughout the American K–12 educational system (Wong 2017). Additionally, in large urban school districts that are under mayoral control, white families have sought out private contributions, for example, through holding community-based fundraisers, to ensure that their schools will be sufficiently funded even if the rest of the schools in the district remain underfunded (Posey-Maddox 2016). They have also supported the proliferation of "Gifted and Talented" schools that have a test-based application process—yet another fortification of racialized educational boundaries (Sattin-Bajaj and Roda 2018).

These examples demonstrate some of the ways that white families have created and exploited racial partitions at every scale of the educational system to give themselves more funding and more power over how the system is managed. Since the founding of the American public education system to the present day, educational boundaries have formed a geography of racial domination through which seemingly objective policies, such as local control and merit-based placements, have been used to conceal the ways that white Americans have balkanized the system to support an anti-Black and white supremacist racial hierarchy.

SUBURBAN SCHOOL SEGREGATION AND THE OPT-OUT MOVEMENT

The racial contestations that gave rise to a system of school segregation in the South during Reconstruction demonstrated how racially segregated spaces in general and segregated schools in particular have been produced by white Americans to preserve their competitive advantage under racial capitalism. This is especially true during times of economic crisis, when white workers have felt the need draw racialized boundaries of exclusion to "protect" themselves from the perceived threat of having to compete with a larger pool of workers for the same jobs and economic opportunities. It was under such conditions that locally funded and racially segregated school districts were developed throughout US suburbs.

As World War II came to an end and soldiers returned to find limited job opportunities and housing shortages in American cities, white city dwellers increased their demands for white-only neighborhoods as a way to gain more economic security (Hayden 2002, 2015; Teaford 2006). Their calls were answered by the federal government, which institutionalized white supremacy in America's new suburban housing market (Baxandall and Ewen 2001). For the first time in the nation's history, the federal government made homeownership a reality for millions of white Americans by offering them long-term, low-interest, federally backed mortgages, which were denied to people of color. The federal government also endorsed the use of racial covenants and enforced a national policy of redlining—denying financing and investments to racially integrated or majority nonwhite neighborhoods (Jones-Correa 2000; Lipsitz 2006, 2011).

While school segregation had always been important for white parents to secure a better education for their children than for children of color, suburban homeownership added another important incentive for maintaining racial homogeneity. In most suburbs, the quality of public education became the most important determinant of a homeowner's property value. Therefore, school quality was not just important for parents, but for every homeowner within the school district boundary.

The connection between school quality and property values is best illuminated through considering the geography of Long Island, New York, which is widely considered the archetype of postwar suburban development (Teaford 1997). On Long Island, there are a dizzying array of local governments, including 126 school districts. In New York City, there is only one centralized school district. Prior to World War II, the vast majority of students in the state were educated under the city's centralized school system, which pools funding together and redistributes it to all of the schools through a central board of education. In contrast, on Long Island, every neighborhood school district has its own local board of education and is responsible for creating a budget and raising funds. While urban school districts have always been marred by various levels of racial segregation—from classroom segregation to intradistrict school segregation—the geography of neighborhood school districts that came to define America's suburbs brought with it a new set of incentives for white residents to maintain racially separate and unequal spaces of education.

Urban historian Jon Teaford (1997) argues that the proliferation of local governments is what made suburbia distinct from the city. In contrast to what they considered the messiness of urban life, suburbanites created an idealized village form of local government and local control. It was at this local level that homeowners had to cooperate out of their shared interest in providing the best services to their community for the least amount of taxes. As the single most expensive local service, public education became one of the most important incentives for community cooperation.

After World War II, white communities worked together to make sure that their schools districts were seen as desirable. They did this not only by making sure that their students had enough resources to do well in school, but also by working to keeping the community all white. The latter was achieved first through overt forms of housing discrimination, such as racial covenants and then, after racial discrimination was outlawed with the Fair Housing Act of 1968, with covert forms of discriminations, such as restrictive zoning. Black suburbanites also worked hard to secure resources for their children, but they had the odds stacked against them. For example, the all-Black community that resided in Long Island's Wyandanch School District had to deal with structural discrimination at every level of government (Koubek 1971). Not only were the county and town negligent in providing them with basic infrastructure, such as water, roads, and public transportation, but the county targeted the community for locating residents who received welfare. Without a way to attract wealthier residents, it became impossible for Wyandanch residents to raise enough funds for their school district. A 1967 lawsuit brought by the NAACP claimed that the Wyandanch school district "does not have the economic resources to provide a basic, minimum educational program."

Suburban development based on a highly fragmented and racialized system of local control has made New York the state with the most racially segregated school system in the nation (Kucsera and Orfield 2014). As competition in the housing market has played out over time, school segregation has been maintained, and through this process wealth has continued to concentrate in New York's majority-white suburban school districts ("2009 Report" 2009; Koch 2017, 95–106). Putting the opt-out movement into context within this uneven geography of local control helps to explain why the largest boycott in the country emerged from New York's affluent, majority-white suburban school districts. As the districts with the most local control, they not only view more state testing as an encroachment on their community's power to govern their own schools, but also as a potential threat to their privileged position in the housing market. These fears are revealed in a 2001 *New York Times* article titled "In Scarsdale, Debate on Tests Masks Much Bigger Issues," which covered the first standardized testing boycott in New York State (Foderaro 2001). It begins: "On the surface, the issue is testing. That is, just how much time schools here should spend preparing for state tests and even whether students should take them. In truth, though, the issue here and in other high-achieving districts is about much more: status, real estate prices, curriculum and all sorts of other matters, real and imagined, that have been wrapped into a debate over standard tests used to measure school districts around the state." Since the results of state tests are used by real estate agents and home sellers to rank communities, top districts have the most pressure to stay at the top. In explaining her opposition to state standardized testing, the president of the Scarsdale Middle School Parent Teacher Association, Melanie Spivak, commented, "Our community expects the best, and rightly so. All people have to go by is a number that's printed in the newspaper, and, you know, it's human nature to look at that box and want to be No. 1. The schools are our industry, and that's what sells the houses, and that's what sells people on Scarsdale." Consequently, the repercussions of bad performance on standardized testing go far beyond the students who take the exam; not only do teachers and school administrators have much to lose through being assessed based on their student's test scores, but entire communities are affected through the spectacle of school rankings that directly affect property values.

Even though the representatives from the New York State Department of Education have claimed that the exams are only for assessing where children need more help, school administrators have called this view "detached from the life of real schools" (Foderaro 2001). As a Westchester superintendent explained, "When we have all of our scores being printed in newspapers with graphics and charts, it's foolish to believe that this doesn't cause a kind of test frenzy" (ibid.). Echoing this point, Thomas Rogers of the New York State Council of School Superintendents blamed the overemphasis on testing on the media, explaining, "The tests get a lot of attention outside the school district, so the school district takes them very seriously" (Gormley 2001).

In addition to requiring more state exams and making the results public, state education policies have heightened competition between school districts by creating "accountability" systems that publicize which school districts are underperforming. In 2015, in compliance with the federal Every Student Succeeds Act, New York State adopted a new accountability system to identify struggling school districts and publicly release a list of districts that are rated as "needing improvement." Making the connection with the state's rating system and property values, Roger Tilles, who represents Long Island on the state's policymaking board of regents, commented, "There are consequences to being placed on the lists, as many superintendents have told me, in the way a district is looked at by its residents and by *those who may be thinking of moving in*" (Hildebrand 2019, emphasis added).

Since highly ranked school districts are already hypersensitive to any factor that can lower their ranking, it did not help that before the Common Core State Standards were released in 2013, the representatives from the New York State Department of Education warned that the new, more rigorous exams would most likely lead to a 30 percent drop in passing rates. Following this announcement, talks of boycotting the exam started bubbling up in majority-white suburban school districts throughout New York state. Refusals started to snowball the following year after the results on the exams were even worse than the state department had predicted (Hildebrand 2013).

The media coverage of the initial testing boycotts that I outlined above reveals a climate of intense cooperation within school district communities and competition between school districts. The interviews with opt-out parents and representatives from suburban Westchester and Long Island, where the boycotts began, demonstrate that concern over testing does not just center around whether individual students will be able to perform well on the exams. Thus, to view the movement as a fight against testing is far too simplistic and masks the underlying motivations. As is clear from comments such as "The schools are our industry, and that's what sells the houses," school performance is important to the entire residential community since it is operationalized in the housing market to sell homes. School district communities, therefore, are incentivized to compete with one another in order to optimize their property values.

While it is unclear whether youth in high-performing districts understand the reasons for the intense external pressures placed on them to do well in school, anecdotes from scholars who have studied highly ranked districts suggests it would be difficult for students to ignore. In his nationwide study of suburban fragmentation, "new regionalist" scholar Myron Orfield (2011) demonstrates how, in an effort to keep their communities competitive in the housing market, homeowners became obsessed with monitoring the quality of education of their local school district. A government official he interviewed commented, "You should see the white homeowners in this city. Whether they have kids or not, they are constantly monitoring the test scores at the school. At the first hint of change, everybody will be out of there. People paid big money for these houses—they have a lot of their saving tied up in them, and if they were threatened in this investment, they would be gone" (Orfield 2011, 40).

In many ways, this competition between school districts is normalized as a necessary part of suburban life and homeownership. However, as I have illustrated through providing an analysis of the history of school segregation, it is this form of competition that privileges majority-white suburban school districts and affords them the economic and political power to challenge the authority of the state. Even deciding to not take the exams is indicative of the uneven geographies of local control. Since affluent suburban school districts can tax themselves enough at the local level to fund their school districts, they can more easily make the decision to opt out of the state-mandated exams compared to less-affluent communities that rely on state and federal funding. In order to deter communities from boycotting, state and federal officials repeatedly warned that districts that fall below a 95 percent participation rate might lose federal and state funds.[2] Additionally, the state reported that high opt-out rates would affect a school district's rating, putting it at risk of being placed on the state's list of low-performing districts and, in the worst case, being taken over by the state. While the state eventually decided not to follow through on withholding funding, in 2018 it passed a plan that lowers the ranking of school districts that have an opt-out rate greater than 5 percent.

Though there are undoubtedly additional factors that can help to explain why the opt-out movement began in affluent majority-white suburban school districts, a critical assessment of school segregation and local control provides important preliminary answers. Although the opt-out movement has largely been framed as a fight against standardized testing, analyzing the uneven geographies of the opt-out movement reveals a more complicated picture. Through placing the movement within New York's history of structural racism and suburban development, I have suggested that the movement is more accurately a fight for local control by districts that have historically had the most local control.

Furthermore, the opt-out movement has been effective in changing educational policies at the state level. In 2015, after the largest testing boycott to date, the state passed a four-year moratorium on using student test scores to evaluate teacher performance—a principal demand of the opt-out movement leaders. Three years later a bill was passed that eliminated a requirement that at least 50 percent of public schoolteachers' ratings be based on their students' scores. These significant wins for the movement exemplify how local control is not just the ability to raise enough money through local taxes to meet the needs of the community, but it is also contingent on community's ability to influence educational policies at larger scales. In a system of racial capitalism, we see how school district boundaries are not neutral partitions, but rather they are lines of exclusion that allow white Americans to maintain their economic and political advantages.

CONCLUSION

This chapter has analyzed why local control over public education was produced and why it continues to be reproduced. In doing so I have illustrated that contrary to the legal framing of local control as a right that is given to every local school district to levy taxes and make decisions at the local level, local control is more accurately a form of economic and political power that privileges majority-white residential communities. This reframing is important to understanding why school segregation persists today. Rather than viewing school segregation as an effect of a racist past—a time when the country had overtly racist policies—or as the effect of racial animosity, a racial capitalism framework allows us to understand it as an important geography for capitalism that continues to provide competitive advantages to white Americans.

As outlined in this chapter, the immense effort by white communities in the United States to create a system of public education that secures material benefits for their school districts was accomplished in a number of ways, including, but not limited to (1) creating separate funding streams for white and Black school districts, (2) steering public and private investments to majority-white neighborhoods while simultaneously divesting in Black neighborhoods, (3) taking control of elected offices and school administration positions so that white officials and administrators could set the terms for what is considered a high-quality education, and (4) using school quality as an important metric in the housing market so that it can help to sell homes and increase property values.

Taken together, these processes have established a system of public education that pits schools in competition with each other while unfairly rewarding majority-white suburban school districts, which are positioned to win in this fight for funding and political power. Furthermore, their rewards are contingent on the losses of other school districts. Thus, the ability of white communities to have control over their school district is directly connected to the inability of communities of color to exercise the same level of control and autonomy. In many ways, the opt-out movement is an expression of these uneven and relational geographies of economic and political power. On the surface the movement appears to be a fight between the state and individual school districts that are rejecting the overuse of testing. Yet, as I demonstrate in this chapter, the decision to refuse state-mandated exams is largely influenced by a school district's level of local control.

Critical to the reproduction of a public school system structured on the competitive advantage of white communities has been the legal and discursive framing of school districts as independent entities. Through treating school districts as autonomous from one another, the successes and failures of each district are attributed to the ability of the residents within that district to provide a quality education for their students. Youth are framed as a product of their residential community. As such, all of the educational reforms that attempt to "help" youth in failing school districts put the onus for change on school administrators, teachers, parents, and students within those school districts. This has been the approach by the federal government and state governments in their quest to implement more standardized testing and accountability systems. The critical point to understand is that these reforms will *never* bring about any meaningful change as long as they are targeted toward individual districts and not the entire system of locally funded and racially segregated schools.

NOTES

1. One significant advantage of the European lower classes is that they had a much longer history of fighting for their freedom with the European ruling classes (Fields 1990). Due to this longer history of class struggle, they came to colonial America voluntarily as indentured servants who could work of their debt and eventually attain freedom (although few of the earliest immigrants actually lived long enough to reach this point). Additionally, European indentured servants were well armed, and they outnumbered

their masters (ibid.). For these and other similar reasons that factored into calculations of risk and reward, the planter class conceded greater material benefits to the European lower classes.
2. Under the federal guidelines, the federal government has the right to impose various sanctions on states that fail to ensure all students are tested, including withholding Title I funds, which are granted based on the number of students in poverty. Under the same law, the state itself can also withhold funds.

REFERENCES

"2009 Report." 2009. Long Island Index. http://www.longislandindex.org/wp-content/uploads/2015/10/2009_Long_Island_Index.pdf.

Ayscue, Jennifer B., and Gary Orfield. 2016. "Perpetuating Separate and Unequal Worlds of Educational Opportunity through District Lines: School Segregation by Race and Poverty." In *Race, Equity, and Education*, 45–74. Springer.

Baxandall, Rosalyn, and Elizabeth Ewen. 2001. *Picture Windows: How the Suburbs Happened*. Basic Books.

Buck, Pem Davidson. 2001. *Worked to the Bone: Race, Class, Power, and Privilege in Kentucky*. Monthly Review Press.

Cox, Oliver Cromwell. 1948. *Caste, Class, and Race: A Study in Social Dynamics*. New York, Monthly Review Press.

Doyle, Denis P., and Chester E. Finn. 1984. "American Schools and the Future of Local Control." *The Public Interest* 77: 77.

Drennon, Christine M. 2006. "Social Relations Spatially Fixed: Construction and Maintenance of School Districts in San Antonio, Texas." *Geographical Review* 96 (4): 567–93.

Du Bois, W. E. B. 1998. *Black Reconstruction in America 1860–1880*. Free Press.

Fields, Barbara Jeanne. 1990. "Slavery, Race, and Ideology in the United States of America." *New Left Review* 181 (1): 95–118.

Foderaro, Lisa W. 2001. "In Scarsdale, Debate on Tests Masks Much Bigger Issues." *New York Times*, April 20, 2001. https://www.nytimes.com/2001/04/20/nyregion/in-scarsdale-debate-on-tests-masks-much-bigger-issues.html.

Gormley, Michael. 2001. "High Tech Stakes for Whom? Parents, Educators Revolt." *The Record*, May 6, 2001. https://www.troyrecord.com/news/high-tech-stakes-for-whom-parents-educators-revolt/article_aac79291-61e1-5f65-a256-ea2b5dadce5c.html.

Harris, Cheryl I. 1992. "Whiteness as Property." *Harvard Law Review* 106: 1707.

Harris, Elizabeth. 2015. "20% of State Students Opted Out of Tests in Sign of a Rising Revolt." *New York Times*, August 13, 2015.

Hayden, Dolores. 2002. *Redesigning the American Dream: The Future of Housing, Work, and Family Life*. W. W. Norton & Company.

———. 2015. "Building the American Way: Public Subsidy, Private Space." In *American Democracy and the Pursuit of Equality*, 70–82. Routledge.

Hildebrand, John. 2013. "LI Schools, Parents Prepare for More Rigorous Tests." *Newsday*, April 7, 2013. https://www.newsday.com/long-island/education/li-students-parents-uneasy-over-more-rigorous-tests-1.5025321.

———. 2018. "Test Boycotts Top 50% on LI as Large Opt-Outs Continue." *Newsday*, April 13, 2018. https://www.newsday.com/long-island/education/state-test-ela-opt-outs-1.18005317.

———. 2019. "NY: District, School Regain Good Academic Standing." *Newsday*, February 12. https://www.newsday.com/long-island/education/freeport-schools-atkinson-intermediate-academic-standing-1.27199629.

Jones-Correa, Michael. 2000. "The Origins and Diffusion of Racial Restrictive Covenants." *Political Science Quarterly* 115 (4): 541–68.
Koch, Tom. 2017. *Ethics in Everyday Places: Mapping Moral Stress, Distress, and Injury*. MIT Press.
Koubek, Richard. 1971. "Wyandanch: A Case Study of Political Impotence in a Black Suburban Ghetto." PhD thesis, Queens College. Department of Political Science.
Kucsera, John, and Gary Orfield. 2014. "New York State's Extreme School Segregation: Inequality, Inaction and a Damaged Future." Available at https://civilrightsproject.ucla.edu/research/k-12-education/integration-and-diversity/ny-norflet-report-placeholder.
Lipsitz, George. 2006. *The Possessive Investment in Whiteness: How White People Profit from Identity Politics*. Temple University Press.
———. 2011. *How Racism Takes Place*. Temple University Press.
Mitchell, Katharyne. 2010. "Pre-Black Futures." *Antipode* 41: 239–61. https://doi.org/10.1111/j.1467-8330.2009.00724.x.
National Commission on Excellence in Education. 1983. "A Nation at Risk: The Imperative for Educational Reform." *Elementary School Journal* 84 (2): 113–30.
Neem, Johann N. 2017. *Democracy's Schools: The Rise of Public Education in America*. JHU Press.
Omi, Michael, and Howard Winant. 2014. *Racial Formation in the United States*. Routledge.
Orfield, Gary, and Erica Frankenberg. 2014. "Increasingly Segregated and Unequal Schools as Courts Reverse Policy." *Educational Administration Quarterly* 50 (5): 718–34.
Orfield, Myron. 2011. *American Metropolitics: The New Suburban Reality*. Brookings Institution Press.
Pizmony-Levy, Oren, and Nancy Green Saraisky. 2016. "Who Opts Out and Why? Results from a National Survey on Opting Out of Standardized Tests."
Posey-Maddox, Linn. 2016. "Beyond the Consumer: Parents, Privatization, and Fundraising in US Urban Public Schooling." *Journal of Education Policy* 31 (2): 178–97.
Ravitch, Diane. 2020. *Slaying Goliath: The Passionate Resistance to Privatization and the Fight to Save America's Public Schools*. Knopf.
Robinson, Cedric J. 2000. *Black Marxism: The Making of the Black Radical Tradition*. University of North Carolina Press.
Roediger, David R. 1991. *The Wages of Whiteness: Race and the Making of the American Working Class*. Verso.
Rooks, Noliwe. 2017. *Cutting School: Privatization, Segregation, and the End of Public Education*. New Press.
Sattin-Bajaj, Carolyn, and Allison Roda. 2018. "Opportunity Hoarding in School Choice Contexts: The Role of Policy Design in Promoting Middle-Class Parents' Exclusionary Behaviors." *Educational Policy* 34 (7). https://doi.org/10.1177/0895904818802106.
Smith, Neil. 2010. *Uneven Development: Nature, Capital, and the Production of Space*. University of Georgia Press.
Strauss, Valerie. 2016. "The Testing Opt-Out Movement Is Growing, despite Government Efforts to Kill It." *Washington Post*, January 31, 2016. https://www.washingtonpost.com/news/answer-sheet/wp/2016/01/31/the-testing-opt-out-movement-is-growing-despite-government-efforts-to-kill-it.
Teaford, Jon C. 1997. *Post-Suburbia: Government and Politics in the Edge Cities*. Johns Hopkins University Press.
———. 2006. *The Metropolitan Revolution: The Rise of Post-Urban America*. Columbia University Press.
Wong, Katarina. 2017. "Racing on Two Different Tracks: Using Substantive Due Process to Challenge Tracking in Schools." *Duke Journal of Constitutional Law and Public Policy Sidebar* 13: 163.

PART 2
YOUTH RESISTANCE AND RESILIENCE

The chapters in the previous part explored intersections of law, youth categorizations, and geographies of power. This part follows these discussions with consideration of the other side of youth interactions with law and politics: youth resistance and resilience. The chapters further showcase the unique vantage points young people gain from their lived experience. Methodologically, these chapters more heavily rely on the experiences of youth directly impacted by the forms of law, policy, and categorization discussed in part 1. Doing so demonstrates how young people themselves are often aware of the realities produced by power relations, and how they push against them.

To open this part, Weissman, Rodriguez, and Weissman link the themes from the first part to the second by discussing both the processes of racialized criminalization of youth and youth resistance to these processes. They analyze the emergence of the "superpredator" narrative, describing how politicians wield this narrative in the service of mass incarceration. Coded racial language was key to "tough on crime" policies, resulting in the further proliferation of the carceral state. The authors center their argument on the firsthand experiences of young people pushed into the school-to-prison pipeline and the realities they face under the pervasive policing and increased surveillance within schools. However, rather than becoming passive victims of policy, youth and others directly impacted by juvenile incarceration lead transformative social change. The chapter highlights the collaborations of young people ensnared in the criminal justice system and formerly incarcerated people who now serve as mentors, or "credible messengers," as they push back against the criminalization of children. Youth and grassroots organizations form strategic coalitions as they resist the created punitive system and its extended consequences. These coalitions reflect the movement building and resilience that are fundamental to move beyond mere reform and toward fundamental structural change.

Continuing the theme of resilience and resistance, Benson explores how queer youth of color are criminalized yet show resilience in pursuit of police reform and community creation. In this case study of queer youth activists in New Orleans, Benson discusses the importance of intersectional alliances. Here, the LGBTQ+ youth of color collective BreakOUT! work with undocumented organizers to further resist criminalization and build liberatory movements. Key here is that BreakOUT! makes intersectionality a vital feature of their organizing, and the resulting collaboration facilitates stronger social movements. The chapter also reveals how deep knowledge of culture facilitates the intersectional work among those of varying positionalities in the South. They acknowledge complexities that move beyond oversimplified narratives of marginalization. Members of the collaborating organizations built a coalition that is attentive to the complicated realities of different community members. The youth highlighted in this case exhibit flexibility and evolution of philosophy as they reorient their understandings of racialized categorizations through their experiences with differently marginalized peoples. They use this knowledge to imagine alternative futures as well as to make concrete suggestions for changes to policing in relation to both communities.

Adding to part 2's emphasis on the experiences of those directly impacted by law and policy, Morris and McGowan center the experiences of young Black students taking part in a desegregation plan in the St. Louis school system. The chapter is an important examination of the effects of policies that attempt to counter structural racism in hyper-segregated cities, highlighting the policies and practices imposed on Black students in school desegregation plans as well as the many ways in which students create spaces and tactics of resistance to these practices. By centering the lived experiences of Black students participating in desegregation plans, the authors show that the harm of segregation does not end with the increased presence of Black students. Instead, the implementation of these desegregation plans often continues to marginalize Black students socially, culturally, and academically. Through interviews, the authors explore the consequences for Black students who took part in the process of desegregating the school system and how Black students name and resist the marginalization they experience. Students demonstrate resilience and resistance in the face of differential course placement of students by race, as well as institutional attempts at deculturalization. Morris and McGowan found that it was Black students, and not necessarily the teachers and district administrators, who took the initiative to resist the academic marginalization and deculturalization that followed the initial push for desegregation. As with previous chapters in this part, young people are shown not to be passive victims; in many cases, they offer their own solutions to the institutional struggles they face.

Finally, Ortiz shows how youth litigants form "a tribunal of the future" in response to climate change. They challenge what he terms the US "petroscape" and the environmental destruction wrought by extractive capitalism. Litigants question entrenched modes of capitalism and the acknowledged effects of climate change. The case study of youth-led litigation against a nebulous and challenging present and future issue speaks to the ways in which youth are making novel claims to rights. They push back against the deliberate shirking of responsibility by older generations who discount the future in exchange for short-term gains for a powerful few. Through these lawsuits, the category of youth is mobilized to expand and intervene into entrenched legal regimes surrounding the problem of climate change and to confront questions concerning generational responsibility. Today's young people, and future generations, will be the ones to face the consequences of climate change, while those currently accelerating it are unlikely to see the long-term negative results of their actions. This case study demonstrates creative claims to rights that reorient the justice system toward care for both young people and the future. This chapter and others reveal how youth grapple with the diffuse net of power shaped by dominant power structures and the limits to current socio-legal framings in dealing with temporal justice.

The chapters in this part show that youth are asking new questions, reshaping discourse, building community, and working to make new presents and futures possible. Youth are frequently aware of the limitations of political and legal structures and actively challenge the unsatisfactory legal frameworks that shape their lives. In doing so, they can both create and reframe movements and strategies for change making, forging new pathways toward just futures. The resistance by youth whose lives are affected by punitive and exploitative practices holds the power to reshape the socio-legal structures of our society and bring fundamental change.

CHAPTER 5

THE COMING OF THE SUPERPREDATORS: RACE, POLICING, AND RESISTANCE TO THE CRIMINALIZATION OF YOUTH

Marsha Weissman, Glenn Rodriguez, and Evan Weissman

By the mid-1990s, the narrative of the "superpredator" had a firm grip on the public discourse about crime, with dire consequences for poor youth of color. Across the nation, state policies pushed children as young as twelve into the adult criminal justice system and, if they were convicted, sent them to large, prison-like institutions[1] far from their homes and communities. The toxic perception of poor children of color as violent and dangerous criminals spread from the criminal justice system into schools and classrooms. Adolescent misbehavior was criminalized, falling under the purview of school-based police rather than teachers and principals, driving young people into what many have called the "school-to-prison pipeline"[2] (Wald and Losen 2003; Weissman 2015).

In this chapter we explore themes of how and why young people of color are fixed in the (white) American imagination as dangerous predators to be feared and caged. The construction of this stereotype dates back to the very founding of the US continuing through the early history of the juvenile justice system. Now contemporary policies such as zero tolerance and policing of schools work to (re)produce capitalist structures, racism, and sexism and extend social control over young Black and Brown bodies. Increasingly, youths' journeys into the criminal justice system begin at school. Drawing upon qualitative interviews with young people ensnared in the criminal justice system and formerly incarcerated people who now serve as "credible messengers"[3] to help guide youth out of this system, we examine how such marginalized people resist this stereotype, reclaim their humanity, and use their redefined personae to dismantle oppressive criminal justice laws and policies.

METHODS

This chapter is based on existing literature on juvenile justice and previous projects, especially interviews conducted from 2010 to 2016. We interviewed young people directly impacted by the juvenile justice system and youth pushed out of school. We also interviewed formerly incarcerated people who, at the time of the interview, were employed as "credible messengers" in a program working with youth in the juvenile justice system. Finally, we draw on the experience of the authors, who have long worked on issues of juvenile justice reform.[4]

MASS INCARCERATION AND JUVENILE JUSTICE: THE TETHER OF RACISM

Race looms large throughout any examination of the juvenile or criminal justice system in the United States. In twenty-first-century America, a criminal record has become a surrogate for race-based discrimination, serving the same function as the Black Codes and Jim Crow laws in earlier times (Alexander 2010). Hyper-aggressive policing in low-income communities of color has led to the overrepresentation of African Americans and Latinos among those with criminal convictions. Under the race neutral rubric of crime control, "tough on crime" became coded language for containment of the largely African American "castaways" of the US population (Wacquant 2009). Incarceration rates vary dramatically for whites and people of color. Although African Americans and Latinos comprise 29 percent of the US population, they make up 57 percent of its prison population. African American adults are 5.9 times more likely to be incarcerated than whites, and Hispanics are 3.1 times as likely (Carson 2018). In 2016, the rate of incarceration was 274 per 100,000 white adults, compared to 856 per 100,000 for Hispanics and a shocking 1,608 per 100,000 for black adults (Gramlich 2018).

These disparities show up in the juvenile justice system as well. African American youth are 4.1 times as likely to be committed to secure placements (a euphemism for juvenile prisons) as whites, "American Indians" [sic] are 3.1 times as likely, and "Hispanics" are 1.5 times as likely (Sickmund et al. 2017). Data from the W. Haywood Burns Institute (2016) show that while youth confinement has declined dramatically, racial disparities in the juvenile justice system have risen during that time.

Much as in the juvenile and criminal justice system, the prisonization[5] of schools is overrepresented in urban schools and directed at students of color. According to the New York Civil Liberties Union (2007), increased law enforcement and security measures are concentrated in the schools whose student body is disproportionately students of color: 82 percent of children attending NYC schools with metal detectors were black and Latino, surpassing their representation in the citywide school population by 11 percent. US Department of Education (2018) data showed that in the 2015–16 school year, more than 291,100 students were referred to law enforcement agencies or arrested throughout the US. Children of color made up 51 percent of enrolled students but represented 64 percent of students who were arrested or referred to police.

The data on the scope of retributive policies in the US are clear, spanning both carceral institutions and schools. In 2018, there were 2.3 million people incarcerated in jails, prisons, and detention facilities. The path of these more than 2 million people often starts with school suspension that in turn pushes young people out of school. In the 2015–2016 school year, 2.7 million children were suspended out of school. The National Center for Education Statistics shows that 31 percent of students who had been suspended three or more times before the spring of their sophomore year did not complete high school, compared to 6 percent of students who had never been suspended (Institute of Education Sciences 2006, table 27-2). Western (2006) found education to have the most profound impact on the likelihood of incarceration, with high school students who drop out or are pushed out of school five times more likely to go to prison than high school graduates regardless of race. The combination of race, gender, and education level is devastating. A 2016 Brookings Institution study reports that black men without a high school diploma who are in their thirties have a 70 percent chance of going to prison (Kearney et al. 2014).

In addition, in 2018, 840,000 people were on parole and 3.7 million people were on probation in the US, bringing the total number people under some form of correctional control to 15 million (Wagner and Sawyer 2018). This enormous number does not include the millions of people who have a past conviction, nor does it include their family members who have been affected by the incarceration of a loved one. But the sheer numbers of young people and adults ensnared in the criminal justice system as well as their families, combined with the stark racial disparities, shape the resistance to these punishing policies and practices; directly impacted people lead resistance to mass criminalization. Opposing the carceral state is a matter of individual, family, and community survival.

A CLOSER LOOK: THE CRIMINALIZATION OF MARGINALIZED YOUNG PEOPLE

The treatment of juveniles who engage in behaviors thought to be criminal or delinquent has been one of the most contentious issues in America's long-running debate about crime and justice. The underlying issue is the question of culpability: is there something different about childhood and adolescence that justifies separate and distinct treatment by the justice system? To be clear, the recognition of distinctions between children and adults has never been about absolving young people of responsibilities for wrongdoing. Rather it is about constructing appropriate responses to youths' intellectual and emotional development—that is, policies and practices that are derived from an understanding of the effects of juvenile justice interventions on adolescent development. Judge Julian Mack, one of the first juvenile court judges, expressed it this way: "The child who must be brought into court should, of course, be made to know that he is face to face with the power of the state, but he should at the same time, and more emphatically, be made to feel that he is the object of its care and solicitude" (Mack 1909).[6] Despite the seeming concern for the well-being of children, the responses to perceived juvenile delinquency have never been class or race neutral. For example, the House of Refuge, America's first juvenile facility, was established in 1824 for the purpose of controlling and containing "the children of poor and often vicious emigrants; from the intemperance of parents, and the frequent want, misery and ignorance of their children" ("Our City Charities" 1860, 2). By the mid-1800s, early reform schools were criticized for their punitive character, and debates about how to handle youth deemed delinquent continued. The perspective of the nascent progressive movement of the time prevailed, and in 1899, the Illinois Juvenile Court Act was passed, establishing the Cook County Juvenile Court as the first juvenile court in the US. Its focus was ostensibly rehabilitation rather than punishment. By 1925, juvenile courts were established in all but two states.

The intent of the early juvenile justice reformers notwithstanding, there is little evidence that their rehabilitative goals were achieved. Despite efforts to distinguish the juvenile justice system from the adult system, the systems were glaringly similar. Young people were removed from their home communities and sent to large harsh and punitive institutions typically located at considerable distance from their families. Ironically, however, young people tried in juvenile courts were subject to these conditions without the due process rights of the adult criminal justice system (Fox 1969).

By the 1960s, the informality of a juvenile justice system with such far-reaching powers was called into question. In 1967, the Supreme Court required that juveniles accused of crimes in delinquency proceedings be afforded the due process rights granted to adults, including the right to counsel (In re Gault, 387 U.S. 1 [1967]). Just as with the creation of separate juvenile justice institutions, the Gault decision did not achieve all the results advocates pushed for (Buss 2003). The scope of the rights that were extended to children remained unclear, including whether the right to attorney meant that indigent children could have an attorney appointed to represent them. Vigorous legal advocacy was often absent in juvenile court, where the culture remained less formal than the adult system. The impact of the Gault decision was also constrained by the punitive policies that came to characterize American criminal justice system for decades to come (Feld 1990).

THE SUPERPREDATORS ARE COMING!

The juvenile justice system has long struggled with its role and purpose, vacillating between punishment and rehabilitation, expanding and restricting juvenile rights, and pondering over notions of culpability. The "get tough" perspectives coalesced in a particularly ugly way in the mid-1990s with the labeling of American children (of color) as "superpredators." The racialization of black children as violent, out of control, and fundamentally threatening was explicitly articulated by the chief proponent of the superpredator brand, John DiIulio, a political scientist and former director of the White House Office of Faith-Based and Community Initiatives under President George W. Bush: "[T]he black kids who inspire fear seem not merely unrecognizable but alien. . . . all that's left of the black community in some pockets of urban America is deviant, delinquent and criminal adults surrounded by severely abused and neglected children, virtually all of whom were born out of wedlock" (1996, 20). The unprecedented punitive turn of the US juvenile justice system actually began before DiIulio unambiguously demonized children, specifically black children. In 1978, NYS passed the first—and harshest—of such laws, the Juvenile Offender Law, allowing youth under the age of sixteen to be treated as adults if charged with certain violent felony offenses. Like most criminal justice policies, it was driven by a combination of one aberrational—albeit terrible—crime[7] and political considerations to avoid being labeled "soft on crime." Other states followed suit, and by the mid-1990s, all states had laws that allowed for youth under the age of eighteen to be treated in the adult criminal justice system for certain crimes involving violence. While the exact number is not known, estimates suggest that as many as 200,000 to 250,000 youth a year are tried as adults in the United States (Marshall Project 2014).

Inflammatory political rhetoric about the threat of a generation of superpredators was relentless and part of the larger American project of mass incarceration. The US carceral state has subsumed the welfare state as a response to social and economic needs of its most marginalized population, a population that is excluded from an ever-shrinking job market (Western and Beckett 1999). The US criminal justice system became the mechanism to contain and disenfranchise communities of color, the latest in a long line of venal racism that includes slavery, the Black Codes, and Jim Crow. It has become the dog whistle (López 2014) of American politics reminding (white) voters what is at stake in elections (Mendelberg 2017).

BRINGING THE CARCERAL STATE TO THE CLASSROOM

By the mid-1990s, these criminal justice policies crept into schools, targeting poor children of color and the labeling those children as violent and dangerous (Weissman 2015). Schools that serve as a pipeline to prison are spatially concentrated, like other aspects of the carceral state, located in the "million dollar blocks"[8] (Kurgan and Cadora 2005) that are the home communities of the majority of people in prison. Fathers and older brothers go to prison while children go to dilapidated, underresourced schools.

Public schools in these neighborhoods reflect the carceral culture in many ways. For example, zero-tolerance suspension policies are analogous to mandatory sentencing. Pervasive police presence, pro-arrest policies, and expanded surveillance and security also mimic prisons. This transformation of schools into prison-like institutions is well captured by Loïc Wacquant: "Public schools in the hyperghetto have similarly deteriorated to the point where they operate in the manner of *institutions of confinement* whose primary mission is not to educate but to ensure 'custody and control'—to borrow the motto of many departments of corrections" (Wacquant 2001, 108; emphasis in original). Police have become a ubiquitous presence in schools. In the late 1970s, there were only one hundred school police officers. By the close of the twentieth century, the number of school resource/police officers was about fourteen thousand (Brady, Balmer, and Phenix 2007). The number of police deployed in New York City schools exceeded the size of the entire Boston police force (Beger 2002). The expanded role of police in schools is disconcerting to students, conveying a sense that they are in a place of danger.

Young people's reactions to police in schools is also informed by their experiences of policing in their communities. One young person interviewed, Kora,[9] said that she found the presence of police in school frightening. Asked why she felt this way, Kora explained that it was because she witnessed her mother's arrest: "[It was] horrible, horrible because it was my mom that got arrested. We watched her get arrested. I was outside watching her in front of the apartment building. It was sad to see my mom get arrested." Kwame likewise viewed the police as problematic: "It's bad. Because you could be just messing with somebody and they acting like they arguing and stuff and then a cop just come out of nowhere and grab you and stuff and start slamming you on the ground and put their knee in your back and stuff."

The carceral culture of schools is not lost on the students who attend such institutions. This is especially apparent for students who are suspended and are removed from the general public school population and sent to so-called "alternative schools," where the levels of security and surveillance are even higher. Daily searches, the use of metal detectors, pat-downs and wanding by security guards, and police presence in halls actualize the metaphor of the "school-to-prison pipeline" (Weissman 2015). The young people subject to these practices well understand that they are in a jail-like setting. Here is what Jay, a tenth grader, had to say: "At Steel alternative school, they treat you like you in jail. When you walked through there [you go through] three searches in one day . . . When they pat you down, then you have to walk up through the metal detector and even if you don't go off, they still wand you. So, I just feel like, wow we're in jail." Another young woman, Janella, elaborated how the searches are even more intrusive for girls and resemble strip searches that prisoners are subjected to:

> Steel is like jail. You got to take off all your stuff when you get in there. You got to take your shoes off and get searched. Then when you go up the stairs, you have to take off all of your like jewelry and stuff and put it in this big old box. And then take your shoes off again and put them in the box. And then walk through the metal detectors and then you get wanded down. Then if you beep, they are going to take you in the bathroom and tell you to empty out all of your pockets. And then they move around and unzip your pants and all that stuff. . . . It makes me feel uncomfortable because they had a lady touching on your butt and everything. They empty out your bra and stuff to see if you have any weapons.

The youth are also aware of how school disciplinary policies and practices, particularly zero-tolerance policies, are rigid and harsh. Roland's experience captures the effect of criminal justice policies. Roland and his younger brother rode a school bus to school each day. One morning, Roland learned that his brother had a pen knife in his pocket: the brother said he needed it to protect himself from bullies. Roland took the knife away from his brother, knowing that it was not the appropriate way to deal with the problem. Roland was well aware of the school's zero-tolerance policy—that is, that having anything that could be considered a weapon would result in out of school suspension. Roland intended to turn the knife in, but before he had an opportunity to do so, was intercepted by the bus aide and teacher. Roland's description of the consequences show resignation to his fate but also confusion about, and alienation from, a system that could not consider the circumstances of his behavior:

> They literally had no choice but to send me to Brig alternative school because it (the knife) was in my possession. They [school administrators] said to me that they know I didn't do nothing wrong, but if my hand touches the knife then they have no choice but to send me out [. . .] But when they said that they were gonna ya' know suspend me, that's what had got me upset. I started crying because I didn't understand the fact that me getting suspended just for taking the knife away from my brother, because if I didn't take it away from him, it could have been, ya' know, a dead student.

Finally, the young people are also well aware that certain bodies are policed and not others. A comment made by Anna highlights this awareness: "why is everyone [white people] always so worried about us [students of color]?"

CREDIBLE MESSENGERS: BRINGING DIRECTLY IMPACTED PEOPLE INTO SERVICE

Notwithstanding the dismal data and narratives above, we are at a moment in history when criminal and juvenile justice reform is touted across the political spectrum. The number of people incarcerated has decreased slightly from a high of 2.3 million in 2008 to 2.1 million in 2018. The changes in juvenile incarceration are more notable, decreasing by 55 percent between 1997 and 2013 (W. Haywood Burns Institute 2016), although the continuing racial disparities in juvenile confinement undermine this achievement. States like New York and Missouri are closing their juvenile justice facilities. Through its "Close to Home" initiative, New York City no longer sends youth adjudicated as juvenile delinquents to state institutions. Instead, they are involved in community-based programs or, if placement is ordered, sent to small group homes near their homes and families (Weissman, Ananthakrishnan, and Schiraldi 2019). The number of out-of-school suspensions and expulsions declined by 20 percent between 2012 and 2014 (Steinberg and Lacoe 2016).

History demonstrates that both transformative social change and more modest reforms are advanced by directly impacted people and their allies. Criminal and juvenile justice advances are no different, although the impediments to their leadership and activism are distinct. The stigmatization of formerly incarcerated people is particularly extreme, often resulting in lifetime social exclusions in a range of domains, including most notably employment as well as voting, housing, education, and other forms of civic participation.

These barriers make the growing involvement of formerly incarcerated people in keeping young people out of the criminal justice system remarkable. Once barred from working with system-involved youth, formerly incarcerated people, called "credible messengers," are now sought after as mentors to youth in the juvenile justice system. The term "credible messenger" is used to describe people who have backgrounds similar to the populations they serve. Such individuals may also be referred to as peer leaders, peer educators, or mentors.

A common background, shared experiences, and authenticity are now considered to be central to meaningful connections with people dealing with a range of problems from addiction, to HIV and AIDS, to community violence. Peers with similar lived experiences help overcome mistrust of formal institutions that address these problems. For juvenile justice programs, credible messengers are individuals who can draw on their past criminal justice system experiences to connect with young people currently involved in the system.

What role, if any, do credible messengers have in resisting mass incarceration? Through their direct service, formerly incarcerated people are presented as leaders and as contributors to programs that aim to prevent the incarceration of youth. This role alone helps to change the conversation: seeing individuals who are often demonized as unredeemable in new—and inspiring—roles provokes debates about our carceral systems and its overreliance on incarceration. It raises questions about the policies of lifelong exclusion that are imposed even once people are released.

Formerly incarcerated men interviewed understand how their experiences in the criminal justice system could lend credibility to their work with young people. Glenn Rodriguez, incarcerated for murder at the age of sixteen in 1990, recognized the power of using his experiences to motivate young people long before his release in 2017. For over a decade of his incarceration (1999–2011), Glenn volunteered for the Youth Assistance Program (YAP). Operating in a maximum-security prison, YAP represents a precursor to what has since become the "credible messenger movement" (Credible Messenger Justice Center n.d.; Maruna 2017).

Glenn and the other individuals interviewed work for an organization that provides alternative-to-incarceration programming for youth in the juvenile justice system, including young people charged with serious crimes involving violence. Youth are released by courts to the program in lieu of incarceration. They must comply with court-ordered conditions such as participating in counseling, obeying a curfew, attending school, and engaging in positive youth development activities. They also meet regularly with their case manager, who reports to the court about the youth's compliance with the terms of their release.

Credible messengers, however, play a different role in the program; they are not part of the mandated requirements, and they have no court reporting obligations. One such person interviewed distinguished his role as credible mentor in this way: "The case manager plays the parent role. We, as mentors, play the brother role."

Credible messengers are motivated by a desire to "give back" to communities they may have harmed and a commitment to redirect young people away from mistakes they have made. One mentor said, "I wanted to work with youth. I had a hand in creating conditions in the community that can lead them astray. I ran those streets ... I can influence these kids without judging them." Being able to unconditionally support young people without being judgmental was a theme reiterated by all of the mentors interviewed. "I have to be there for them, not judge them" was offered by another mentor.

Becoming a credible messenger is also a mechanism for formerly incarcerated people to reintroduce themselves to their communities, families, and even themselves. One person reflecting on his role as a credible messenger said, "I never thought I could do this out here." He found it therapeutic for him to tell his life story to young people and a way to reinforce his personal commitment to desistance.[10]

Emerging research on the impact of credible messengers is showing promising results. An evaluation of the Arches Transformative Mentoring Program in New York City found that youth who participated in Arches had felony reconviction rates that were 69 percent lower after twelve months and 57 percent lower after twenty-four months than a comparison group (Lynch et al. 2018). Further, and consistent with the discussion above, credible messengers themselves benefit from being able to service in this manner. A pilot study by Lopez-Humphreys and Teater (2019) found a statistically significant improvement in mentors' self-esteem, level of hope, and self-identity change behaviors from pretest to posttest.

However, the engagement of directly impacted people is not without risks, including shoehorning formerly incarcerated people into the role of credible messenger. One individual interviewed cautioned that individuals with criminal justice experience may be tracked into the credible messenger role as one of their only available employment opportunities. Credible messengers are vulnerable to being used to perform tasks that might otherwise be done by higher-paid, full-time professional employees.

Equally if not more concerning is the possibility that the credible messenger movement, now popular in the not-for-profit sector, may be used as a mechanism to depoliticize and coopt social justice movements. Criticism of the not-for-profit sector points to its role as a "shadow state"[11] established to cushion the blows of increasing inequality and economic destitution of marginalized populations (Gilmore 2007). Not-for-profit organizations, including those run by social justice advocates, get caught up in the competition for scarce resources provided by a philanthropic sector whose wealth is derived from the very economic structure that causes the stark inequities driving mass incarceration (Mananzala and Spade 2008). It may be used to attract funding from foundations that are enamored with the credible messenger concept as the latest fashion and have made this a required element for projects they support.

Despite these concerns, credible messengers whose service contributions are grounded in their lived experiences are better positioned to resist cooptation by the "not-for-profit industrial complex" (Smith 2007). Not only can they influence service delivery, but they also play a role in advocacy efforts. Maruna (2017) likens the efforts of credible messengers to a social movement similar to the civil rights movement, achieving victories such as "ban the box," restoration of voting rights, bail and sentencing reform, and prison closures.

RESISTANCE AND REFORM

Incarcerated and formerly incarcerated people, others with criminal records, and their families have pushed back against social exclusion produced by of a criminal record and play critical leadership roles in reform. Examples of community-level struggles date back to the very emergence of mass incarceration. The national community-organizing effort Attica Is All of Us began in 1971, led by the people who were charged in the aftermath of the rebellion. Joined by allies around the country, the organizing effort resulted in the dismissal of all but one of the indictments against the sixty-two men who were charged in the prison uprising (Weissman 2009). The protests did more than achieve some modicum of justice for those indicted; they also sparked the grassroots movements and activities to counter mass incarceration that continue to this day. For example, in the early 1970s, Eddie Ellis, a member of the Black Panther Party, founded the Think Tank while incarcerated in a NYS maximum security facility. Its research was the first to identify the geographic concentration of incarceration in poor communities of color (Clines 1992). The Attica rebellion sparked interest in prison conditions, and the growing use of incarceration spurred the creation of organizations devoted to prisoners' rights (e.g., Prisoner Legal Services) as well as groups challenging the prison-industrial complex (e.g., Critical Resistance).

In recent years, the leadership of directly impacted people has become more visible in changing public opinion and promoting criminal justice policy reforms. The Dignity in Schools Campaign (DSC) is one of the best examples of the ways that youth and parent-led grassroots organizations push back against the criminalization of children. DSC and its roughly one hundred organizational members lead reforms of school discipline policies, including the adoption of policies that limit the use of suspension. In Syracuse, New York, for example, new policies and practices resulted in a 71 percent decrease in suspensions between 2014 and 2018 (Atkinson 2018). The decline in suspensions was accompanied by a 14-point increase in the District's graduation rate over the same time period (New York State Department of Education 2019).

Similarly, organizations led by parents and youth spearhead reforms in the juvenile justice system. Families and Friends of Louisiana's Incarcerated Children played a major role in efforts to close the notorious Swanson Correctional Center for Youth, and in New York, youth and parent voices were at the forefront of the decades-long struggle to "raise the age" of criminal responsibility from sixteen to eighteen, resulting in legislation that passed in 2016.

Directly impacted people disrupt and challenge the dominant paradigm by sharing their stories and demanding and designing solutions based on their experience. The strategies employed vary from street actions such as protests and marches, to bearing witness and testifying, to voter mobilization. In one notable example from our own work, in 2008, youth participated with the US Human Rights Network in its report to the UN Convention on Ending Racial Discrimination in All Forms. One of four youth invited to testify, Jenna, spoke eloquently about the school-to-prison pipeline and racial disparities in the juvenile justice system. Reflecting on their experience, Jenna emphatically asserted, "We are all activists now!"

When directly impacted parents testify, they reveal the horror of the system as evident by this statement from a parent in California, whose son was incarcerated: "My son has made mistakes in his life. But he wasn't sentenced to be tortured. He wasn't sentenced to sit in a cold cell by himself all day with no help. And he wasn't sentenced to be viciously beaten by guards" (Justice for Families 2012, 23).

By telling their stories, young people become uncontroverted advocates for reform. Ismael Nazario became a major spokesperson for Raise the Age New York. His story brought more people into the campaign and was hard for policy makers to ignore:

> We need to change the culture in our jails and prisons, especially for young inmates . . . I know firsthand. Before I ever turned 18, I spent approximately 400 days on Rikers Island, and to add to that I spent almost 300 days in solitary confinement, and let me tell you this: screaming at the top of your lungs all day on your cell door or screaming at the top of your lungs out the window . . . you start pacing back and forth in your cell, you start talking to yourself, your thoughts start running wild, and then your thoughts become your own worst enemy. Jails are actually supposed to rehabilitate a person, not cause him or her to become more angry, frustrated, and feel more hopeless. (Nazario 2014)

The cumulative effect of these narratives has been the driver behind justice system reforms; directly impacted people have challenged and educated the public and the policy-making and political elites. The 2020 presidential campaign shows the strength of this collective voice. Through the activism of Black Lives Matter, the criminal justice reform has become a central concern that can no longer be avoided.

CONCLUSION

The organized resistance of youth caught up in the school-to-prison pipeline and people whose lives have been upended by the extraordinarily punitive policy of America's carceral state are essential to moving beyond meager reforms to more fundamental structural change. While centering their activism on criminal justice reform, groups like DSC recognize the intersectionality with the other mechanisms of dominance such as racism, homophobia, Islamophobia, and other fundamental social conditions under which the policies of carceral control emerged. JustLeadership, an organization founded and led by formerly incarcerated people that has been active in the successful effort to close the notorious Rikers Island jail, has turned its attention to challenging the toxic social conditions that go hand in hand with mass incarceration. Through #buildCOMMUNITIES, a coalition of health, mental health, education, and housing advocacy groups, along with criminal justice organizations, created an organizing platform calling for the reinvestment of the estimated $7.3 billion spent on the various criminal justice agencies in public health, housing, economic development, schools. #buildCOMMUNITIES further calls for investments to support grassroots groups rooted in their communities.

The young people and the credible messengers interviewed are the very leaders who will sustain what will be a difficult struggle to end the criminalization and incarceration that has so dominated our social policies. As Barbara Ransby (2003) summarized Ella Baker's message, "Oppressed people, whatever their level of formal education, have the ability to understand and interpret the world around them, to see the world for what it is, and move to transform it."

NOTES

1. States differ in the names they use for institutions that confine children convicted of criminal/delinquent behavior; names include juvenile centers, training schools, and juvenile correctional facilities.
2. Editor's note: While there are critiques of the phrase "school-to-prison pipeline," the authors choose to use it based on consultation with a number of community advocates. They note that the term, however imperfect, is most commonly used by those who work on dismantling school push-out, removing police from schools, and ending the criminalization of minors.
3. The term "credible messenger" refers to individuals with relevant life experiences, notably criminal justice system involvement, who connect with young people facing similar circumstances. Credible messengers may also be referred to as mentors or "wounded healers" (LeBel 2007; Maruna 2017). They may also assist formerly incarcerated adults in adjusting to release.
4. Marsha Weissman was the founding executive director of the Center for Community Alternatives, a not-for-profit organization working to end mass incarceration through research, advocacy, and services, and wrote *Prelude to Incarceration*, about youth experiences of school policing. Glenn Rodriguez volunteered for the Youth Assistance Program while incarcerated in a New York State maximum security prison. The Youth Assistance Program was founded by incarcerated people in an effort to share their life experiences with young people in nearby communities. Evan Weissman was a food justice activist-scholar and works with youth impacted by the criminal justice system. Dr. Weissman died in April 2020 at the beginning of the COVID-19 pandemic.
5. The term "prisonization" first appeared in a book by Donald Clemmer (1940), referring to the taking on of the culture and practices of penitentiaries by other social institutions. It has since been applied to schools: see for example Ahranjani (2016) and Payne and Welch (2010).
6. The creation of the juvenile court system was part of a larger nineteenth-century social reform movement concerning the treatment of children who came into conflict with the

law. Reformers focused on the need to separate children from adults and on rehabilitation rather than punishment. Juvenile courts were based on the doctrine of *parens patriae* (Latin for "parent of the country"), which gives the state the authority to act as the guardian of juveniles. Support for distinct juvenile justice institutions and practices has waxed and waned. In the 1990s calls for a punitive response to juvenile crime peaked, followed by a resurgence of interest in rehabilitation that surged in the early 2000s and continues to this day (see McCarthy, Schiraldi, and Shark 2016).

7. The case in point involved a fifteen-year old boy, Willie Bosket, who killed two men on a New York City subway. Then governor Hugh Carey, facing formidable reelection challenges, called a special session of the state legislature to pass the Juvenile Offender Law of 1978. Willie Bosket's life is detailed in *All God's Children* by Fox Butterfield (2008). Willie Bosket remains incarcerated in a New York State prison.
8. This term captures the relationships between poverty, race, prison admissions, and prison expenditures revealing government expenditures that can exceed a million dollars to incarcerate poor people of color living within one census block.
9. The names of the youth interviewed as well as the schools have been changed to preserve confidentiality.
10. Within the study of criminology, "desistance" refers to the cessation of criminal behavior. See for example Kazemian and Maruna (2009).
11. The term connotes the use of nongovernmental organizations to deliver social services previously offered by government agencies.

REFERENCES

Ahranjai, Maryam. 2016. "The Prisonization of America's Public Schools." *Hofstra Law Review* 45: 1097.

Alexander, Michelle. 2010. *The New Jim Crow: Mass Incarceration in the Age of Colorblindness*. New Press.

Atkinson, C. 2018. "Progress Report: Syracuse City School District AOD Priority Areas 2017–2018 School Year."

Beger, Randall R. 2002. "Expansion of Police Power in Public Schools and the Vanishing Rights of Students." *Social Justice* 29 (1/2): 119–30.

Brady, Kevin P., Sharon Balmer, and Deinya Phenix. 2007. "School–Police Partnership Effectiveness in Urban Schools: An Analysis of New York City's Impact Schools Initiative." *Education and Urban Society* 39 (4): 455–78.

Buss, Emily. 2003. "The Missed Opportunity in Gault." *University of Chicago Law Review* 70: 39–54.

Butterfield, Fox. 2008. *All God's Children: The Bosket Family and the American Tradition of Violence*. Vintage.

Carson, E. Ann. 2018. *Prisoners in 2016*. NCJ 251149. US Department of Justice, Bureau of Justice Statistics.

Clemmer, Donald. 1940. *The Prison Community*. Holt, Rinehart and Winston.

Clines, Francis X. 1992. "Ex-Inmates Urge Return to Areas of Crime to Help." *New York Times*, December 23.

Credible Messenger Justice Center. N.d. "Focal Point for Justice." https://cmjcenter.org.

DiIulio, John J., Jr. 1996. "My Black Crime Problem, and Ours." *City Journal* 6 (2): 14–28.

Feld, Barry C. 1990. "The Transformation of the Juvenile Court." *Minnesota Law Review* 75: 691.

Fox, Sanford J. 1969. "Juvenile Justice Reform: An Historical Perspective." *Stanford Law Review* 22: 1187–240.

Gilmore, Ruth Wilson. 2007. "In the Shadow of the Shadow State." In *Incite! The Revolution Will Not Be Funded: Beyond the Nonprofit Industrial Complex*: 41–52. South End Press.

Gramlich, John. 2018. "The Gap between the Number of Blacks and Whites in Prison Is Shrinking." *Pew Research Center*. http://www.pewresearch.org/fact-tank/2018/01/12/shrinking-gap-between-number-of-blacks-and-whites-in-prison.

Institute of Education Sciences. 2006. *The Condition of Education 2006 in Brief*. US Department of Education, National Center for Education Statistics.

Justice for Families. 2012. "Families Unlocking Futures: Solutions to the Crisis in Juvenile Justice." Oakland, CA: Justice for Families.

Kazemian, Lila, and Shadd Maruna. 2009. "Desistance from Crime." In *Handbook on Crime and Deviance*, 277–95. Springer.

Kearney, Melissa S., Benjamin H. Harris, Elisa Jácome, and Lucie Parker. 2014. *Ten Economic Facts about Crime and Incarceration in the United States*. Hamilton Project.

Kurgan, Laura, and Eric Cadora. 2005. "Million Dollar Blocks." http://countermapcollection.org/collection/million-dollar-blocks.

LeBel, Thomas P. 2007. "An Examination of the Impact of Formerly Incarcerated Persons Helping Others." *Journal of Offender Rehabilitation* 46 (1–2): 1–24.

López, Ian Haney. 2014. *Dog Whistle Politics: How Coded Racial Appeals Have Reinvented Racism and Wrecked the Middle Class*. New York: Oxford University Press.

Lopez-Humphreys, Mayra, and Barbra Teater. 2019: " 'It's What's on the Inside That Counts': A Pilot Study of the Subjective Changes among Returned Citizens Participating in a Peer-Mentor Support Initiative." *Journal of Social Service Research* 46 (6): 1–15.

Lynch, Matthew, Nan Marie Astone, Juan Collazos, Micaela Lipman, and Sino Esthappan. 2018. *Arches Transformative Mentoring Program: An Implementation and Impact Evaluation in New York City*. Justice Policy Center.

Mack, Julian W. 1909. "The Juvenile Court." *Harvard Law Review* 23 (2): 104–22.

Mananzala, Rickke, and Dean Spade. 2008. "The Nonprofit Industrial Complex and Trans Resistance." *Sexuality Research and Social Policy* 5 (1): 53–71.

Marshall Project. 2014. *The Willie Bosket Case: How Children Became Adults in the Eyes of the Law*. December 29. https://www.themarshallproject.org/2014/12/29/the-willie-bosket-case.

Maruna, Shadd. 2017. "Desistance as a Social Movement." *Irish Probation Journal* 14: 5–20.

McCarthy, Patrick, Vincent Schiraldi, and Miriam Shark. 2016. *The Future of Youth Justice: A Community-Based Alternative to the Youth Prison Model*. New Thinking in Community Corrections Bulletin. U.S. Department of Justice, National Institute of Justice.

Mendelberg, Tali. 2017. *The Race Card: Campaign Strategy, Implicit Messages, and the Norm of Equality*. Princeton University Press.

Nazario, Ismael. 2014. "What I Learned as a Kid in Jail." TEDxNewYork. October. https://www.ted.com/talks/ismael_nazario_what_i_learned_as_a_kid_in_jail/transcript.

New York Civil Liberties Union. 2007. *Criminalizing the Classroom: The Over-Policing of New York City Schools*.

New York State Department of Education. 2018. *NY Graduation Rate Data 4 Year Outcome as of August*. https://data.nysed.gov/gradrate.php?year=2018&state=yes.

"Our City Charities: The New York House of Refuge for Juvenile Delinquents." 1860. *New York Times*. January 23.

Payne, Allison Ann, and Kelly Welch. 2010. "Modeling the Effects of Racial Threat on Punitive and Restorative School Discipline Practices." *Criminology* 48 (4): 1019–62.

Ransby, Barbara. 2003. *Ella Baker and the Black Freedom Movement: A Radical Democratic Vision*. University of North Carolina Press.

Sickmund, M., T. J. Sladky, W. Kang, and C. Puzzanchera. 2017. "Easy Access to the Census of Juveniles in Residential Placement." Office of Juvenile Justice and Delinquency Prevention. http://www.ojjdp.gov/ojstatbb/ezacjrp.

Smith, Andrea. 2007. "Introduction: The Revolution Will Not Be Funded." In *The Revolution Will Not Be Funded: Beyond the Non-Profit Industrial Complex*, ed. Incite! Women of Color against Violence, 1–18. Duke University Press.
Steinberg, Matthew P., and Johanna Lacoe. 2016. "What Do We Know about School Discipline Reform?" *Education Next* 17 (1). https://www.educationnext.org/what-do-we-know-about-school-discipline-reform-suspensions-expulsions.
———. 2018. "2015–16 Civil Rights Data Collection: School Climate and Safety." https://www2.ed.gov/about/offices/list/ocr/docs/crdc-2015-16.html.
W. Haywood Burns Institute. 2016. "Stemming the Rising Tide: Racial and Ethnic Disparities in Youth Incarceration and Strategies for Change." https://www.burnsinstitute.org/blog/new-bi-report-highlights-troubling-trends-in-youth-of-color-incarceration.
Wacquant, Loïc. 2001. "Deadly Symbiosis: When Ghetto and Prison Meet and Mesh." *Punishment and Society* 3 (1): 95–133.
———. 2009. *Punishing the Poor: The Neoliberal Government of Social Insecurity*. Duke University Press.
Wagner, Peter, and Wendy Sawyer. 2018. *Mass Incarceration: The Whole Pie 2018*. Prison Policy Initiative. https://www.prisonpolicy.org/reports/pie2018.html.
Wald, Johann, and Daniel F. Losen. 2003. *Defining and Redirecting a School-to-Prison Pipeline*. Jossey-Bass.
Weissman, Marsha. 2009. "Aspiring to the Impracticable: Alternatives to Incarceration in the Era of Mass Incarceration." *NYU Review of Law and Social Change* 33 (2): 235.
———. 2015. *Prelude to Prison: Student Perspectives on School Suspension*. Syracuse University Press.
Weissman, Marsha, Vidhya Ananthakrishnan, and Vincent Schiraldi. 2019. *Moving beyond Youth Prisons: Lessons from New York City's Implementation of Close to Home*. Columbia University Justice Lab.
Western, Bruce. 2006. *Punishment and Inequality in America*. New York: Russell Sage Foundation.
Western, Bruce, and Katherine Beckett. 1999. "How Unregulated Is the US Labor Market? The Penal System as a Labor Market Institution." *American Journal of Sociology* 104 (4): 1030–60.

CHAPTER 6

BREAKOUT!: QUEER AND TRANS OF COLOR ACTIVISM IN NEW ORLEANS

Krista L. Benson

Analysis of youth contact with police and the justice system often focuses on the space of juvenile justice centers or juvenile justice courts. However, it is important to acknowledge that the juvenile justice system, much like the adult criminal justice system, is "not some building 'over there' but a set of relationships that undermine rather than stabilize everyday lives everywhere" (Gilmore 2007, 242). These sets of relationships and their impacts include instances when police profile youth—especially transgender girls of color—which aren't always reflected in data. Not every incident of police interaction results in arrest, but the threat is always there, as outlined later in the chapter. When comparing juvenile contact with the police by race in 2017 (Office of Juvenile Justice Detention and Prevention 2017) with 2010 US Census data (2011), it appears that juvenile justice officers detain or charge Asian American, Black, and Native youth at similar rates to their percentage of the population.[1] However, lesbian, gay, bisexual, transgender, and questioning (LGBTQ) youth of color are at much higher risk of coming into contact with police or the juvenile justice system than white LGBTQ youth or heterosexual youth of color. Therefore, as my analysis of the policing of youth in Louisiana demonstrates, these statistics are better understood in the context of the city of New Orleans and the parish practices of policing and detention in Louisiana more broadly. In this chapter, I analyze the activist work of BreakOUT!, a youth-lead organization that "seeks to end the criminalization of... [LGBTQ] youth to build a safer and more just New Orleans" (BreakOUT! n.d.). BreakOUT! has been working since its establishment in 2011 to bring critical attention to these issues, work for social change, and resist the criminalization and surveillance of LGBTQ youth from the grassroots. Later in the chapter, I explore the evolution of the ways that members of BreakOUT! articulate intersections of race, gender identity, gender expression, and sexuality in their major publications and reports and in their coalitional work with the Congress of Day Laborers/Congreso de Jornaleros (hereafter Congreso), who focus on advocating for immigrants who are undocumented or presumed undocumented.

This chapter is based in analysis of reports and documents created by BreakOUT!, both in collaboration with Congreso and alone. I am not a member of either organization, though I have been in communication with current and former members of both organizations. I was most interested in examining the resources that BreakOUT! produces for their community and to disseminate publicly, as this provides a view into the ways that the organization has evolved and the ways that their resources and analysis have developed over the last ten years.

BreakOUT! was started in 2011 by six founding members, including "5 Black transgender young women and 1 Black gay-identified young man" (BreakOUT! 2014, 12). Members founded the organization when they shared their stories with one another about police surveillance, harassment, and experiences of marginalization in New Orleans. From the beginning, BreakOUT! was taking the experiences of young people as the starting point of how to produce knowledge and create change. Since then, BreakOUT! secured the adoption of New Orleans Police Department Policy 402, which prohibits profiling by the police on the basis of gender expression, gender identity, or sexual orientation. The organization has also launched a GED program for BreakOUT! members, produced a theater performance that shares the lives of five transgender performers, launched the *Get Yr Rights* youth network in collaboration with Streetwise and Safe (NYC), and amplified LGBTQ youth voices (BreakOUT! 2014). They also produced their own tool kits and reports regarding race, gender, and sexuality and police contact. As described by BreakOUT!'s then healing justice coordinator[2] Nate Faulk, "BreakOUT! just seeks to be a safe place for trans black women, mostly, and, through that, the rest of the community overall" (McCann 2016, 101). This highlights a common radical organizing technique, wherein the fight for rights centers on the safety of the most vulnerable people. As the most vulnerable benefit, everyone else benefits.

In much of this work, BreakOUT! members talk about centering the experiences and safety of queer and trans people of color. "People of color" is a term that is widely used in other spaces, often in a way that tries to foster inclusivity. That said, when "queer and trans people of color" refers to only or primarily Black queer and trans people, there comes a troubling conflation of "people of color" and "Black people." Interestingly, this works *against* the ways that "people of color" is popularly used, often to erase Blackness. However, both rhetorical moves blur ways of understanding race and contact with police that can conflate differential racialized experience with police. This conflation allows for a Black/white racial binary that erases other people of color in its construction. The conflation of people of color with Black people is especially striking considering where the term "women of color" originated. In 1977, at the National Women's Conference, a group of Black women brought the "Black Women's Agenda" in response to a weak three-page "Minority Women's Plank" written by the conference organizers. When other racialized women and Indigenous women wanted to sign on to this agenda, it became clear that the name would need to change. There, those women created the political coalition term "women of color" (Ross 2011). Though earlier publications operate along this binary, this rhetoric shifts significantly in BreakOUT!'s publications with Congreso.

In this piece, I analyze the ways that BreakOUT's work is centered in a youth-centered Southern queer of color analysis and how that analysis has expanded through their work with Congreso, including with the families of Congreso members. To contextualize the national numbers of detentions and arrests of youth of color, BreakOUT! members write in collaboration with Congreso that

> Louisiana is the state with the highest rate of incarceration in the country [at the time of the report]; and New Orleans has the highest incarceration rate in Louisiana ... Louisiana has the highest deportation rate per capita than anywhere else in the country and New Orleans has the highest incarceration rate per capita than anywhere else in the world. Louisiana is also home to the highest per capita immigration arrest rate in non-border states and new data continues to show the disproportionate arrest of LGBTQ youth ... (BreakOUT! and Congreso 2016, 12).

As indicated by the attention to intersectional issues, we must consider issues of police practices, arrests, and court decisions both in juvenile courts and in immigration courts in the context of the South generally and New Orleans in particular.

I argue that BreakOUT! builds upon strong Southern queer and trans of color frameworks in their discourse and organizing. These discourses both center queer and trans youth of color and call into question the frameworks that are used to criminalize them. As their work has developed in deep collaboration with immigrant organizers, their materials further nuance the coalitional possibilities for Southern justice-based organizations to impact change.

SOUTHERN QUEER AND TRANS YOUTH OF COLOR'S EXPERIENCES OF CRIMINALIZATION

This section of the chapter outlines two literatures that I combine when considering the work of advocacy agencies for queer and trans youth of color in Louisiana. Literature on incarceration and policing systems and the experiences of people of color in the South come into play in this analysis, yet they rarely overlap. I consider both conversations vital to any analysis of BreakOUT!. As the carceral systems in the US continue to grow, much critical carceral theory has analyzed incarceration and criminalization through the lenses of race (e.g., Davis 2003), gender and heteronormativity (e.g., Harris 2011; Haney 2010), and nation-state relations to globalization (e.g., Gillmore 2007; J. Mallory 2006; Parenti 2000). Additionally, many scholars and activists are engaging in important work that is attentive to the ways that LGBT people experience harassment and discrimination from law enforcement and the ways that systems of incarceration are set up to not recognize and to harm LGBT people, especially LGBT people of color (e.g., C. Mallory, Hasenbush, and Spears 2015; Spade 2015; Stanley and Smith 2015).

However, the vast majority of this research has focused on analyzing adult incarceration and criminalization. Of those scholars examining the criminalization of youth, some draw attention to the ways that gender, sexuality, and race impact how youth come into contact with policing and confinement and how they are treated within the connected systems. This focus is not only on official confinement and involvement in court systems, but also on the ways that spaces such as schools act as feeding lines into incarceration and supervision. Since the early 1990s, schools have enacted increasingly punitive policies about school code violations, leading to increasing numbers of suspensions and expulsions from school. Alongside these policies, increased use of high-stakes testing has led to higher drop-out rates among of youth of color (Wald and Losen 2003). According to a study from the Public Policy Research Institute at Texas A&M University (2005), a history of disciplinary referrals at school is the greatest predictor of juvenile justice involvement. Within the juvenile justice literature, scholars are particularly attentive to the ways that social control over youth of color impacts how they come into contact with the juvenile justice system (Kempf-Leonard 2007; Morris 2016; Nicholson-Crotty, Birchmeier, and Valentine 2009). Meda Chesney-Lind explains that common perception about heightened violence among girls isn't based in real increased rates of violence. She writes that the "pattern suggests that the social control of girls is once again on the criminal justice agenda, with a crucial change. In this century, the control is being justified by girls' 'violence' " (Chesney-Lind 2010, 60). This same pattern emerges for boys, wherein zero-tolerance policies combined with what Victor Rios terms "the youth control complex" of criminalization of non-illegal behaviors such as "talking back" to teachers can lead to boys of color being referred to systems that criminalize their non-illegal behaviors (Rios 2011, 27).

It is also necessary to consider the cultural and geographic places of the American South when considering the work of BreakOUT!. In his analysis of Black queer experiences, Black queer scholar E. Patrick Johnson argues that it is vital to "debunk the myth that the South is a place where it is *more* difficult to be a black gay man, in part because—according to common myth—black folks, in general, are more homophobic than whites . . . Many black communities around the South and especially those in rural towns, accommodated sexual dissidence in ways unimaginable" (Johnson 2008, 6). As Johnson highlights throughout his book, queer cultures and communities have been and continue to be important parts of Southern culture. He also seats his own understanding of Black queerness in an understanding of queerness as "quare"—a term that he imports from his grandmother's pronunciation of queer.

> [O]ne might wonder, though, what, if anything, can a poor, black, eighty-something, southern, homophobic woman teach her educated, middle-class, thirty-something, gay grandson about queer studies? Everything. Or *almost* everything. On the one hand, my grandmother uses "quare" to denote something or someone who is odd, irregular, or slightly off-kilter—definitions in keeping with traditional understandings and uses of "queer." On the other hand, she also deploys "quare" to connotate something excessive—something that might philosophically translate into an excess of discursive and epistemological meanings grounded in African American cultural rituals and lived experience . . . It is this culture-specific positionality that I find absent from the dominant and more traditional use of "queer" . . . (Johnson 2001, 2)

Considering these "culture-specific" positionalities is key to considering the intersections of Blackness, queerness, and the South.

This matters not just at the level of language, but also at the level of lived experience. Latoya E. Eaves (2017) focuses on Black geographies that center a Black sense of place as one way to undermine a limited identity politics framework of the American South (see also McKittrick and Woods 2007; Wilson 1992; Shabazz 2014; Bailey and Shabazz 2014). She concludes that "Queer Black South geographies exist" (Eaves 2017, 86) and that they require "understanding space and place requires a more nuanced regard for social location" (88). Eaves explores the complex lived experience of a queer Black woman to nuance social location and to produce a different spatial understanding of the American South for Black queer people.

There is an important connection and distinction between Black queer studies and transgender studies. As Treva Ellison, Kai M. Green, Matt Richardson, and C. Riley Snorton assert, "If we ask what is new about Black queer studies, the answer is 'trans.' There is an attempt not simply to grapple with the presence of noncis subjects but also, again, to return to this question: what will become of the commonsense intellectual and political genealogies of transgender studies?" (2017, 163). This question, they say, must always be answered not just in the abstract, but also in tangible ways which "disrupt the violent machinations and accumulation imperatives of racial capitalism that position those considered surplus as killable and cageable" (163–64). These demands are not only issued in academic trans* studies spaces[3] but also in activist spaces. Southerners on New Ground (SONG)—based out of Atlanta, Georgia—issued a report from research they conducted with transgender Southerners in 2010, with the majority of respondents being transgender people of color. SONG reports that "by far, there were 3 issues that participants named as most important: Employment/money, Violence and Safety, and Access to healthcare" (SONG 2010, 3). These needs are material and connected to Ellison et al.'s "violent machinations and accumulation imperatives" (2017), which put transgender people of color especially at risk of violence and precarity. It seems that the solutions that come from Black transgender studies—both in the academy and on the ground—are fundamentally connected to real systemic change.

Gender, race, and sexuality in the South in general and in New Orleans in particular are complex and do not reflect any of the simple narratives of progression or repression that are so common to hear outside of these spaces. Placing this analysis firmly within these frameworks is necessary for understanding the impact and the impetus of the work done by BreakOUT!. Here, I need to note that this literature centers Black voices and experiences, which cannot speak for all people of color and racialized people in the South. It is inarguable that it is different to be a Latinx, Asian American, or Native queer or transgender person than to be a Black queer or transgender person in the South. All these youth are racialized within the juvenile justice system in ways that are too rarely recognized in the literature on both the juvenile justice system and queer experiences in the South. While I do not argue that Black Southern experiences are the experiences of all youth of color in Louisiana, this literature around Black queer and trans experience does resonate with the ways that BreakOUT! members advertise their organization and frame their work.

In the next section, I turn to BreakOUT! as an organization and the ways that their members, training materials, and public documents discursively invoke queer and trans of color perspectives in a way that is rooted in Black queer and trans perspectives in the South and the lives of queer and trans youth. I consider the educational materials and research produced by BreakOUT! as central texts to understand the ways that LGBTQ youth of color experience policing in New Orleans. Additionally, as BreakOUT! continued to work more closely with Congreso, their articulation of issues impacting people of color became more complex and moved away from discussing race on a Black/white binary.

EVOLUTION OF THE WORK OF BREAKOUT!

BreakOUT!'s members developed their work across a number of different programs and media produced for and by these programs since their founding in 2011. Importantly, youth act as organizers and researchers in all of the programs run by BreakOUT!. This is not only an organization for youth; it is one that centers youth. In this section, I analyze two of their longest and most research-intensive publications: *We Deserve Better: A Report on Policing in New Orleans by and for Queer and Trans Youth of Color* (2014) and *From Vice to ICE Toolkit* (2016). *Vice to ICE* was co-written by Congreso members. Even though BreakOUT! members issued these reports within two years of one another, there is a significant shift in the ways that BreakOUT! members use language such as "people of color." In *We Deserve Better*, the report focuses on policing of queer and trans youth of color and highlight important findings. In this publication, they also sometimes have some slippage between "youth of color" and "Black youth" in both their images and rhetoric. In contrast, the *From Vice to ICE Toolkit*, which was co-authored by Congreso members, uses language about "people of color" in ways that highlight the connections between policing of queer and trans youth and surveillance of workers who are undocumented or presumed to be undocumented.

We Deserve Better Report

BreakOUT! members produced *We Deserve Better* through a three-year mixed-methods research program in New Orleans launched shortly after BreakOUT! was formally established. In the course of this project, BreakOUT! members conducted surveys and semi-structured interviews, resulting in eighty-six survey respondents aged fifteen to sixty-six and ten semi-structured interviews. BreakOUT! members' goals for this project were to educate, maintain pressure on New Orleans to implement policing reform, measure effectiveness of current reforms, document their stories and strategies, work to improve BreakOUT! members' research and data collection skills, "establish ourselves as experts on our issues and solutions," and "prove to ourselves we could do it" (BreakOUT! 2014, 8). These latter goals are an important part of this project—BreakOUT! members articulated the importance of both developing formal research skills for the youth researchers and being a part of the proposals for solutions.

The report was always intended to have multiple impacts and audiences. This can be seen through the ways that the authors mix formal reporting of statistics and analysis of qualitative interviews with manifesto-like language, such as the passage that directly followed their articulation of their research methods:

> This document is a manifestation of love, hard labor/research, bravery, and vulnerability of BreakOUT! members and the entire community. This report is a call for equal treatment and creating or strengthening support structures which promote mobility in the areas of safety, housing, health, education, and employment. We hope this report will help you rise to action—or at least support the young people who are organizing against forces which continue to exploit, harm, and overall enslave us in the criminal justice system. (BreakOUT! 2014, 9)

These goals and their clear articulation in a research report connect directly to many of the calls within trans* studies for material solutions to the experiences of violence and marginalization that trans people experience. BreakOUT! members are not merely representing the violence that they already knew they were experiencing. Instead, they focus on how this research supports their existing knowledge and position it as a call to power for other marginalized young people.

These commitments also inform how BreakOUT! members position their research methods for the report. In a section titled "Why Peer Researchers?" BreakOUT! members write, "We live it everyday. Our Black youth are being taken off the streets. The criminal justice system is working and doing what it was designed to do from the beginning. I have a family member doing 150 years in prison—it's something that isn't new to us. And we're the experts on what needs to change" (BreakOUT! 2014, 15). This means that it is vital that the researchers include BreakOUT! youth and young people. They also emphasize that one of the reasons that their study was always going to include qualitative analysis of interviews is because "it is important that personal stories are told to illustrate the crisis of harsh and discriminatory policing in New Orleans" (BreakOUT! 2014, 19). The humanizing effect of including personal narratives is highlighted in combining quantitative data with stories like that of Wednesday when she talks about her experiences with the New Orleans Police Department (NOPD).

> Wednesday [pseudonym], 20, informed BreakOUT! that NOPD always stops her for no reason. . . . Wednesday says that when one of the officers that usually harasses her sees her walking, "He stops me just to %*@ with me." Wednesday said that NOPD officers would talk negatively about her to others in her presence. When she attempts to correct the officers, they respond with, "What is your punk ass gonna do about it?" (BreakOUT! 2014, 20)

This story gives a human face to some of the survey results presented in the report, including that 50 percent of transgender respondents reported police officers referring to them with a slur, while only 22 percent of cisgender LGBQ people report NOPD officers using a slur about them. In terms of race, 73 percent of LGBTQ people of color report being stopped by the police, and 57 percent of white LGBTQ report being stopped by police. The mix of the qualitative analysis of interviews with the quantitative findings helps bring faces to the numbers and reminds the readers that the survey respondents are more than numbers.

These quantitative findings are also an important place where "people of color" starts to enter into BreakOUT!'s analysis in an important way. Though BreakOUT! materials often refer to youth or people of color broadly, the cover of the report has five Black-appearing young people with a variety of gender presentations. It is in their summary of survey findings where BreakOUT!

members articulate how they are using the term "people of color" in the report:

> For purposes of this report, since most respondents were either Black or white and few were Latin@, Native American/American Indian, or mixed race, we use the category "people of color" when we want to include those respondents but did not have enough respondents in either category to reliably break the data down further by race/ethnicity. We recognize that more research needs to be done to accurately capture the experiences of people of color communities who are not Black/African American. (BreakOUT! 2014, 18)

This highlights the necessity to think in complex ways about how race operates in LGBTQ people's experiences of criminalization—though there are connected issues across different racial groups, there are also differences, which aren't as apparent in this report.

Throughout this report, from design of the study through the reporting of findings, BreakOUT! members are very attentive to the specific space of New Orleans. They do not simply call for changes in policing; they have specific suggestions and calls for change for the NOPD. This report is an important contribution to youth-led and youth-developed sustained research about the use of policing and surveillance on LGBTQ youth within New Orleans and the ways that those experiences map along lines of gender identity and race.

From Vice to ICE Toolkit

This kind of very local work situated in the context of New Orleans in particular, and the South in general, developed in particular ways by the time BreakOUT! published the *From Vice to ICE Toolkit*, which BreakOUT! and Congreso published online in both English and Spanish (2016). The program Vice to ICE also began shortly after the founding of BreakOUT! and was used as a name for the relationship between BreakOUT! and Congreso as they connected the policing of LGBTQ youth of color as presumed sex workers by vice squads and the surveillance that immigrant workers experienced due from Immigration and Customs Enforcement (ICE). In 2011, when this relationship was first forming, vice police squads were targeting LGBTQ homeless youth's hotel rooms and profiling young Black transgender women as sex workers. At the same time, police "were using ICE as translators for domestic violence calls and collaborating for huge sweeps and raids of Latinx people targeted as being undocumented" (BreakOUT! and Congreso 2016, 4). Although Congreso does not have an exact duplication of the structure of BreakOUT!, they do refer to themselves as "an organization of immigrant workers and families founded by the day laborers who helped rebuild New Orleans after Hurricane Katrina" (New Orleans Workers' Center for Racial Justice n.d.). This includes children in the families, which emphasizes that both movements are either led by or inclusive of children in ways that are unusual in these kinds of movements.

As of 2016, both organizations used "Vice to ICE" as a term for the campaigns or areas that recognize the overlap of their respective projects, "as well as our intentional building with those whose lives are at the intersections of these identities—LGBTQ undocumented communities in New Orleans" (BreakOUT! and Congreso 2016, 4). The evolution of this collaboration highlights the ways that solidarity work can help organizations expand the scope of their work in ways that strengthen their existing goals. When people outside of both organizations asked them how they overcame what some people might see as different base populations—LGBTQ youth of color and immigrants and their families—the authors wrote that in "typical Southern fashion, we shared a meal, grabbed an interpreter, and sat in a circle and talked. Everything after that is just the magic that happens when directly impacted bases come together to organize!" (BreakOUT! and Congreso 2016, 6). This magic produced the shared understanding that vice policing of transgender Black women and police collusion with ICE connected the issues. This led to movements that highlighted ways members could collaborate and share power.

Members of both organizations do this work through formal events and programs, but also through intentional relationship-building. Congreso and BreakOUT! members write that

> In the South, we understand that it's impossible to organize without deep, personal relationships with one another. And at the same time, it's hard to develop those relationships across language and cultural barriers. Cultural barriers impact everything we do—from how we greet each other to how we approach our work. We acknowledge these differences—sometimes meeting in the middle and sometimes laughing at ourselves and the vast gulf of both spoken and unspoken barriers that can keep us apart. (BreakOUT! and Congreso 2016, 28)

This building of relationships has benefited the work of both organizations, according to the report.

This collaboration has also benefited particularly marginalized members of both organizations, including connecting Kenisha and Rixi. Both young women became involved with juvenile justice systems and with BreakOUT! and Congreso, respectively, as teenagers. Rixi is a young transgender Latina woman who was facing seven years of incarceration in a Louisiana prison and immediate deportation after her sentence was complete. Rixi writes, "Despite the challenges, thanks to the support of Congreso and BreakOUT! and the power of community showing up on behalf of one another, my sentence was reduced to twenty-three months in prison. Eventually, they were able to stop my deportation, too" (BreakOUT! and Congreso 2016, 54). At the same time that Rixi's case was being addressed by the combined efforts of the two organizations, they also set her up with a pen pal outside of the prison and introduced her to Kenisha. Kenisha is a founding BreakOUT! member and, at the time of the report, was incarcerated at the same institution as Rixi. They were the only two transgender women incarcerated at the all-male institution. In the report, they write that their relationship with one another and their ability to support one another inside prison inspired "alliances on the inside as well as on the outside with their families and friends" (BreakOUT! and Congreso 2016, 14).

Congreso and BreakOUT! members collaborated on a number of projects, but two of the most notable were story circles and the organizing and educational activities they share for organizing across language differences. Story circles were developed in the mid-1960s by the New Orleans–based Free Southern Theater (FST). The FST and the use of story circles formed out of Freedom Summer[4] "as the theatrical branch of the civil rights movement. John O'Neal, another movement elder in New Orleans, is legendary for his work as co-founder of the Free Southern Theatre (FST) and for his lifetime at the intersection of social justice and performance" (Flaherty, Goodman, and Washington 2010, 43). These story circles provide structured opportunities for participants to share their experiences, their life stories, and the stories that others entrusted to them. The report authors acknowledge that "[m]uch of organizing in the South and within our communities relies on stories—both the stories we share with one another to find connection, the stories our textbooks ignore that we pass down in oral tradition, and the stories we lift up in our organizing and movement building work to move others to action" (BreakOUT! and Congreso 2016, 32). Story circles are open to participants of all ages, and all stories are carried together, which encourages youth to share their stories and experiences. These story circles allow a place for members to share experiences, to heal, to build relationships, and to lift up resiliency and resistance of communities.

The From Vice to ICE Toolkit is also notable in its attentiveness to bringing in a range of organizers and activists in the activity examples they give about coalitional work. In the section "Navigating Language Barriers through Ice-Breakers," the organizers highlight some effective exercises and practices that they have used to navigate language barriers among members of both groups. In their explanation of the activity "Privilege Train," a common activist activity where participants navigate physical spaces to highlight the ways that systemic privilege can move someone "forward" or "back" in the world, the instructions include a disclaimer: "For youth or people who are just becoming politicized, the game can also feel disempowering if not facilitated properly and they find themselves at the end of the line with the odds stacked against them" (BreakOUT! and Congreso 2016, 20). They encourage adequate time to unpack the activity for all participants. I am particularly interested in the way that "youth" is combined with "or people who are just becoming politicized," as it is one way to acknowledge that some youth might be very politicized and not frustrated with the exercise. Also, older people who are just becoming politicized might feel disempowered. This focuses attention on experience with political mobilization, not on age. In another icebreaker, the facilitators write down each person's name, pronouns, and years in the field of activism. The facilitator totals the years of experience and shares it with the participants, which "represents the total of years of collective experience, knowledge and wisdom in the room. This is a good way to bring youth into the space, along with elders, and honor this collective wisdom" (BreakOUT! and Congreso 2016, 27). Here, it is acknowledged that youth may come in with *or* without organizing experience and the collective wisdom is a benefit to all participants and not something a single person "owns."

This report's clear attention to issues of racialization which acknowledge the connections and differences of the racialized attention of police and immigration officers for both Black and Latinx community members shows a nuancing of BreakOUT!'s language around race and police attention. This goes beyond the level of language and into strategy. The report begins by acknowledging that "immigrant and LGBTQ communities of color in New Orleans are and have been heavily criminalized in their ability to move safely and freely in our own communities, faced with tremendous, and very real, fear of law enforcement" (BreakOUT! and Congreso 2016, 13). The strong connections between these communities are evident, as is their commitment to one another's freedom.

COALITION BUILDING AND EVOLUTION OF BREAKOUT!

The clarity of what it might mean to discuss issues that impact people of color and the ways that BreakOUT! has integrated much of the mission and goals of Congreso is a clear example of how coalition building through youth activist organizations actually strengthens the effectiveness of their work. Through situating strategies and goals in specifically Southern and New Orleans–based contexts, this work more strongly advocates for New Orleans as a place that is safe and supportive for all of these communities. This is because of, not despite, the collaboration between these organizations. Because of their work together, both groups built on the intellectual and activist work of LGBTQ people of color through BreakOUT! and on the insights of immigrants through Congreso.

NOTES

1. According to the Orleans Parish 2010 Census, New Orleans residents were approximately 33 percent white, 60 percent Black, 0.3 percent American Indian, and 3 percent Asian. In the OJJDP reports on 2017 youth contact with the police, the youth were 35 percent white, 61 percent Black, 0.4 percent American Indian, and 3 percent Asian. However, I have written previously about the mistake of classifying Native youth as only a racial category (Benson 2019; Benson 2017).
2. This position is now held by Kwan Moonlite and is described as a position in which the person works to "coordinate healing and wellness work at the organization and works to integrate a healing justice analysis into the organization's campaigns and movement building work" (BreakOUT! n.d.).
3. The asterisk in trans* studies serves the same way that it does in a search capacity—to include all related terms that start with "trans-," from "transgender" to "transsexual" to "trans." However, beyond the linguistic function, it recognizes that "trans" encompasses a wide-ranging use of terms and vocabulary, which is always evolving, includes and is not limited to the terms above, and also includes terms that don't linguistically connect, such as "non-binary" or "genderqueer."
4. Freedom Summer (1964) was a voter registration drive coordinated by many civil rights organizations that aimed to increase Black voter registration in Mississippi and was met with threats and violence. Two of the organizing committees were Student Nonviolent Coordinating Committee and Congress of Racial Equality, and each had a strong chapter in New Orleans that was involved in the Mississippi voter drive (Flaherty, Goodman, and Washington 2010).

REFERENCES

Bailey, Marlon M., and Rashad Shabazz. 2014. "Gender and Sexual Geographies of Blackness: New Black Cartographies of Resistance and Survival (Part 2)." *Gender, Place, and Culture* 21 (4): 449–52.

Benson, Krista L. 2017. "Generations of Removal: Child Removal of Native Children in Eastern Washington State through Compulsory Education, Foster Care, Adoption, and Juvenile Justice." PhD diss., Ohio State University.

———. 2019. "What's in a Pronoun? Trans Kids and Misgendering in Juvenile Justice Systems in Washington State." *Journal of Homosexuality* 67 (12): 1691–712.

BreakOUT! n.d. "Vision, Mission, & History." http://www.youthbreakout.org/mission.

———. 2014. *We Deserve Better: A Report on Policing in New Orleans by and for Queer and Trans Youth of Color*. https://www.scribd.com/document/334018552/We-Deserve-Better-Report.

BreakOUT! and Congress of Day Laborers/Congreso de Jornaleros (Congreso). 2016. *From Vice to ICE Toolkit*. New Orleans: BreakOUT!

Chesney-Lind, Meda. 2010. "Jailing 'Bad Girls': Girls' Violence and Trends in Female Incarceration." In *Fighting for Girls: New Perspectives on Gender and Violence*, ed. Meda Chesney-Lind and Nikki Jones, 57–79. Albany: State University of New York Press.

Davis, Angela Y. 2003. *Are Prisons Obsolete?* New York: Seven Stories Press.

Eaves, Latoya E. 2017. "Black Geographic Possibilities: On a Queer Black South." *Southeastern Geographer* 57 (1): 80–95.

Ellison, Treva, Kai M. Green, Matt Richardson, and C. Riley Snorton. 2017. "We Got Issues: Toward a Black Trans*/Studies." *TSQ* 4 (2): 162–69. https://doi.org/10.1215/23289252-3814949.

Flaherty, Jordan, Amy Goodman, and Tracie Washington. 2010. *Floodlines: Community and Resistance from Katrina to the Jena Six*. Chicago: Haymarket Books.

Gilmore, Ruth Wilson. 2007. *Golden Gulag: Prisons, Surplus, Crisis, and Opposition in Globalizing California*. Berkeley: University of California Press.

Haney, Lynna Allison. 2010. *Offending Women: Power, Punishment, and the Regulation of Desire*. Berkeley: University of California Press.

Harris, Angela P. 2011. "Heteropatriarchy Kills: Challenging Gender Violence in a Prison Nation." *Washington University Journal of Law and Policy* 37: 12–65.

Johnson, E. Patrick. 2001. " 'Quare' Studies, or (Almost) Everything I Know about Queer Studies I Learned from My Grandmother." *Text and Performance Quarterly* 21 (1): 1–25.

———. 2008. *Sweet Tea: Black Gay Men of the South: An Oral History*. Chapel Hill: University of North Carolina Press.

Kempf-Leonard, Kimberly. 2007. "Minority Youths and Juvenile Justice: Disproportionate Minority Contact after Nearly 20 Years of Reform Efforts." *Youth Violence and Juvenile Justice* 5 (1): 71–87.

Mallory, Christy, Amira Hasenbush, and Brad Spears. 2015. *Discrimination and Harassment by Law Enforcement Officers in the LGBT Community*. Los Angeles: Williams Institute.

Mallory, Jason L. 2006. "Globalization, Prisons, and the Philosophy of Punishment." *Women's Studies* 35 (6): 529–43.

McCann, Bryan J. 2016. "Holding Each Other Better: Discussing State Violence, Healing, and Community with BreakOUT!." *QED: A Journal in GLBTQ Worldmaking* 3 (1): 98–116.

McKittrick, Katherine, and Clyde Woods. 2007. "No One Knows the Mysteries at the Bottom of the Ocean." In *Black Geographies and the Politics of Place*, ed. Katherine McKittrick and Clyde Woods, 1–13. Cambridge, MA: South End Press.

Morris, Monique. 2016. *Pushout: The Criminalization of Black Girls in Schools*. New York: New Press.

New Orleans Workers' Center for Racial Justice. N.d. "Congress of Day Laborers/Congreso de Jornaleros." http://nowcrj.org/our-work/congress-day-laborerscongreso-de-journaleros.

Nicholson-Crotty, Sean, Zachary Birchmeier, and David Valentine. 2009. "Exploring the Impact of School Discipline on Racial Disproportion in the Juvenile Justice System." *Social Science Quarterly* 90 (4): 1003–18.

Office of Juvenile Justice and Detention Prevention. 2017. *Easy Access to Juvenile Populations: 1990–2017, Race by County in Louisiana—2017*. https://www.ojjdp.gov/ojstatbb/ezapop/asp/comparison_display.asp?display_type=counts&export_file=&printer_friendly

=&selState=22&col_var=v03&submit=SHOW+TABLE&selLowerYear=1&selUpperYear=1&selLowerAge=1&selUpperAge=1.

Parenti, Christian. 2000. *Lockdown America: Police and Prisons in the Age of Crisis*. New York: Verso.

Public Policy Research Institute. 2005. *Study of Minority Overrepresentation in the Texas Juvenile Justice System Final Report*. College Station, TX: Public Policy Research Institute.

Rios, Victor M. 2011. *Punished: Policing the Lives of Black and Latino Boys*. New York: NYU Press.

Ross, Loretta. 2011. "The Origin of the Phrase 'Women of Color.'" https://www.youtube.com/watch?v=82vl34mi4Iw.

Shabazz, Rashad. 2014. "Masculinity and the Mic: Confronting the Uneven Geography of Hip-Hop." *Gender, Place, and Culture: A Journal of Feminist Geography* 21 (3): 370–86.

SONG. 2010. *"In Your Face and in the Trenches": Southern Trans People Speak Out*. Atlanta: Southerners on New Ground.

Spade, Dean. 2015. *Normal Life: Administrative Violence, Critical Trans Politics, and the Limits of Law*. Durham, NC: Duke University Press.

Stanley, Eric A., and Nat Smith. 2015. *Captive Genders: Trans Embodiment and the Prison Industrial Complex*, 2nd ed. Oakland, CA: AK Press.

United States Census. 2011. *Profile of General Population and Housing Characteristics: 2010, New Orleans City, Louisiana*. https://www.census.gov/quickfacts/neworleanscity louisiana.

Wald, Johanna, and Daniel J. Losen. 2003. "Defining and Redirecting the School-to-Prison Pipeline." *New Directions for Youth Development*, no. 99: 9–15.

Wilson, Bobby M. 1992. "Structural Imperatives behind Racial Change in Birmingham, Alabama." *Antipode: A Radical Journal of Geography* 24 (3): 171–202.

CHAPTER 7

BLACK YOUTH RESISTANCE TO POLICIES, PRACTICES, AND DOMINANT NARRATIVES OF THE ST. LOUIS VOLUNTARY DESEGREGATION PLAN

Jerome E. Morris and Wanda F. McGowan

St. Louis sits at an important historical, geographical, cultural, political, and social crossroads of the United States. It is located within Missouri, which borders six states and was admitted as a slave state under the Missouri Compromise of 1820. A historic site for landmark cases pertaining to civil rights, housing, and schooling, more recently, St. Louis served as the setting for the largest voluntary desegregation plan undertaken in the US.[1] Despite billions of dollars supporting this plan for almost four decades, the geospatial reality for the Black poor in the city has been largely unaltered (Gordon 2008; Strauss 2017). For example, St. Louis has been consistently rated as one of America's most hyper-segregated cities, which means not only that Black and White people are physically isolated from one another, but that opportunity and opportunity structures for Black people are elusive in the areas of housing, schooling, employment, etc.[2] Moreover, hyper-segregation within a city means that racial integration can be achieved only if at least 70 percent of Black people were to move into predominately White neighborhoods (Goodman, 2016).

St. Louis's significance is further illustrated by the impending termination of the desegregation plan, Missouri's takeover of "failing" school districts (overwhelmingly Black), and the 2014 Ferguson unrest that was spurred by the killing of an unarmed Black youth, Michael Brown, by Darren Wilson, a White police officer. A plethora of lingering remnants of institutionalized apartheid remains in the St. Louis region, making the region central to national conversations about the education of poor and Black students within the context of public school desegregation.

The corpus of the scholarship on public school desegregation has overwhelmingly focused on the transferring of Black students into predominantly White school contexts, without carefully considering the lived experiences of Black students once they are in these contexts. In particular, what have been the lived experiences of Black students who participated in the St. Louis voluntary desegregation plan? Moreover, in what ways have Black participants resisted policies and practices that could result in their schooling marginalization, and what are the dominant narratives about their experiences?

Emanating from an in-depth analysis of qualitative interviews with former and present Black participants in the St. Louis voluntary desegregation plan since its inception in 1983, we provide insights about Black high school students' experiences and capture how they pushed back against both the marginalizing efforts within predominantly White schools and the dominant narratives of their experiences. The "voluntary" aspect of the plan is that Black students from the city of St. Louis could do one of the following: (a) attend their assigned neighborhood schools, (b) participate in a lottery with the possibility of being selected for the magnet schools in the city (which had a racial-balancing goal), or (c) apply to and "transfer" into the public schools in one of sixteen participating predominantly White suburban school districts. White students from the predominantly White school districts, on the other hand, could apply for and would automatically be guaranteed attendance in of the city's magnet schools. Capturing former (and current) Black participants' perspectives at this time is important due to the fact that the transferring of Black students into the predominantly White school districts is scheduled for termination at the end of the 2023–2024 school year.

The findings presented within this chapter stem from a larger investigation that sought to include the "forgotten voices" of Black people within policy conversations around public school desegregation (Morris 2016, 2001). Researchers and policy analysts have written extensively about how educational reforms, policies, and practices have shaped the experiences of Black students. However, rarely do we get a sense of Black people's perspectives on educational policies (Morris 2001). This is especially the case with public school desegregation, which arguably has been one of the most significant educational policies to affect the schooling of Black people during the latter part of the twentieth century (Delmont 2016; Heaney and Uchitelle 2004; Morris 2016, 2009, 2004). The few studies that feature Black students' voices note how Black students' attendance in predominantly White schools as a result of their participation in desegregation programs often resulted in Black students' ostracism (Jacoway 2007; Lit 2009). Moreover, Black students recalled being labeled by their White peers and teachers as disruptive (Butler-Barnes et al. 2016; Lewis and Diamond, 2015), and often felt racially marginalized (Butler-Barnes et al., 2016; Stevenson and Arrington 2009).

A body of research attests to the benefits of public school desegregation plans, particularly in terms of enhanced academic and social outcomes for Black youth in addition to long-term social gains (Johnson 2015; Wells 2009; Wells and Crain 1997). Proponents of desegregation plans that place Black students into predominantly White school settings specifically note the presence of better facilities and resources in comparison to many predominantly Black schools. Although some Black students benefit from these resources, such benefits, however, would come at a cost.

In this chapter, we present an overarching theme that emerged from the Black participants profiled in our research: a constant resistance to the policies and practices imposed on Black students. The imposition of these policies represented an attempt—although some might say it was unintended—to marginalize Black students socially, culturally, and academically. The importance of Black students' insight must not be understated, given the promises implied in *Brown v. Board of Education (1954)*. Upon entering predominantly White school settings, Black students too often find themselves in educational environments that do not appreciate their personhood, culture, or race (Lit 2009). As O'Connor noted, "[O]nce inside the schools, Black students find these schools to be culturally, socially, and institutionally organized in ways that amplify and reify their subordination" (2016, 421–22).

HISTORICAL CONTEXT OF THE ST. LOUIS VOLUNTARY DESEGREGATION PLAN

In 1954, *Brown v. Board of Education* declared that separate public schools for Black and White students were inherently unequal. Symbolically, the *Brown* case represented an end to legalized racism and offered two promises: (1) the eradication of legalized segregation with the hope of promoting integrated schooling, and (2) the promotion of quality schooling for Black children who had been disenfranchised educationally (Morris 2004, 2019). Despite decades of White resistance to implementing *Brown*, *Brown*'s promises would compel Minnie Liddell, a Black mother, to sue the St. Louis Board of Education in 1972 due to her children being forced to attend segregated schools (*Liddell v. Board of Education* 1972; Norwood 2012). In 1979, however, the judge that presided over the case, Judge Meredith, said there was not sufficient evidence that the city of St. Louis purposefully discriminated against Black children. The United States Court of Appeals for the Eighth Circuit would disagree with Judge Meredith and assert there was adequate evidence that the Board of Education of the city of St. Louis and the state of Missouri discriminated against Black children.

In the summer of 1980, in an effort to foster school desegregation efforts in the St. Louis region, officials from the National Association for the Advancement of Colored People (NAACP), the city of St. Louis, and a number of the predominantly White county school districts approved a voluntary settlement that would allow Black St. Louis students to attend schools in these districts (*Liddell v. Board of Education* 1980). By 1982, dissatisfied with the efforts of the settlement, Black plaintiffs and St. Louis's Board of education members would come together and sue for the establishment of a metropolitan system-wide school district. Rather than go to court, a day before the scheduled trial in 1983, lawyers for the Black plaintiffs, officials from the twenty-three county districts, and the St. Louis Board of Education entered into a settlement. Officials from the twenty-three predominantly White county school districts would agree to a settlement that included a dual transfer program under threat of being told how their districts would be desegregated.

Under this final settlement, Black children from the city of St. Louis could attend sixteen of the participating predominantly White county school districts with the goal of achieving a 25 percent Black student population. Seven of the twenty-three county school districts had already achieved at least a 25 percent Black student population and, consequently, did not participate in the voluntary transfer part of the settlement (Morris 2009). This resulted in the inclusion of sixteen predominantly White county school districts in the voluntary desegregation plan. Key components of the settlement included the provision of free transportation for Black students to attend the participating county schools as well as for White students to enroll in magnet schools within the city of St. Louis. Educators in participating school districts could screen children for special needs, behavior, and attendance records prior to admission. A Voluntary Interdistrict Coordinating Council was created during the settlement in order to coordinate the transfer program and oversee other components of the settlement.

As the increase in funding was provided to build magnet schools within the city of St. Louis, money was allocated to develop new programs and facilities within the city's public school system. The state also paid the host county school districts for each Black student that was accepted while giving half the per-pupil expenditure to the St. Louis city school district for each Black student that left. If participating school districts were found to be compliant for five years, the original lawsuit would be dropped.

During the 1997–1998 school year, a total of 14,224 students enrolled in the transfer program between the city and the county school districts. Of these, 12,746 Black students from the city transferred to county schools, whereas 1,478 White students from the sixteen participating county districts transferred to magnet schools in St. Louis. As part of the settlement, the court mandated that the composition of magnet schools have at least a 40 percent White student enrollment. During 1997–1998, the racial composition of White students in magnet schools was 46 percent.

By 1999, the state of Missouri and the St. Louis Public School Board had paid almost $2 billion into the voluntary desegregation plan.[3] The state of Missouri paid $160 million into the plan during the 1998–1999 academic year. Approximately $70 million went into funding the St. Louis Public School District's portion of the plan. Examples of enhancements included mandating a maximum student-teacher ratio of twenty to one. Sixty million dollars went toward funding the student per-pupil cost for transferring students into the county schools, and the remaining funds paid for the city and county transportation costs. By then, the state wanted to end the desegregation plan by declaring that the city district had achieved unitary status—a legal term that meant that the state and the city have done all that is necessary to eliminate the vestiges of legal segregation and will not return to these illegal and discriminatory practices. On the other hand, lawyers representing the NAACP argued that the interdistrict transfer plan should continue because of the possible resegregation that would result if the plan ended. A panel of judges, at the request of the state of Missouri, began hearing the court case in March 1996 to establish a deadline for settlement negotiations.

On March 12, 1999, the judges on the case signed the order officially ending the 1983 settlement in St. Louis. In removing the case from federal supervision, they agreed to the following: (a) the continuation of the interdistrict transfer plan during the following three years for Black students who wished to transfer into the county schools and a referendum at the end of the third year in which citizens from each participating county school district would vote on whether to continue or to end the plan in their respective school districts; (b) additional state funds to the St. Louis Public School District from a change in the state funding formula and the tax increase that allowed for the expansion of magnet school opportunities to White and Black students in the city; and (c) money for capital improvement in the city schools during the following ten years. To facilitate the new transfer plan, a nonprofit agency, the Voluntary Interdistrict Choice Corporation (VICC), would replace the Voluntary Interdistrict Coordinating Council, which had previously managed the plan and had to provide annual reports to the court.

Thus, the new settlement allowed for new Black students to be admitted to the voluntary transfer plan and the St. Louis magnet schools through the 2008–2009 academic year. Over this period, enrollment goals were established that allowed specified percentages of students to continue participating in the plan. During the first three years after the new settlement, the districts collectively agreed to maintain at least an 85 percent enrollment of those previously in the plan, which decreased to an agreed-upon 70 percent enrollment through the 2004–2005 academic year.

From 2005 on, no minimum enrollment had to occur. Beginning September 2008, 6,774 Black students from the city of St. Louis transferred into county schools, and only 171 White students from the participating county schools attended the magnet school programs in the city of St. Louis. Two of the districts originally participating in the St. Louis interdistrict transfer plan no longer participated because of the increase of minority student presence in the district. This increase of Black students resulted from the intrametropolitan Black migration in the once predominantly White suburbs and subsequent White flight, which resulted in some of these areas becoming predominantly Black (Gordon 2008).

To reduce busing costs, and in a response to the criticism about the long bus rides the Black students had to endure, four attendance zones were created in the city with links to specific suburban school districts. VICC received $50 million to cover the transportation costs associated with facilitating the transfer of students within the new attendance zones.

In June 2007, the VICC board approved a five-year extension that allowed Black transfer students to be enrolled in the county districts until the 2013–2014 school year. This was followed by a November 2016 agreement to extend the transferring of Black students for a five-year period, in which about one thousand new students would be permitted to enroll in county school districts through the 2023–2024 school year. Priority would be given to students with siblings already enrolled. Students enrolled may continue through graduation from the district in which they are enrolled. In other words, if a student begins during the 2023–2024 school year, that student can finish out their studies in the county district even if they enter as first-year students in the last year of the extension.

CENTERING BLACK STUDENTS' VOICES AND RESISTANCE USING CRITICAL RACE THEORY

A sociohistorical backdrop regarding Black students' resistance in the United States becomes useful for centering contemporary Black students' voices within contemporary educational reforms and policies. The courage demonstrated by Claudette Colvin and the Little Rock Nine during the modern civil rights movement provides a historical reference point for understanding Black youth resistance to their marginalization. In May 1955, Colvin, a Black female teenager, refused to give up her seat to a White passenger in Montgomery, Alabama—months before Rosa Parks did so during the famous Montgomery bus boycott (Hoose 2009). Furthermore, in 1957, a group of Black teenagers, known as the Little Rock Nine, braved the vile racism in order to integrate Central High School in Little Rock, Arkansas (Beals 1994). Black youth have always had a perspective on their experiences, even if their views and voices have been ignored in conventional narratives of resistance. For the purposes of this paper, we utilize Ginwright's (2004, 2007) definition of resistance to include the ways that Black youth ignore, confront, and challenge power structures.

We couple the above definition of resistance with a critical race theoretical (CRT) framework as a way of centering Black students' voices (see Bell 1992; Dixson and Rousseau 2005; Ladson-Billings 2014; Ladson-Billings and Tate 1995). A key tenet of CRT is the *interest-convergence dilemma* originally posited by Bell (1980), which states that significant progress for Black people is achieved only when their goals are consistent with the needs of White people. The desegregation plan's design resonated with this theorem. For example, Black students were allowed to attend schools in the predominantly White county districts with the condition that these districts would receive a per-pupil financial incentive for each enrolled Black transfer student.

Another aspect of CRT relevant to this paper is the use of counter-narrative or counter-story to the dominant narrative. Solórzano and Yosso (2002) defined the counter-narrative or counter-story as a "method of telling the stories of those people whose experiences are not often told (i.e., those on the margins of society)." A counter-story serves as a "tool for exposing, analyzing, and challenging the majoritarian stories of racial privilege" (32). In this chapter, we elevate the voices of those on the racial margins by giving value to their perspectives and experiences given how such counter-stories have the power to amplify voices and challenge marginalization (Morris and Parker 2018).

Utilizing an ethnographic interview protocol, the three members of our research team (all Black) interviewed thirty-nine Black participants in the desegregation plan.[4] Given the longevity of the plan (1983 to present), we organized the interview data into four discrete waves: Wave 1 (1983–1989), Wave 2 (1990–1999), Wave 3 (2000–2009), and Wave 4 (2001 to present). We identified participants using the snowball sampling technique, which allowed interviewees to identify other participants. These referrals were then contacted and asked to provide information about other participants. The interviews conducted were generally from transfer participants who had completed the program. In the data analysis, we searched for patterns and conducted a cross-case comparison among the themes and participants.

FINDINGS

Race, Tracking, and Resisting Inequitable Disciplinary Actions

The schooling contexts that children attend send messages about race and racial socialization at every level of students' schooling experiences (Nasir, Jones, & McLaughlin 2011; Pollock 2005; Van Ausdale and Feagin 2001). Despite significant variation in the extent to which educators explicitly discuss or address issues of race, racial boundaries become maintained and conveyed to even young students in schools. For example, Pollock (2005) found that while teachers and administrators were reluctant to talk about race (a phenomenon she calls "colormute"), school policies and practices tended to recreate racial hierarchies and leave students poorly equipped to name and cope with the racism they encountered in school contexts. Moreover, the differential course placement of students by race sends messages about race and what it means to be Black, White, Latino, or Asian. For example, students become tracked by race and social class (Lewis and Diamond 2015; Oakes 2005; Tyson 2011), Black students are underrepresented in advanced placement and gifted education programs (Grantham 2004), and they are disproportionately disciplined in school (Gregory and Roberts 2017; Morris and Goldring 1999). Black males experience these inequities at particularly high rates (Monroe 2005). Finally, extracurricular activities and sports reinforce racial and social class identities and often become sources of racial group identity (Hodge et al. 2008; Ogden and Hilt 2003).

One of the realities of Black students' attendance in predominantly White school settings has been the persistence of within-school segregation in the form of academic tracking (Lewis and Diamond 2015; Oakes 2005; Tyson 2011). Data across every participating county school district revealed that Black students are less likely than White students to be placed into advanced academic tracks. Black student participants in the voluntary transfer plan discussed their disproportionate placement into lower academic tracks, as well as their inequitable treatment as far as disciplinary actions. The following quote from a Black male participant from Wave 1 captured an awareness of the level of academic tracking experienced Black students. This awareness, we assert, also represented a form of resistance: "There's tracks in school. All the kids who were bussed in from the city, it was only a handful of us [Black students] that were in the advanced track in terms of the college prep courses. It was really just me, my cousin, and one other girl. There were three of us. We weren't in class with all the other city kids" (Andrew, Wave 1).

Beyond academic tracking, racial inequities persisted in other areas. Yet, Black students described how school personnel avoided discussing this omnipresence of racial inequities as illustrated by Walter, a Black male student from Wave 2:

> Nobody wanted to say race or talk race or deal with race . . . Race festered behind the scenes of everything. Like I said, there was always a perception, particularly among Black students, that there were disparate treatment going on or in terms of particularly behavior and discipline; in academic placements, that there were just ways that were small and subtle that Black kids, particularly Black kids from the city, weren't being treated like everybody else was . . . It's [racial inequity] embedded in disciplinary action. It's embedded in teachers' treatment and expectations of people, especially when you're in a school setting when there are so few African Americans who live there . . . You are a foreigner . . .

A common assumption held by some was that the longer the voluntary transfer plan is in existence, the less likely racial inequities would be evident. However, two decades after the plan had been in existence, a Black female student from Wave 4 described the disproportionate policing of Black students in the county schools:

There was this [school] officer ... and he, like he targeted Black students all the time ... But there's this one time that I, um, there was a group of us, all Black students and one White girl actually, sitting at a table during lunch. And our table was apparently making too much noise in his opinion. So he made the entire table stand up, and he made us go to the front of the room and then he sat us down at a table and he started screaming at us. He was like, "This is not the city. This is a privilege to be at this school!" Like all of this different stuff. And I remember like being super, super mad. Like we went to the principal's office, and we like told the principal on him, because we were like that's unacceptable. And they [school administrators] were trying to like say, "He didn't mean any of this." Like no! He actually meant what he said. Then they just tried to diffuse the situation, but nothing was ever done to that security guard. (Mary, Wave 4)

While Mary further stated that she and the other Black students did not argue with the school officer during the incident, their reporting of the officer to the school's principal demonstrated their resistance to their mistreatment by the school officer.

Resistance to Assimilation

Educational policy makers have historically (Adams 1995; Anderson 1988; Spring 2016; Watkins 2001) and contemporarily (Lewis 2003; Morris 2009; Nasir 2011) ensured that schools functioned as deculturalizing institutions. The manner in which desegregation plans became implemented often continued this deculturalization. For example, the overwhelming majority of desegregation plans throughout the United States involved the disproportionate bussing of Black students into predominantly White schools, where they are often taught by educators of the dominant culture. The framing of the St. Louis voluntary transfer plan, as described by Black students, reflected this pattern, as we will explore throughout this section.

Black students' attendance in schools in which they are a racial minority does not mean these students automatically acquiesce to deculturalizing efforts. For example, Black participants in our investigation described how they resisted assimilation into Eurocentric school culture by creating spaces that would maintain and affirm their identities as Black people. This resistance would take on many forms: creating student organizations, such as the African-American Culture Club and Black Student Union that were culturally centered and affirming; using their own transportation to attend athletic events to support Black students who played sports; creating culturally affirming spaces in the schools' cafeteria, such as the "Black lunch tables"; participating in Black student-led protests; and building solidarity with other Black youth from across the various St. Louis neighborhoods. These efforts and organizations, initiated by the Black youth at the time, served as safe havens, and provided opportunities for them to socialize with other Black peers and to learn about Black American culture.

Malcolm, a student from Wave 4, described his efforts to create affirming spaces for Black students at the high school he attended:

> *Interviewer:* Were you involved in any student groups? You mentioned speech and debate. I thought I heard you say band?
>
> *Interviewee:* Yeah. I was in a band. Speech and debate also. I played football in high school all four years until I got hurt my senior year. Um, I was also a part of—I was president of the Black Student Union my senior year.
>
> *Interviewer:* Black Student Union at the high school?
>
> *Interviewee:* Yeah, at the high school.
>
> *Interviewer:* They created a Black Student Union?
>
> *Interviewee:* Yeah. We had a Black Student Union. Yeah, I ran it my senior year.

Researchers have described how it is essential that school personnel in predominantly White schools create equitable educational settings for all students—settings in which Black students feel not only tolerated but welcomed (Darling-Hammond and Friedlaender 2008; Ladson-Billings 2014). During the earlier years of the voluntary transfer plan, a key criticism was the lack of preparation of the educators (overwhelmingly White) to effectively teach the Black transfer students from the city of St. Louis. Jerry, a student from Wave 2, discussed his efforts to create a culturally affirming program at the high school where he attended due to school administrators' not fully orientating the White teachers and students, as well as the Black students, about the expectations and experiences that each group might incur: "Actually, while I was at the school I created a program. [Our group] called the American Mentors did exactly that. That was my sophomore going into my junior year. I started that program. I don't even know if they still have it anymore . . . I don't recall there being any—no other than some type of orientation of some sort. I don't remember there being any prep for it [the experiences of the transfer plan]" (Jerry, Wave 2).

Mary, from Wave 3, described the creation of a high school step team as a way to provide Black girls with opportunities beyond the predominantly White cheerleading squads.

> We had a step team and we came up with that on our own because we needed something that represented us . . . Our step team wasn't at the games or anything like that. We probably went to maybe a few games . . . But we didn't have the same opportunities that the cheerleaders had to be on the sidelines. So like, we would have a halftime step show or during our pep rally or something like that where we would perform at the school. And then we had, like stuff that we did around the neighborhood. We performed in the [Annie Malone] May Day Parade.

The Black students' incorporation of stepping into their extracurricular experiences at the high school represented a deliberate effort to maintain their cultural identity. Stepping is a form of African American dance that combines rhythmic movements, chanting, foot stepping, gymnastics, and hand clapping. It is associated with Black American fraternities and sororities and emerged out of African culture, Black American folk culture, and military step drills (Fine 2003; Ross 2001). Although the Black students were afforded few opportunities to step at the high school, their participation in the Annie Malone Parade allowed them to display their culture as well as connect with the larger St. Louis Black community. The Annie Malone Parade, based in St. Louis, is the second largest Black parade in the United States. The parade is named after Annie Turnbo Malone, a St. Louis–based businesswoman and philanthropist who focused on Black beauty products and was one of the first African American women to become a millionaire (Phillips 2003).

How students identify reflects an interaction between the student and the unique social settings where they live and go to school. Whereas students' racial identities become shaped earlier in their lives than previously thought, researchers continue to note how adolescence is a period of time in which young people attempt to gain an integrated sense of self (Erikson 1968). For Black youth, this process can be further complicated by race, gender, and class status (Adeyemo and Morris 2021; Pattillo-McCoy 1999; Morris and Woodruff 2015; Phinney 1990). Adolescence in particular is a time in which young people are beginning to think extensively about identity related issues and to engage in practices that reinforce racial identity and boundaries such as where they sit together in school cafeterias (Tatum 2003). Amari, a Black female student from Wave 4, described these patterns as follows: "The Black kids basically sat with the Black kids, and the White kids sit with the White kids. I mean like for me I kinda—I got along with everybody. I talked to everybody, but acting the same when it comes—when it's at lunch or something or when school's over I would like, go with Black friends" (Amari, Wave 4).

Black student participants in the voluntary transfer plan carved out spaces of resistance by building relationships with peers from other communities in the city of St. Louis. Even though the Black youth came from various communities across the city and attended different county schools, they forged friendships during the bus rides. Amari further described how structures within the schooling process (whether tracking, athletics, or riding a school bus together) can reinforce racial identities among students who initially may have not embraced such identities: "There was so little of us [Black students] that we—and we all knew each other cuz we rode the bus to school, we rode the bus home. So that also gave us time to like to get close to—closer to each other. The bus ride was always like an hour long."

Another Black student, from Wave 3, specifically described how the voluntary desegregation program united Black students racially:

> I can honestly say the reason why I loved [the county school district] so much is not because of the White staff, not because of the White students, but there was a sense of unity with the Black students that I never got in my own neighborhood. We [Black students] knew that we were somewhere else and that we had to stick together. And so, we came together and we were so close. I loved these people, loved, loved, loved them . . . I've never experienced anything like that where I had people who cared about me as much as I cared about them despite the fact that we lived in different gang territories. We didn't bring that stuff to school. We didn't bring that with us. (Mary, Wave 3)

CONCLUSION

Almost six decades since the passage of *Brown v. Board of Education*, Black children in the St. Louis region continue to experience what W. E. B. Du Bois (1935) termed the "separated black school–mixed school paradox." This refers to a situation in which (a) Black children attending predominantly Black schools lacked the necessary resources that lead to an optimized education, and (b) Black children attending predominantly White schools become ignored and marginalized culturally and educationally. In his analysis of this paradox, Du Bois (1935) asserted that no matter the context (predominantly Black, predominantly White, or mixed), educators within schools should provide Black children with the academic, cultural, and psychological sustenance for their educational and social development. In an earlier article focusing on St. Louis's desegregation plan, the first author, Jerome Morris, captured how twenty-one Black educators in St. Louis—much like the former students who participated in the desegregation plan as noted in this chapter—critiqued the plan and embraced views that resonate with what is being defined today as critical race theory (Morris 2001). Through rich and detailed accounts, Black educators described how the desegregation plan ultimately protected the overall interests of White people. More recent scholars have extended Du Bois's and Morris's thinking and some of the work related to Black children's experiences with desegregation (Dumas 2014; Horsford 2010). Specifically, Michael Dumas's influential piece on Black school leaders' critique of desegregation in Seattle, Washington, further details what Black students lost by attending predominantly White schools. Collectively, these scholars and the interviews of former student participants that are shared in this chapter capture the Black community's tensions, contradictions, and losses experienced through efforts to achieve desegregation in US public schools.

Despite the push for and the backlash against desegregation efforts, today Black children continue to attend schools that are overwhelmingly minority and underresourced, which has grave consequences for their academic experiences and outcomes (Morris 2009). On the other hand, Black children attending racially diverse or predominantly White schools continue to experience academic marginalization, deculturalization, and dehumanization, which may have consequences for their racial and ethnic identity and school performance (Carter Andrews 2009; Chapman 2013; Dumas 2014; Morris 2009; Nasir 2011).

To minimize the dissonance they experienced as participants in the St. Louis voluntary transfer plan, we found that Black students would make deliberate efforts to push back against actions by adults and peers who sought to relegate them to the academic and social margins. Rather than becoming victims of social structures, policies, reforms, or practices that could contribute to their marginalization and dehumanization, the Black students demonstrated a sense of agency in ensuring that they could benefit from some of the resources within predominantly White schooling contexts. As we have demonstrated in this chapter, the Black students—not necessarily the teachers and district administrators—would take the initiative to ensure that their backgrounds, identities, and perspectives became a part of their experiences in the predominantly White, and often hostile, schooling context. They accomplished this by creating spaces and activities that affirmed their humanity.

NOTES

1. Key court cases with national implications include *Dred Scott v. Sandford* (1857), *Gaines v. Canada* (see *Missouri ex rel. Gaines v. Canada* 1938), *Shelley v. Kraemer* (1948), and *Liddell v. City of St. Louis Board of Education* (1972). The Liddell case would become the impetus for the St. Louis voluntary desegregation plan.
2. Massey and Denton (1989) developed the concept of hypersegregation to describe metropolitan areas that segregated Black and White people among four of five dimensions: unevenness focuses on their uneven distribution across metropolitan neighborhoods, isolation refers to the extent to which Black people live in predominately Black neighborhoods, clustering measures the degree to which predominately Black neighborhoods are clustered together, concentration involves the physical space occupied by Black people, and centralization is the extent to which Black people live near a metropolitan area's center.
3. From 1999 to the present, the exact accounting related to funding after the 1999 settlement has not been fully transparent and has not been readily accessible by members of the research team.
4. Members of the data collection team included Jerome Morris, Wanda McGowan, and Melissa Garcia, a graduate student. Data analysis team members included Jerome Morris, Wanda McGowan, graduate students Zori Paul and Tiffany Simon, and Bryson Mahari, a current high school student who provided invaluable insights from a Black youth perspective.

REFERENCES

Adams, David Wallace. 1995. *Education for Extinction: American Indians and the Boarding School Experience, 1875–1928*. Lawrence: University Press of Kansas.

Adeyemo, Adeoye O., and Jerome E. Morris. 2021. "Place, Another Dimension: Researching the Neighborhood and Schooling Experiences of Black Male High-School Students Who Play Sports in Atlanta and Chicago." *Teachers College Record* 122 (8).

Anderson, James D. 1988. *The Education of Blacks in the South: 1860–1935*. Chapel Hill: University of North Carolina Press.

Beals, Melba Pattillo. 1994. *Warriors Don't Cry: A Searing Memoir of the Battle to Integrate Little Rock's Central High*. New York: Simon & Schuster.

Bell, Derrick. 1980. "*Brown v. Board of Education* and the Interest-Convergence Dilemma." *Harvard Law Review* 93 (3): 518–33.

———. 1992. *Faces at the Bottom of the Well: The Permanence of Racism*. New York: Basic Books.

Brown v. Board of Education of Topeka, Kansas, 347 U.S. 483 (1954).

Butler-Barnes, Sheretta T., Charles H. Lea, Seanna Leath, and Rosa Colin. 2016. "Voluntary Interdistrict Choice Program: Examining Black Girls' Experiences at a Predominantly White School." *Urban Review* 51 (2).

Carter Andrews, Dorinda J. 2009. "The Construction of Black High-Achiever Identities in a Predominantly White High School." *Anthropology and Education Quarterly* 40 (3): 297–317.

Chapman, Thandeka K. 2013. "You Can't Erase Race! Using CRT to Explain the Presence of Race and Racism in Majority White Suburban Schools." *Discourse: Studies in the Cultural Politics of Education* 34 (4): 611–27.

Darling-Hammond, Linda, and Diane Friedlaender. 2008. "Creating Excellent and Equitable Schools." *Reshaping High Schools* 65 (8): 14–21.

Delmont, Matthew F. 2016. *Why Busing Failed: Race, Media, and the National Resistance to School Desegregation*. Oakland: University of California Press.

Dixson, Adrienne D., and Celia K. Rousseau. 2005. "And We Are Still Not Saved: Critical Race Theory in Education Ten Years Later." *Race, Ethnicity, and Education* 8 (1): 7–27.
Dred Scott v. Sandford, 60 U.S. 393. 1857.
Du Bois, W. E. B. 1935. "Does the Negro Need Separate Schools?" *Journal of Negro Education* 4 (3): 328–35.
Dumas, Michael J. 2014. " 'Losing an Arm': Schooling as a Site of Black Suffering." *Race Ethnicity and Education* 17 (1): 1–29.
Erikson, Erik H. 1968. *Identity, Youth, and Crisis*. New York: W. W. Norton.
Fine, Elizabeth C. 2003. *Soulstepping: African American Step Shows*. Urbana: University of Illinois Press.
Ginwright, Shawn A. 2004. *Black in School: Afrocentric Reform, Urban Youth, and the Promise of Hip-Hop Culture*. New York: Teachers College Press.
———. 2007. "Black Youth Activism and the Role of Critical Social Capital in Black Community Organizations." *American Behavioral Scientist* 51 (3): 403–18.
Goodman, Melody. 2016. "White Fear Creates White Spaces and Exacerbates Health Disparities." Racial Disparities of the Institutes for Public Health at Washington University. https://publichealth.wustl.edu/white-fear-creates-white-spaces-and-exacerbates-health-disparities.
Gordon, Colin. 2008. *Mapping Decline: St. Louis and the Fate of the American Dream*. Philadelphia: University of Pennsylvania Press.
Grantham, Tarek C. 2004. "Multicultural Mentoring to Increase Black Male Representation in Gifted Programs." *Gifted Child Quarterly* 48 (3): 232–45.
Gregory, Anne, and Gabrielle Roberts. 2017. "Teacher Beliefs and the Overrepresentation of Black Students in Classroom Discipline." *Theory Into Practice* 56 (3): 187–94.
Heaney, Gerald W., and Susan Uchitelle. 2004. *Unending Struggle: The Long Road to an Equal Education in St. Louis*. St. Louis: Reedy Press.
Hodge, Samuel R., Joe W. Burden, Leah E. Robinson, and Robert A. Bennett III. 2008. "Theorizing on the Stereotyping of Black Male Student Athletes: Issues and Implications." *Journal for the Study of Athletes in Education* 2: 203–26.
Hoose, Phillip. 2009. *Claudette Colvin: Twice Toward Justice*. New York: Square Fish.
Horsford, Sonya Douglass. 2010. "Mixed Feelings about Mixed Schools: Superintendents on the Complex Legacy of School Desegregation." *Educational Administration Quarterly* 46 (3): 287–321.
Jacoway, Elizabeth. 2007. *Turn Away Thy Son: Little Rock, the Crisis That Shocked the Nation*. New York: Free Press.
Johnson, Rucker C. 2015. "Long-Run Impacts of School Desegregation and School Quality on Adult Attainments." National Bureau of Economic Research, Working Paper No. 16664.
Ladson-Billings, Gloria. 2014. "Culturally Relevant Pedagogy 2.0: a.k.a. the Remix." *Harvard Educational Review* 84 (1): 74–84.
Ladson-Billings, Gloria, and William F. Tate. 1995. "Toward a Critical Race Theory of Education." *Teachers College Record* 14 (1): 7–15.
Lewis, Amanda. 2003. *Race in the Schoolyard: Negotiating the Color Line in Classrooms and Communities*. New Brunswick, NJ: Rutgers University Press.
Lewis, Amanda, and John B. Diamond. 2015. *Despite the Best Intentions: How Racial Inequality Thrives in Good Schools*. Oxford: Oxford University Press.
Liddell v. Board of Education of City of St. Louis, Mo., No. 72C100(1) (Complaint) (E.D. Mo. 1972).
Liddell v. Board of Education of the City of St. Louis, Mo., 505 F. Supp. 654 (1980).
Lit, Ira W. 2009. *The Bus Kids: Children's Experiences with Voluntary Desegregation*. New Haven, CT: Yale University Press.
Massey Douglas S., and Nancy A. Denton. 1989. "Hypersegregation in U.S. Metropolitan Areas: Black and Hispanic Segregation along Five Dimensions." *Demography* 26: 373–93.
Missouri ex rel. Gaines v. Canada, 305 U.S. 337 (1938).

Monroe, Carla R. 2005. "Why Are "Bad Boys" Always Black? Causes of Disproportionality in School Discipline and Recommendations for Change." *Clearing House* 79 (1): 45–50.

Morris, Jerome E. 2001. "Forgotten Voices of African American Educators: Critical Race Perspectives on the Implementation of a Desegregation Plan." *Educational Policy* 15 (4): 575–600.

———. 2004. "Can Anything Good Come from Nazareth? Race, Class, and African American Schooling and Community in the Urban South and Midwest." *American Educational Research Journal* 41 (1): 69–112.

———. 2009. *Troubling the Waters: Fulfilling the Promise of Quality Public Schooling for Black Children*. New York: Teachers College Press.

———. 2016. *The St. Louis Desegregation Plan: Gains, Losses, and Community Recommendations for Future Success*. Research investigation funded by the St. Louis Public Schools.

———. 2019. "Black Participants' Experiences and Perspectives in the St. Louis Desegregation Interdistrict Transfer Plan: Lessons Learned and Insights for Quality Schooling." Presentation to St. Louis Public Schools superintendent and Special Administrative Board.

Morris, Jerome E., and Ellen B. Goldring. 1999. "Are Magnet Schools More Equitable? An Analysis of the Disciplinary Rates of African-American and White Students in Cincinnati Magnet and Nonmagnet Schools." *Equity and Excellence in Education* 32 (3): 59–65.

Morris, Jerome E., and Benjamin D. Parker. 2018. "Understanding Critical Race Research Methods and Methodologies: Lessons from the Field." In *Understanding Critical Race Research Methods and Methodologies: Lessons from the Field*, eds. Jessica T. DeCuir-Gunby, Thandeka K. Chapman, and Paul A. Schultz. New York: Routledge.

Morris, Jerome E., and Sara E. Woodruff. 2015. "Adolescents' Perceptions of Opportunities in the U.S. South: Postracial Mirage or Reality in the New Black Mecca?" *Peabody Journal of Education* 90 (3): 404–25.

Nasir, Na'ilah Suad. 2011. *Racialized Identities: Race and Achievement among African-American Youth*. Stanford, CA: Stanford University.

Nasir, Na'ilah Suad, Amina Jones, and Milbrey McLaughlin. 2011. "School Connectedness for Students in Low-Income Urban High Schools." *Teachers College Record* 113 (8): 1755–93.

Norwood, Kimberly Jade. 2012. "Minnie Liddell's Forty-Year Quest for Quality Public Education Remains a Dream Deferred." *Washington University Journal of Law and Policy* 40 (1): 1–66.

Oakes, Jeannie. 2005. *Keeping Track: How Schools Structure Inequality*. New Haven, Ct: Yale University Press.

O'Connor, Carla. 2016. "Black Agency and the Ongoing Struggle for Black Educational Opportunity." *Du Bois Review: Social Science Research on Race* 13 (2): 413–24.

Ogden, David C., and Michael L. Hilt. 2003. "Collective Identity and Basketball: An Explanation for the Decreasing Number of African-Americans on America's Baseball Diamonds." *Journal of Leisure Research* 35: 213–27.

Pattillo-McCoy, Mary. 1999. *Black Picket Fences: Privilege and Peril among the Black Middle Class*. Chicago: University of Chicago Press.

Phillips, Evelyn Newman. 2003. "Ms. Annie Malone's Poro: Addressing Whiteness and Dressing Black-Bodied Women." *Transforming Anthropology* 11 (2): 4–17.

Phinney, Jean S. 1990. "Ethnic Identity in Adolescents and Adults: A Review of Research." *Psychological Bulletin* 108: 499–514.

Pollock, Mica. 2005. *Colormute: Race Talk Dilemmas in an American School*. Princeton, NJ: Princeton University Press.

Ross, Lawrence, Jr. 2001. *The Divine Nine: The History of African American Fraternities and Sororities*. New York: Kensington Publishing.

Shelley v. Kraemer, 334 U.S. 1 (1948).
Solórzano, Daniel G., and Yosso, Tara J. 2002. "Critical Race Methodology: Counter-Story-Telling as an Analytical Framework for Education Research." *Quarterly Inquiry* 8 (1): 23–44.
Spring, Joel. 2016. *Deculturalization and the Struggle for Equality: A Brief History of the Education of Dominated Cultures in the United States*, 8th ed. New York: McGraw Hill.
Stevenson, Howard C., and Edith G. Arrington. 2009. "Racial/Ethnic Socialization Mediates Perceived Racism and the Racial Identity of African American Adolescents." *Cultural Diversity and Ethnic Minority Psychology* 15 (2): 125–36.
Strauss, Valerie. 2017. "The Sad Story of Public Education in St. Louis." *Washington Post*, September 7. https://www.washingtonpost.com/news/answersheet/wp/2017/09/07/the-sad-story-of-public-education-in-st-louis.
Tatum, Beverly Daniel. 2003. *Why Are All the Black Kids Sitting Together in the Cafeteria? And Other Conversations about Race*. New York: Basic Books.
Tyson, Karolyn. 2011. *Integration Interrupted: Tracking, Black Students, and Acting White after Brown*. New York: Oxford University Press.
Van Ausdale, Debra, and Joe Feagin. 2001. *The First R: How Children Learn Race and Racism*. New York: Rowman & Littlefield.
Watkins, William Henry. 2001. *The White Architects of Black Education: Ideology and Power in America, 1865–1954*. New York: Teachers College Press.
Wells, Amy Stuart. 2009. *Both Sides Now: The Story of School Desegregation's Graduates*. Los Angeles: University of California Press.
Wells, Amy Stuart, and Robert L. Crain. 1997. *Stepping over the Color Line: African American Students in White Suburban Schools*. New Haven, CT: Yale University Press.

CHAPTER 8

THE TRIBUNAL OF THE FUTURE: YOUTH, RESPONSIBILITY, AND TEMPORAL JUSTICE IN US CLIMATE CHANGE LITIGATION

Mark Ortiz

On International Youth Day in August 2015, the Oregon-based legal advocacy organization Our Children's Trust filed a constitutional climate lawsuit against the US federal government. Our Children's Trust represented twenty-one children, teenagers, and young adults from across the United States. The ongoing lawsuit—*Juliana v. United States*—alleges that the federal government has violated the constitutional rights of young people and future generations by knowingly destabilizing the climate system through decades of policies and practices promoting the exploitation of fossil fuels. The lawsuit asks federal courts to compel the US government to design and implement a climate recovery plan that would rapidly phase out fossil fuels from the domestic energy mix and set the US on a trajectory to stabilize the climate system. *Juliana* is part of a growing global wave of youth-led and rights-based climate litigation, which has seen some success, achieving favorable court rulings mandating government authorities in Colombia, the Netherlands, Pakistan, and other jurisdictions to act on climate change (Peel and Osofsky 2017).

As activists litigate climate change in national courts and international policy processes, they increasingly articulate claims to atmospheric rights and responsibilities that stress and stretch existing legal orders (Fisher, Scotford, and Barritt 2017). Asserting novel claims to rights, such as to a stable climate system or healthy atmosphere, young climate change litigants are creating what I call a tribunal of the future by bringing long-term atmospheric processes with bearing on their future livelihoods and successors into the foreground of legal thought and action. Through a focused case study of *Juliana v. United States*, this chapter explores the political possibilities and potentialities engendered by this case and similar youthful interventions into the legal regimes taking shape around the problem of climate change. Specifically, in analyzing key legal exchanges and judicial rulings in the *Juliana* case, it examines how the category of "youth" is mobilized to make visible and contestable the legal geographies naturalizing the US petrostate and the spacetimes underpinning US gerontocracy—what I collectively term the petrolawscape—by gesturing to more-than-human conceptions of temporality and responsibility.[1] Differentially enveloped by a warming atmosphere compared to other generations, youth plaintiffs utilize their generational positionality to articulate claims to temporal justice, rebuking the short-termism of the market economy while challenging state institutions to reimagine responsibility in intergenerational and ecological time. To establish a theoretical foundation, the next section offers a brief literature review situating this contribution in relation to contemporary legal geographies and scholarship in the interstitial field of law and literature.

UNSETTLED LAWSCAPES IN TIMES OF ATMOSPHERIC DISRUPTION: SPECULATIVE LEGAL GEOGRAPHIES OF CLIMATE CHANGE

Legal geographers have long investigated the co-constitution of law, space, and nature. Law "draws from and organizes space" (Blomley 2015, 3), structuring power relations on and across land, water, and airscapes. The project of legal geography has involved "becoming spatial detectives," inquiring into the "the *where* of laws, social spaces, lived places and landscapes which are inscribed with legal significance" and interrogating the power relations encoded in dominant spatio-legal arrangements while illuminating other possible configurations (Bennett and Layard 2015, 409).

To this end, legal geographers have developed a rich conceptual vocabulary for characterizing the interrelations of law, space, and nature, and for describing the fusion of the spatial and legal or normative. Geographer David Delaney (2004, 851), for example, uses the neologism "nomosphere" to refer to the "cultural-material environs" produced in the reciprocal process of law becoming material (e.g., the construction of a fence to designate private property) and the social-spatial taking on legal significance (e.g., a site of religious importance being declared a national monument under federal jurisdiction). Building on the notion of the nomosphere, Andreas Philippopoulos-Mihalopoulos's (2013, 2015) work offers the portmanteau "lawscape." He defines the lawscape as the inseparable enmeshment of law and space in which, though "constantly conditioned by each other," the legal and spatial dimensions are more or less *visible* at different times and under different conditions (2015, 4). Thus, within the lawscape, certain legal operations become naturalized and rendered invisible even as they actively work to subjugate and obscure other possible arrangements. Law, in other words, though present, fades into the background. Philippopoulos-Mihalopoulos (2013) distinguishes the lawscape from other conjunctive formulations, like the "nomosphere," by assigning significance to a range of non-human forces and agencies (such as the climate system) alongside human processes in the making of law.

Central to Philippopoulos-Mihalopoulos's framing of the lawscape is his notion of "atmospheres of law." Atmospheres, as he understands them, are a means of seeing "affective occurrences as collective, spatial, and elemental," composed of and co-created by the relations among human and non-human forces and materialities (2013, 36). He sees law as engineering atmospheres, partially determining what "sensory options" are highlighted or suppressed in a space and thus shaping the experience of that space for the bodies that interact with it (ibid., 36). Inspired by and extending Philippopoulos-Mihalopoulos's work, McCormack (2018, 4) explains atmospheres as "elemental spacetimes that are simultaneously affective and meteorological," linking the elemental with the social and somatic. Critically, McCormack argues that bodies are "enveloped" in shared atmospheres and that different bodies—human or otherwise—are differentially capable of sensing and recreating the conditions of the atmospheres in which they are immersed (ibid.). Scholarly attention to atmospheres, he argues, must explore "how these spacetimes become the focus of intervention, action and experiment" and with what effects (6). Coupling McCormack's sharp definitional work with Philippopoulos-Mihalopoulos's emphasis on law as a key site of atmospheric intervention, this chapter further develops an atmospheric perspective on law and a legal understanding of the emergent atmospheres of climate crisis.

This chapter also relies upon insights from the interdisciplinary field of "law and literature." Law and literature scholarship conceptualizes legal development as an "iterative response to recurrent and competing stories" which convey different visions of the world and disparate senses of value (Burger 2013, 3). According to this framework, popularly circulating narratives and imagery, such as those of climate apocalypse, are central to processes of legal reasoning, litigation, and lawmaking (Weaver and Kysar 2017). Such narratives frame the terms of legal debate, the tone of legal interventions, and, often, the shape of judicial rulings. Law, in this perspective, is both an instrumental and expressive practice: it builds and puts into circulation narratives that confer legal and material significance to otherwise desultory events or causal chains.

In the context of building a progressive politics of climate change, the narrative dimensions of law are particularly significant. Literary theorist Rob Nixon (2011) describes climate change as a form of "slow violence." In contrast to the "spectacular" events that are typically recognized as violence, climate change appears "incremental" and "anonymous," creating "representational obstacles that can hinder our efforts to mobilize and act decisively" and assign responsibility for climate change and its impacts (2). Nixon stresses the importance of storytelling from below as way to address this representational problem, a form of narrative making that allows disenfranchised, or what he calls "unimagined communities," to mobilize against the slow violence of climate change and name those responsible (150).

Youth climate justice organizations like Our Children's Trust place high priority on storytelling as a mode of prefigurative politics and a means of challenging dominant narratives that stress individual responsibility for climate change and promoting accounts that stress the roles of powerful major polluters and governments. This chapter thus builds upon Nixon's conceptual foundations with an emphasis on youth legal activism in the *Juliana* lawsuit as a form of storytelling from below, in which the youth plaintiffs articulate visions of hopeful and/or dreadful futures and link these visions to demands for government accountability in protecting the intergenerational community of which they are part. Young people form one of the critical "unimagined communities" most at risk from, and least responsible for, climate change: they face a future defined by a dramatically altered climate yet have limited formal power because of age-based restrictions on political participation and the gerontocratic makeup of governance institutions in the United States and elsewhere.

This chapter aims to offer a speculative legal geography of climate change suited to a moment of atmospheric upheaval when long-relied-upon climate signals and processes are shifting. Bridging scholarship in legal geography, atmospherics, and law and literature, I aim to develop an analytic sensitive to the atmospheres of law, the dynamics of (in)visibilization characteristic of lawscapes and the speculative and political possibilities of storytelling from below through the medium of law. Climate change and the dynamic materiality of the atmosphere it highlights are driving contingent destabilizations of spatio-legal orders and opening avenues for intervention, potentially perforating the legal power of states and capital and empowering different actors to intervene in the making of legal-atmospheric worlds. As states and international institutions like the United Nations scramble to define rights and delineate responsibilities in a mutating atmosphere, they do so across vastly uneven global geographies of responsibility and vulnerability and an intergenerational situation that positions young people currently living and future generations as the inheritors of a potentially disastrous climate future of their predecessors' making. These tense dynamics, coupled with the stress placed on legal business-as-usual, create openings for compelling and transformative claims-making on otherwise sclerotic institutions. The youth plaintiffs involved in *Juliana v. United States* locate these opportunities for influence, emphasizing the differential nature of how youthful bodies experience the spacetimes of atmospheric disruption, in order to make visible the mutability of existing legal common sense and venture new claims to rights and responsibilities. Understanding unsettled lawscapes in times of atmospheric disruption demands imaginative, experimental, and speculative approaches that stress the dynamic and unstable interrelations of emergent legal-atmospheric worlds. In the sections that follow, I hope to offer such an approach to understand the *Juliana v. United States* lawsuit.

JULIANA V. UNITED STATES: OVERVIEW AND BACKGROUND

In 2015, the legal advocacy organization Our Children's Trust filed the *Juliana v. United States* constitutional climate lawsuit against the federal government in the Federal District Court of Oregon. Centered around the climate harms faced by twenty-one young people, aged ten to twenty-one at the time of filing, from around the United States, the lawsuit claims infringement to young people and future generations' fundamental and constitutionally enshrined rights to life, liberty, and property through the federal government's creation and continued promotion of the nationwide fossil fuel energy system. Our Children's Trust's case is supported by several legal declarations by leading experts in glaciology, climatology, economics, atmospheric science, and other disciplines, which collectively establish the role of fossil fuels in driving climate change and its associated biophysical, health, and economic impacts.[2] In the more than seven years since the case was filed, oral arguments from the youth plaintiffs and government defendants have been heard in the Federal District Court of Oregon and the Ninth Circuit Court of Appeals and written arguments have been evaluated by the Supreme Court. The case was expected to go to trial beginning in October 2018. However, on the eve of trial, the federal government implored the Supreme Court and the Ninth Circuit Court of Appeals, which oversee the District Court of Oregon, to intervene and halt the case pending additional review. The Ninth Circuit Court exercised its power to halt proceedings in the District Court of Oregon and asked both sides of the controversy to present oral arguments. At the time of writing in 2022, the status of the case is uncertain as plaintiffs await a court ruling permitting them to update their original complaint. The case analysis presented in the following sections take as their basis key legal documents, exchanges from oral arguments, and judicial rulings which took place between 2015 and 2019. Apart from the brief chronology above, documents and examples will be in no particular chronological order.

THE US PETROLAWSCAPE AND THE DISSOLUTION OF STATE RESPONSIBILITY

> This is no ordinary lawsuit . . . This lawsuit challenges decisions defendants have made across a vast set of topics—decisions like whether and to what extent to regulate CO_2 emissions from power plants and vehicles, whether to permit fossil fuel extraction and development to take place on federal lands, how much to charge for use of those lands, whether to give tax breaks to the fossil fuel industry, whether to subsidize or directly fund that industry, whether to fund the construction of fossil fuel infrastructure such as natural gas pipelines at home and abroad, whether to permit the export and import of fossil fuels from and to the United States, and whether to authorize new marine coal terminal projects. Plaintiffs assert defendants' decisions on these topics have substantially caused the planet to warm and the oceans to rise. They draw a direct causal link between defendants' policy choices and floods, food shortages, destruction of property, species extinction, and a host of other harms.[3]

So wrote Oregon Federal District Court Judge Ann Aiken in a November 2016 opinion finding that the *Juliana v. United States* youth plaintiffs had raised legitimate legal claims requiring a public trial to resolve. Although at the time of writing this trial has not happened and may not happen at all, Judge Aiken's opinion nevertheless crystallizes the stakes of the case.

In the above excerpt, Aiken describes how defendants—in this case US federal government agencies with relationships to energy, environment, and land management—have promulgated a particular type of lawscape, which I term the US petrolawscape. I use this term to signify the interactions of a set of legal rules (e.g., the Energy Policy Act) and administrative structures (e.g., the Department of Energy) with space and nature in the production of landscapes of fossil fuel extraction, refining, and circulation. In the act of describing these landscapes and the political choices through which they are produced, Aiken renders visible and denaturalizes the US petrolawscape as a spatio-legal project suffused by the interests of the powerful. The youth plaintiffs and, in turn, Aiken point to the gargantuan latticework of oil and gas transport pipelines that snake across the country and continent, the refinery infrastructure agglomerated in a toxic mass in the Gulf of Mexico, the extractive land and waterscapes leased by the federal government and denuded by private actors, and so forth, revealing these petrolawscapes as sites of struggle and competing claims (Purdy 2018). The petrolawscape is not confined to the technological armatures of the fossil fuel economy and the landscapes slated for extraction and disuse; rather, it infiltrates airsheds, waterscapes, and atmospheres both proximate and far-flung. It is this spatio-legal project in its entirety, which in the *Juliana* lawsuit is referred to as the "energy system," that perpetrates the temporal and spatial injustices of climate change.

A particular temporality and sense of value governs the petrolawscape. It is constructed with reference to a set of abstract mathematics that financially discount the future in relation to the present, deeming future considerations less important in decision-making practices. Writing in his expert report submitted to the court on behalf of the *Juliana* plaintiffs, eminent economist Joseph Stiglitz decries the financial discounting of the future in the context of climate change. He writes, "Defendants' policies that discount the future of Youth Plaintiffs and Affected Children at inappropriately high rates continue to steer America on the path of incalculable losses . . ."[4] Similarly, in an early round of oral arguments in the lawsuit, Judge Thomas Coffin—another Oregon District Court Judge presiding over *Juliana*—framed the discount rate in biblical terms as a case of "robbing Peter to pay Paul."[5] The discount rate spatializes a presentist mathematics of short-term capital gains, inscribing itself onto landscapes as a constellation of fossil fuel facilities and technologies whose impacts are assessed in terms of near-term profit generation rather than long-term climatic destruction. Landscapes themselves are imagined in short-term and discrete timelines as they become host sites of extractive machinery with productive rather than ecological or geological life spans. These calculations are made part of everyday bureaucratic normalcy and industry regimentation in the forms of quarterly earnings reports and projected returns on investments. Fitz-Henry (2017, 5) refers to this (neoliberal) institutional singularization of temporality as a form of "ontological flattening" that erases the alternative tempos and lifespans of non-human others and, in this case, young and future people unfolding across the same land/lawscapes as the fossil fuel economy.

Within this mathematical matrix, a deeper sense of future hardly has room to breathe, choked by toxic fumes and discounted by economic legerdemain.

Soon after Aiken issued her landmark opinion making visible the US petrolawscape and clearing the way for trial, the US government was mandated to submit a legal brief contesting the plaintiffs' allegations. Far from it, the government admitted in its reply brief that the emission of carbon dioxide from the combustion of fossil fuels was "placing our nation on an increasingly costly, insecure, and environmentally dangerous path."[6] Likewise, the government acknowledged that "for over fifty years some officials and persons employed by the federal government have been aware of a growing body of scientific research concerning the effects of fossil fuel emissions on atmospheric concentrations of CO_2—including that increased concentrations of atmospheric CO_2 could cause measurable long-lasting changes to the global climate, resulting in an array of severe deleterious effects to human beings, which will worsen over time."[7]

However, in a rhetorical move worth analyzing, the reply brief then states that "the term 'United States,' as used in the Complaint is vague, ambiguous and Federal Defendants cannot attribute knowledge to it."[8] The government's reply displays the "organized irresponsibility" that has long complicated the (inter)national politics of climate change, in which foundational notions of accountability and proof central to modern legal and moral regimes break down (Beck 2010). Driven by accumulations of gaseous molecules from every corner of the earth from at least the industrial revolution onward, locating responsibility and placing blame for climate change is contentious. Many affluent states and high-emitting corporations seek to insulate themselves from blame behind the geophysical dynamics of anonymity characterizing climate change, arguing that specific impacts, the result of collective accumulations, cannot be attributed directly to their emissions. In the US legal system and many others, so-called generalized grievances, problems like climate change that affect collectives rather than individuals, do not constitute legally recognizable or remediable harm. As author Wen Stephenson (2017), thinking with Arendt's trenchant observations on the "banality of evil," notes, dominant accounts of climate change traffic in terms of a "collective guilt spread so thin that it evaporates into air and disappears." In the government's account, guilt, along with the accountability of the state, become lost in atmospheric expanse.

The plaintiffs, by contrast, insist on the artifice of the petrolawscape and the relational construction of territory. Rather than a physical space itself, they construct the "United States" as a web of negligent bureaucratic bodies, practices performed with "deliberate indifference" to the future, and gerontocrats incapable of thinking of time and temporality outside of neoliberal parameters. The youth plaintiffs have come of age in unsettled atmospheres wondering, as the recent school strikes for climate have shown, why they are studying for a future that may not exist in any recognizable form. They have composed what I call a "tribunal of the future," seeking temporal justice—urgent action that recognizes and dignifies their futures—in the face of what writer and climate activist Alex Steffen (2016) calls "predatory delay." While this section has placed its emphasis on the defendants, I turn now to the interventions of this tribunal of the future.

ARTICULATING SLOW VIOLENCE: THE YOUTHFUL BODY AND TEMPORAL JUSTICE IN *JULIANA V. UNITED STATES*

> He can find no way to say what so badly needs saying. Our home has been broken into. Our lives are being endangered. The law allows for all necessary force against unlawful and imminent harm. His face turns the color of sunset, scaring her. Her arm goes out to calm him. "No worries, Ray. It's just words. Everything's fine." In mounting excitement, he sees how he must win the case. Life will cook; the seas will rise. The planet's lungs will be ripped out. And the law will let this happen, because harm was never imminent enough. Imminent, at the speed of people, is too late. The law must judge imminent at the speed of trees. (Powers 2018, 498)

The above passage, from Richard Powers's towering novel *The Overstory*, follows the thought process of a lawyer nearing the end of his life. In a revelatory moment, he realizes that law is, in a sense, always already too late to arrest the planetary harm of climate change, with its long and bent roots stretching far back and its quickly budding offshoots and extensions reaching far forward in time. To this eloquent passage, I add the words of an eighteen-year old *Juliana* plaintiff who told me an in interview that "the warning signs of impending doom aren't always as obvious as an exploding train." In comparison to the up-tempo geological time of the Anthropocene, an epoch in which planetary change now occurs in the span of a single human lifetime or a few generations, the temporality of law can appear sluggish, unable to keep pace with protean planetary dynamics (indeed, language itself appears to lag; see Nixon 2018). After all, the *Juliana* lawsuit has wound its way through the federal courts for over seven years now, as wildfires, hurricanes, and other climate impacts have proceeded at frightening speeds. Yet, contrarily, the law is also impatient and hasty: it seeks consequences which are not far removed in time and/or space from their causes and seems unable to comprehend the diffuse and deferred webs of harm characteristic of "slow violence" woven across vast spans of time (Nixon 2011). The law is simultaneously slow and circumspect yet hurried and slipshod. The youth plaintiffs, like the moribund lawyer in Powers's book, imagine what the law might look like if it were to "judge imminent at the speed of trees" and take seriously the climate change they are projected to inherit from today's decisionmakers.

The tribunal of the future and their attorney allies narrate climate change through the lens of youthful positionality, foregrounding generational vulnerability and the ways in which youthful bodies are uniquely situated in disrupted atmospheres. The plaintiffs' complaint speaks of young people growing up within or adjacent to moribund ecosystems with dying wildlife, land so parched it can no longer support local food production, tree canopies blackened by drought and West Coast wildfire seasons of infernal intensity. Others describe worsened seasonal allergies and aggravated asthma as their young bodies encounter polluted atmospheres and disrupted climates differentially from older population segments.

The youngest plaintiff, who lives on a barrier island a short distance from the coast of Florida, describes his nightmares about climate change and fears of losing his home to sea level rise. In a declaration to the court, he says,

> I have had recurring nightmares about the impacts of climate change on my home. In these nightmares, the barrier island and beaches are destroyed, and I can't figure out where I am or where I should go. It's dark and there are piles of leaves, sticks, and broken cars. I'm on the beach and there's nobody around me. I see rubble and wonder where my family and everyone else is. I wake up with a feeling of falling, and only then realize that I'm not standing on the beach and that it was just a dream . . . Without changes, I'm afraid I will lose my home and that my nightmares will become real. *These Defendants may not have to wake up to that reality, but me and my future children will be forced to live with their bad choices if we don't do something to stop climate change soon.*[9] (Emphasis mine)

This episode imagines the youth plaintiff as a prism through which to grasp the atmospheric drama of climate change. The child's nightmare becomes prophetic, presaging the world to come, a trope common within imagery and rhetoric of environmental crisis (Sheldon 2016). The nightmarish dreamscape is framed as continuous with the reality in creation. The last sentence is of particular importance, for it directly speaks truth to the power of gerontocratic governance. In a similar vein, during a round of oral arguments that I watched at the Ninth Circuit Court of Appeals, the following exchange took place between a lead attorney for Our Children's Trust and one of the circuit judges:

> *Attorney:* What the complaint alleges is that the federal defendants collectively and through the fossil fuel energy system are affirmatively depriving these young people (gestures to the plaintiffs) of their rights to life, liberty, and property.
>
> *Judge:* But no different than anybody else. Whatever harm they are suffering is the same as everybody else in the country . . . These happen to be children plaintiffs, but they're no different from anybody else in the country; whatever harm they're suffering they're suffering the same as everybody else.
>
> *Attorney:* Actually, they are suffering different harm, and the federal defendants have admitted in various documents that children are disproportionately experiencing the impacts of climate change and will going forward. In addition, Your Honor, they will live far longer than you. They will live to late in the century, when the seas are projected by these federal defendants to be ten feet higher, and in the evidence that's before you in Dr. Wanless's declaration, he explains that the seas could actually rise as much as thirty feet. So, the significance of the harm, the monumental threat that these injuries pose to these plaintiffs, is very distinguishable from the rest of the country.

The child here is figured as a gauge of atmospheric disruption, hypersensitive to the manifestations and ruptures of a changing climate. The attorney appeals to the notion of life span, or "intergenerational time," to humanize the ravages of climate change, but in so doing gestures to temporalities well beyond the human, such as the ecological time of oceanic change (Whyte 2018).

In addition to the critique of generational power and gestures to intergenerational time established by the plaintiffs' arguments, the legal and public discussions this lawsuit has generated also highlight the differential ways in which climate change impacts marginalized communities in the here and now. Describing conceptual connections between the Black Lives Matter movement and the Our Children's Trust lawsuit, one youth plaintiff observed the following in a piece for the *Guardian*: "Just as police, our supposed protectors, perpetuate violence on black bodies . . . our federal government is perpetuating violence on these same bodies through its policies that create and maintain our nation's fossil fuel-based energy system and cause catastrophic climate change." As the plaintiff further notes, "young people from marginalized demographics are especially vulnerable" to the harms of climate change and the systemic neglect of federal authorities (Barrett 2019). Many of the youth plaintiffs involved in the lawsuit describe similar intersections of their embodied experiences of race and gender with the uneven effects of climate change through legal testimony and personal storytelling, linking their efforts for climate recovery with other movements for social and racial justice. Moreover, and taken together, the plaintiffs' legal testimonies, their interventions in the public sphere, and Our Children's Trust's organizational engagements point to a broad analysis of power that frames gerontocratic power and adultism as interwoven with patriarchy, racism, and the present environmental injustices such forms of power perpetrate and normalize.

Against the disembodied "slow violence" of administrative neglect and organized irresponsibility, the claims-making of the youth plaintiffs sketches an urgent constitutional corporeality with roots in civil rights litigation (Nixon 2011). This temporality links their undeniable and urgent "here and now" as young people coming of age in a warming world with alternative visions of temporalities and futures. The words "with all deliberate speed," a phrase that first gained prominence in the *Brown v. Board of Education* case to desegregate schools, have now come to frame this case in judicial interpretation (it has been used repeatedly by Aiken in her rulings). If, for Philippopoulos-Mihalopoulos (2015, 5), "spatial justice" refers to the "conflict between bodies that are moved by a desire to occupy the same space at the same time," I define temporal justice as the conflict between bodies occupying time differently or differentially. I see the claims-making of the plaintiffs as efforts to reclaim or open what geographer Elizabeth Olson (2015, 521–23) refers to as the "deliberative power of urgency," sparking a "debate about whose world is being saved, when and at what cost."

Even as the youth plaintiffs bring claims of temporal (in)justice into the courtroom, they face the institutional inertia of the legal process. For government attorneys, judges and other professionals involved in this case, the time elapsed may carry no special significance. For the youth plaintiffs, however, it is a different story. The same plaintiff quoted earlier describing his recurring nightmares also says the following in his declaration:

> I was only 8 years old when I filed this case and I am so frustrated that we haven't had our trial yet. I am impatient because I'm a kid, and I have spent almost a quarter of my life working on this case, something that should have been done before I was even born because my government has known

about climate change for so long . . . I don't think it's fair that we have to wait so long when every year the climate change impacts I am experiencing are getting worse.[10]

This statement, coupled with the earlier portions of his declaration, exhibit an intergenerational caring agency that envisions past, present, and future communities of humans and non-humans as bound together and interdependent (Kallio and Bartos 2017). This political agency aims to "hold open space in the world for other living beings" (Van Dooren 2014, 5). The temporal imaginary it expresses stands in stark contrast to neoliberal "short-termism" (Fitz-Henry 2017), with its trajectories of progress and infinite growth, and also to masculinist and adultist strands of climate change ethics, which anticipate an "intergenerational arms race" as the planetary situation worsens (see Gardiner 2011, chap. 6). Moreover, this sense of intergenerational caring agency and concern for non-human others and intergenerational time is common across youth climate movements. Youth activists often rhetorically link "planetary life" to their own "subjective life," framing political dreams and nightmares in terms of the exhaustion of a planetary commons and their situatedness in relations of atmospheric intimacy (Yusoff 2018).

From the standpoint of narrative and genre, Weaver and Kysar (2017) argue that the *Juliana* lawsuit and in particular the personal accounts of youth plaintiffs are classic examples of the "environmental apocalyptic" narrative at work. Within the apocalyptic storyline as it is typically told, catastrophe brings normative disorder, a suspension of rules and norms, which is summarily followed by "normative reconstruction" (349). Certainly, the *Juliana* plaintiffs' personal accounts of nightmarish scenarios are consistent with this description, but the perspective elaborated in this chapter through the framing of "slow violence" slightly complicates Weaver and Kysar's assertion. Climate change is a form of slow violence precisely because it does not come naturally outfitted with the spectacular garb characteristic of apocalypse. Species quietly pass on, and the already intensifying harms of climate change are normalized as they bear down on human and non-human bodies already sacrificed and made disposable (Yusoff 2018). Rather than the "cinematic apocalypse" characteristic of this storyline, the "slow violence" of climate change is better understood as a myriad of "endings" of different intensities and scales (Purdy 2017). The work of the *Juliana* plaintiffs and other youth climate activists draws attention to these endings, amplifying them as they attempt to repair what is broken.

Yet, apocalyptic narratives are also defined by temporal rupture and the opening of avenues of possibility for normative reordering (Weaver and Kysar

2017). One such political possibility the *Juliana* case explores and invokes is the Public Trust Doctrine. Though perhaps apocryphal, many accounts date the origin of the Public Trust Doctrine to ancient Rome with the recognition that certain resources, such as navigable waterways and air, were to be preserved for the common use of present and future generations (Sagarin and Turnipseed 2012). Despite limited previous attention in US federal law, the *Juliana* plaintiffs contend that the Public Trust Doctrine forms the bedrock of the US Constitution and prohibits the government from jeopardizing the well-being of posterity by compromising entrusted resources. Potentially powerful interventions into the lawscape like this one often take unexpected forms, reflecting the fact that Western legal regimes are internally pluralistic assemblages, composed of various minor lines buried by precedent that can be, and often are, (re)activated in response to legally disruptive events like climate change (Valverde 2015). The Public Trust Doctrine reflects an interest in reclaiming both a resource and a temporal commons and resisting the temporal injustice of the petrolawscape.

CONCLUSION: CLIMATE IMAGINATION AND THE LAW

Kim Stanley Robinson's (2017) novel *New York 2140* offers profound meditations on the legal characteristics of a world inundated by sea level rise. Commuters in Robinson's twenty-second-century New York must take sea vessels to navigate the sunken city, yet business goes on largely as it did before. Bullish hedge fund investors still play the markets and devise clever schemes to short the next, impending asset bubble, while real estate moguls maneuver to eke value anew out of eroding infrastructure. But in Robinson's terraqueous metropolis, the cartographies of power, the geographies of law, and, consequently, the landscapes of political possibility change with the tide.

As is happening presently in the context of real-world institutions, in Robinson's telling, courts and the very tenability of law as a stabilizing force were pressed to their limits by rapid periods of climate change. The first of these periods of dramatic sea level rise—what he terms "pulses"—rearranged the geography of New York and the greater Eastern Seaboard of the United States such that some areas were completely submerged while others alternated in intertidal limbo. After much legal argument and many hourly fee invoices, the courts of law in Robinson's tale determined that the ancient Roman doctrine of *res communis* (things in common) was most appropriate for governing the intertidal zones. The courts ceded ownership of the intertidal to the "unorganized public," if not completely thwarting at least severely hampering the possibility for private investors to obtain exclusive development rights.

Neither private nor public, in the traditional sense of government ownership, this resurgence of the commons in Robinson's narrative ignites fierce battles between intertidal squatters and the forces of capital that seek to enclose and redevelop the zone. Investors see the intertidal as a new frontier of accumulation, a volatile area of potentially "high-reward" opportunity, while intertidal denizens see it as a space of social experimentation and egalitarian possibility. Under normal circumstances, law would serve to mediate between these divergent visions in order to arrive at a stable settlement involving established rights and clearly defined responsibilities (most likely involving the violent eviction of intertidal squatters and the enclosure of the zone under business as usual). However, the protean dynamics of Robinson's nature appear to militate against this outcome, suspending law in a state of indefinite unsettlement and creating the conditions of possibility for alternative arrangements to emerge.

It is more than coincidental that Robinson's work of climate fiction mirrors aspects of the *Juliana* case, even invoking the very same Public Trust Doctrine that the youth plaintiffs argue is an integral part of the US Constitution. Seeing law as not only an instrumental political device but also an expressive literary production enriches our understanding of the legal geographies of climate change. So too does thinking with literary texts that deal with the political and legal issues raised by climate change. The *Juliana* case has made surprising headway in cutting through the Kafkaesque atmosphere of the courtroom by centering the narrative and expressive qualities of law and conceptualizing temporalities alternative to those of the petrolawscape. Law is practiced by Our Children's Trust and the youth plaintiffs as a form of poesis—of poetic creation. For Amitav Ghosh (2016) and many of the preeminent climate authors, this imaginative work in the political domain is central to meeting the paradigm-shattering challenge of climate change. Despite the sluggishness of legal process and the liberal individualism embedded deeply in US settler colonial law, at least a handful of judges are proving receptive to the "pokes and prods" of the youth plaintiffs (Weaver and Kysar 2017). For the first time in US legal history, environmental rights were found to be fundamental to domestic law when Judge Aiken wrote the following: "Exercising my reasoned judgement, I have no doubt that the right to a climate system capable of sustaining human life is fundamental to a free and ordered society."[11] Similarly, in a round of oral arguments that took place in July 2018, she put it even more conclusively: "the endgame is survival . . . It's survival so that the plaintiffs in this case have the opportunity to life, liberty and the pursuit of happiness."[12]

NOTES

1. I use the term "gerontocracy" to describe the generationally homogenous makeup of US governance institutions, which tend to be dominated by old decisionmakers, and the ways in which this representational uniformity shapes the concerns, outlooks, and practices of these institutions.
2. For a summary of these expert declarations, see Urgent Motion Under Circuit Rule 27-3(b) For Preliminary Injunction, *Juliana v. United States*, No. 18-36082 (Ninth Circuit Court of Appeals Feb. 7, 2019).
3. Opinion and Order at 3–4, *Juliana v. United States*, No. 6:15-cv-1517-TC (D. Or. Nov. 10, 2016).
4. Expert Report of Joseph E. Stiglitz at 46, *Juliana v. United States*, No. 6:15-cv-1517-TC (D. Or. Jun. 28, 2018).
5. Reporter's Transcript of Proceedings at 25, *Juliana v. United States*, No. 6:15-cv-1517-TC (D. Or. Mar. 9, 2016).
6. Federal Defendants' Answer to First Amended Complaint for Declaratory and Injunctive Relief at 35, *Juliana v. United States*, No. 6:15-cv-1517-TC (D. Or. Jan. 13, 2017).
7. Federal Defendants' Answer at 1.
8. Federal Defendants' Answer at 1.
9. Declaration of Levi D. in Support of Plaintiffs' Urgent Motion Under Circuit Rule 27-3(b) for Preliminary Injunction at 15–16, *Juliana v. United States*, No. 18-36082 (Ninth Circuit Court of Appeals Feb. 7, 2019).
10. Declaration of Levi D. in Support of Plaintiffs' Urgent Motion Under Circuit Rule 27-3(b) for Preliminary Injunction at 6, *Juliana v. United States*, No. 18-36082 (Ninth Circuit Court of Appeals Feb. 7, 2019).
11. Opinion and Order at 32, *Juliana v. United States*, No. 6:15-cv-1517-TC (D. Or. Nov. 10, 2016).
12. Reporter's Transcript of Proceedings, *Juliana v. United States*, No. 6:15-cv-1517-TC (D. Or. Jul. 18, 2018).

REFERENCES

Barrett, Vic. 2019. "Yes, I'm Striking over the Climate Crisis. And Suing the US Government, Too." *The Guardian*. September 20.
Beck, Ulrich. 2010. "Climate for Change, or How to Create a Green Modernity." *Theory, Culture, and Society* 27 (2–3): 254–66.
Bennett, Luke, and Layard, Antonia. 2015. "Legal Geography: Becoming Spatial Detectives." *Geography Compass* 9 (7): 406–22.
Blomley, Nicholas. 2015. "The Territory of Property." *Progress in Human Geography* 40 (5): 1–17.
Burger, Michael. 2013. "Environmental Law / Environmental Literature." *Ecology Law Quarterly* 40 (1): 1–57.
Delaney, David. 2004. "Tracing Displacements: Or Evictions in the Nomosphere." *Environment and Planning D: Society and Space* 22 (6): 847–60.
Fisher, Elizabeth, Eloise Scotford, and Emily Barritt. 2017. "The Legally Disruptive Nature of Climate Change." *Modern Law Review* 80 (2): 173–201.
Fitz-Henry, Erin. 2017. "Multiple Temporalities and the Nonhuman Other." *Environmental Humanities* 9 (1): 1–17.
Gardiner, Stephen M. 2011. *A Perfect Moral Storm: The Ethical Tragedy of Climate Change*. Oxford: Oxford University Press.
Ghosh, Amitav. 2016. *The Great Derangement: Climate Change and the Unthinkable*. Chicago: University of Chicago Press.

Kallio, Kirsi P., and A. E. Bartos. 2017. "Children's Caring Agencies." *Political Geography* 58: 148–50.

McCormack, Derek. 2018. *Atmospheric Things: On the Allure of Elemental Envelopment*. Durham, NC: Duke University Press.

Nixon, Rob. 2011. *Slow Violence and the Environmentalism of the Poor*. Cambridge, MA: Harvard University Press.

——. 2018. "The Swiftness of Glaciers: Language in a Time of Climate Change." *Aeon*, March 19, 2018. https://aeon.co/ideas/the-swiftness-of-glaciers-language-in-a-time-of-climate-change.

Olson, Elizabeth. 2015. "Geography and Ethics I: Waiting and Urgency." *Progress in Human Geography* 39 (4): 517–26.

Peel, Jacqueline, and Hari M. Osofsky. 2017. "A Rights Turn in Climate Change Litigation?" *Transnational Environmental Law* 11: 1–31.

Philippopoulos-Mihalopoulos, Andreas. 2013. "Atmospheres of Law: Senses, Affects, Lawscapes." *Emotion, Space, and Society* 7 (1): 35–44.

——. 2015. *Spatial Justice: Body, Lawscape, Atmosphere*. New York: Routledge.

Powers, Richard. 2018. *The Overstory*. New York: W. W. Norton & Company.

Purdy, Jedediah. 2017. "Thinking Like a Mountain." *n+1*, no. 29. https://nplusonemag.com/issue-29/reviews/thinking-like-a-mountain.

——. 2018. "Trump's Nativism Is Transforming the Physical Landscape." *The Atlantic*. July 3, 2018. https://www.theatlantic.com/ideas/archive/2018/07/trumpian-nativism-is-transforming-the-american-landscape/564026.

Robinson, Kim S. 2017. *New York 2140*. New York: Orbit.

Sagarin, Raphael D., and Mary Turnipseed. 2012. "The Public Trust Doctrine: Where Ecology Meets Natural Resources Management." *Annual Review of Environment and Resources* 37 (1): 473–96.

Sheldon, Rebekah. 2016. *The Child to Come: Life after the Human Catastrophe*. Minneapolis: University of Minnesota Press.

Steffen, Alex. 2016. "Predatory Delay and the Rights of Future Generations." *Medium*. April 29. https://medium.com/@AlexSteffen/predatory-delay-and-the-rights-of-future-generations-69b06094a16.

Stephenson, Wen. 2017. "Learning to Live in the Dark: Reading Arendt in the Time of Climate Change." *LA Review of Books*. September 22. https://lareviewofbooks.org/article/learning-to-live-in-the-dark-reading-arendt-in-the-time-of-climate-change.

Valverde, Mariana. 2015. *Chronotopes of Law*. New York: Routledge.

Van Dooren, Thom. 2014. *Flight Ways: Life and Loss at the Edge of Extinction*. New York: Columbia University Press.

Weaver, R. Henry, and Douglas A. Kysar. 2017. "Courting Disaster: Climate Change and the Adjudication of Catastrophe." *Notre Dame Law Review* 93 (1): 295–356.

Whyte, Kyle P. 2018. "Indigenous Science (Fiction) for the Anthropocene: Ancestral Dystopias and Fantasies of Climate Change Crises." *Environment and Planning E: Nature and Space* 1 (1–2): 224–42.

Yusoff, Kathryn. 2018. "Politics of the Anthropocene: Formation of the Commons as a Geologic Process." *Antipode* 50 (1): 255–76.

CONTRIBUTORS

EDITORS

Gloria Howerton is an assistant professor in the Department of Geography and Anthropology at the University of Wisconsin–Eau Claire. As part of her service to the university, she works on the implementation team for the forthcoming Center for Racial and Restorative Justice. Her academic work investigates the political and legal discourses and strategies used to center white nationalist narratives in K–12 curriculum. She is especially concerned with attempts to produce whitened citizen-subjects through historical and cultural erasures in the classroom. Observing how politicians strategically dismissed the concerns of students, painting them as "rude" or mere puppets of their teachers when they protested, prompted the conversations that led to the development of this volume.

Leanne Purdum has her PhD in geography from the University of Georgia. Her research examines the complicated interplay of discourses of care, violence, and law to think through US immigration policies and the violence of detention and deportation. She has been a frequent volunteer legal assistant in the South Texas Family Residential Center in Dilley, Texas. She considers the family detention center and lawsuits over licensing them as "child-care facilities" as a case study to contribute to broader discussions of rights, refugees, and migration, and to understand the spread of structures and procedures that perpetuate worldwide detention regimes. She served as the lead of the Law and Policy Committee for the Athens Immigrant Rights Coalition. She is currently teaching in the Law, Politics, and Society Department at Drake University.

CONTRIBUTORS

Krista L. Benson is an assistant professor in the Integrative, Religious, and Intercultural Studies Department at Grand Valley State University and one of the managing editors of *Feral Feminisms*. Their research and teaching interests center on the interconnections between colonialism, sexuality, gender identity, racism, and supporting marginalized youth. They have published or have writing forthcoming in *Sexualities*; *Frontiers: A Journal of Women's Studies*; *Journal of Homosexuality*; *Reproductive Justice and Sexual Rights: Transnational Perspectives* (Routledge); *Sexuality, Human Rights, and Public Policy* (Farleigh Dickson University Press); and *Expanding the Rainbow: Exploring the Relationships of Bi+, Trans, Ace, Polyam, Kink, and Intersex People* (Brill). Before reentering academia, they worked in student affairs in universities, in communications for nonprofits, and with youth who were homeless on their own.

Kristina M. Campbell is a career public interest attorney, specializing in civil litigation on behalf of immigrants and low-wage workers. After representing farmworkers in Virginia and Arizona, Kristina was a staff attorney with the Mexican American Legal Defense and Educational Fund in Los Angeles, California, where she engaged in impact immigrants' rights litigation in Arizona and California. In 2010, Kristina founded the Immigration and Human Rights Clinic at the University of the District of Columbia, of which is currently the co-director. Since 2014, Kristina has focused her advocacy, litigation, and scholarship on the right of Central American women and children to seek asylum based on their well-founded fear of persecution by private actors on account of their gender, youth, or membership in other vulnerable particular social groups.

Meghan Cope, AB (Vassar) 1989, MA (Colorado) 1992, PhD (Colorado) 1995, is a professor in the Department of Geography at the University of Vermont. She identifies as an urban social/cultural geographer, with a focus on social inequality vis-à-vis children and youth. Her work has always reflected a sustained interest in the everyday, particularly for marginalized groups. Meghan's current research project, Mapping American Childhoods, is a historical geography of childhood in the early twentieth-century United States, which includes projects on children's work and schooling, health, migration, and the cultural constructions of an "ideal" childhood. Meghan also writes and teaches about research methods, including story maps, qualitative research with geographic information systems, and digital geographies.

Olivia Ildefonso, PhD, is a geographer and critical cartographer. She studies K–12 public school segregation with a focus on school funding and local control. She has worked with several community organizations on Long Island to address school segregation in the region. From 2010 to 2013 she was the housing project coordinator for civil rights organization ERASE Racism. Since 2013, she has served on the board of directors for S.T.R.O.N.G. Youth, a youth, family, and community development organization specializing in youth and gang violence prevention and intervention. She holds a BA in ethnic studies from Brown University and a PhD in earth and environmental sciences from CUNY Graduate Center.

Wanda F. McGowan serves as a consultant and has served as the co-director of the St. Louis Desegregation Study. She has a PhD in political science, and her research and teaching interests have focused on non-electoral political participation such as civil disobedience. Her research on *NAACP v. Claiborne County Hardware, et.al.*, 458 U.S. 886 (1982), examined social unrest in the African American community. McGowan has served as advisor or ad hoc advisor for undergraduate students completing senior theses in political science and graduate students completing dissertations in sociology, social work, educational leadership, and history. Her previous experience includes working as an assistant professor at Prairie View Agricultural and Mechanical University (Texas) and Rust College (Mississippi). McGowan works primarily with African American youth and college students. Her experiences include research associate and grant writer at Meharry Medical College and program director of a Kellogg Foundation grant at Tennessee State University. She has served as a field reader for the Foundation for the Improvement of Postsecondary Education. McGowan previously worked at Vanderbilt University as the assistant dean of the Graduate School in admissions, recruitment, retention, and student affairs.

Jerome E. Morris is the E. Desmond Lee Endowed Professor of Urban Education (in conjunction with St. Louis Public Schools) at the University of Missouri–St. Louis. Morris's interdisciplinary and empirically based scholarship examines the institutional structure and culture in schools, provides innovative conceptual frameworks to effectively study marginalized communities, and cultivates meaningful partnerships with communities and schools. The nexus of race, social class, and the geography of educational opportunity represents a major theme of his scholarship as a social scientist. Morris has been at the forefront of highlighting the centrality of the US South in African Americans' experiences, examining achievement-gap issues in Black suburban contexts, and researching the meaning of St. Louis's decades-old desegregation plan for racial and educational opportunity in the region. He served as principal investigator and director of the St. Louis Desegregation Study. Research awards have recognized him for cultivating an "outstanding body of nationally and internationally recognized scholarly activities in the social and behavioral sciences." From 1997 to 2015, Morris was a faculty member in the College of Education and a research fellow at the University of Georgia's Institute for Behavioral Research, rising from assistant to full professor. He is also a co-founder of Education for Liberation—a national coalition of teachers, community activists, researchers, youth, and parents.

Mark Ortiz is a postdoctoral fellow in the Department of Geography at Pennsylvania State University. He has a PhD in geography from the University of North Carolina, Chapel Hill. He received his BA in 2015 from the University of Alabama, where he majored in environmental politics and religious studies. Since 2013, Mark has been involved in a range of social, environmental, and climate justice work spanning local, national, and international scales. During this time, he has worked on international workers' rights issues with United Students Against Sweatshops, the AFL-CIO, and the Worker Rights Consortium, and on intergenerational climate justice issues with CliMates and the International Youth Climate Movement. He also serves as a Leadership Team member for the North Carolina Climate Justice Collective.

Glenn Rodriguez is an innovative leader and advocate for criminal justice reform. Glenn's passion for this work derives from his personal experience with the criminal justice system. Glenn was incarcerated at the age of sixteen and served twenty-six years in prison. Glenn's inspiring tale of redemption and fight for freedom have captured mainstream media attention and facilitated debate on the responsible and ethical use of technology in the correctional system. Since obtaining parole in 2017, Glenn has been employed at the Center for Community Alternatives. In his current role as program director at the Horizon Juvenile Center, a secure detention facility located in the South Bronx, Glenn is responsible for developing the program vision, implementation, and evaluation protocol for the Career Exploration Program.

Evan Weissman was an associate professor and director of undergraduate programs in food studies in the Department of Nutrition and Food Studies in the Falk College at Syracuse University. His work as researcher and teacher explored grassroots efforts to address food disparities in urban America through community engagement. Evan was a co-founder of Syracuse Grows, a grassroots network that cultivates food justice through advocacy, education, and resources in support of urban food production. Dr. Weissman died in April 2020 at the beginning of the COVID-19 pandemic.

Marsha Weissman is the founder of the Center for Community Alternatives (CCA) and served as its executive director for thirty-four years. While at CCA, she developed the first alternatives-to-incarceration program to divert young people charged with crimes of violence, from incarceration. She currently is a professor of sociology at the Maxwell School of Citizenship and Public Policy at Syracuse University, where she currently teaches courses on race, social control, and mass incarceration. She holds a PhD in social science from the Maxwell School and a MPA from Syracuse University as well as the Wagner School of New York University. Her book, *Prelude to Prison: Student Perspectives on School Suspension*, was published by Syracuse University Press in 2015.

INDEX

Note: An f, m, or t following a page number indicates a figure, map, or table, respectively.

ACLU (American Civil Liberties Union), 70
Acosta standard, 47, 49–50, 55–56, 59, 60
adults and adulthood, 4, 5, 12, 171, 172
    See also families
African Americans. *See* Black; juvenile justice system; race
age
    overviews, 3–4, 10–11
    "child" and "adult" and, 4, 5–6
    children of color and, 22
    climate change resistance and, 164, 168
    criminal justice system and, 13
    future and, 10–11
    "immutable characteristic" and, 47–48, 53, 60, 60n3
    intersecting identities and, 11, 13
    juvenile justice system and, 113–14, 117, 120, 121, 127
    "particular social group" and, 47–48
    people of color and, 13, 22
    persecution of youth and, 60n3
    political mobilization and, 138
    political participation and, 163
    school shooting experience and, 9
    See also "teenager"; temporality; work and schooling; youth, categorized and managed
agency, 4, 5, 6–7, 9, 13, 14, 155, 156, 172
    See also resistance and resilience
agricultural workers, 23, 35–38, 37f, 38, 38f
AIC (American Immigration Council), 63, 66
Aiken, Ann, 165–66, 171, 174
Aitken, Stuart, 4, 5, 9, 13
Alabama, 38f, 148
All God's Children (Butterfield), 123n7
Alphonso, Gwendoline, 41–42
American Academy of Pediatrics, 72, 73–74
American Civil Liberties Union (ACLU), 70
American Immigration Council (AIC), 63, 66
American Mentors, 152
anti-standardized testing movement. *See* opt-out movement and segregation (New York)

Arches Transformative Mentoring Program, 118–19
Arendt, Hannah, 167
Arkansas, 24t, 26m, 32m, 38f, 44n5, 148
Asian Americans, 126, 131–32, 139n1, 149
assimilation, 27, 151–54
asylum law. *See* deportation practices; family separations; "particular social group"
Asylum Lawyers Project (UNHCR), 49, 61n6
atmosphere of law, 163–64
Attica Is All of Us, 119–20

"banality of evil," 167
"ban the box," 119
Barr, William, 48–49, 58–60
Beker, Ella, 122
Bell, Derrick, 148
belonging. *See* inclusion and exclusion
Ben-Arieh, Gayla, 47, 60–61n3, 61nn14–15
BIA (Board of Immigration Appeals). *See* "particular social group"
BIPOC youth, 4
Black
    "people of color" versus, 127–28, 132–33, 134–35
    sense of place and, 131
    See also desegregation plan, voluntary (St. Louis, 1983–2024); juvenile justice system; race; race and policing in schools; white supremacy
Black Codes, 110, 114
Black families, 38
Black Lives Matter, 170
"Black lunch table," 148, 150, 151, 154
Black Panther Party, 120
Black/white racial binary, 127–28
    See also race
"Black Women's Agenda" report, 128
Blaisdell, Carolyn, 5
Board of Immigration Appeals (BIA). *See* "particular social group"

Boomers, 10
Bordessa, Ronald, 8
Bosket, Willie, 123n7
Braz, Rose, 72
BreakOUT! (queer and trans resistance)
    overviews, 106, 126–29, 132
    coalition building and, 127, 139
    lived experience and, 127, 129–38
    From Vice to Ice Toolkit, 132, 135–38
    We Deserve Better report, 132–35
Briggs, Laura, 80
Brookings Institution, 111
Brown, Michael, 143
Brown v. Board of Education (1954), 144–45, 171
#buildCOMMUNITIES, 122
Bunge, William, 4, 8
Burridge, Andrew, 72, 78
G. W. Bush administration, 113
bussing, 148, 150, 151, 154
Butterfield, Fox, 123n7

California, 38, 44n5, 121
Campbell, Clio (Black child worker), 37f, 38
Cantarero v. Holder, 61n11
capitalism
    anti-standardized testing movement and, 12
    climate change and, 163–64
    extractive, 107
    global, 7–8, 77–78 (*See also* international law)
    racial, 91–95, 100–101, 131
    work and schooling and, 23, 34–35
    See also industrialization; racial capitalism
care and protection for youth, 30, 73, 76, 78–79, 80, 81, 107, 112, 154, 177
    See also moral arguments
Carey, Hugh, 123n7
Catholic Church, 44n5, 74
CBP (Customs and Border Protection Agency), 65, 68, 77, 82n7, 83n16
Center for Community Alternatives, 122n4
Central American youth, 12, 18, 43–44, 49, 52, 57–60, 61n6, 68, 178
    See also "particular social group"
Chambers, Deborah, 6
Chesney-Lind, Meda, 129–30
"child" and "childhood"
    overviews, 2–8, 20
    age and, 5–6, 13, 53
    categorized and managed, 17
    contemporary ideal, 21–22
    criminal justice system and, 13
    discipline and, 22
    emotional development versus punishment and, 112–13, 123n6
    funding for spaces and, 8
    gendered and classed, 43
    ideals of, 43
    in place, 43
    right to childhood, 30
    right to education and, 41–42
    social institutions and, 11
    youth geographies compared, 4
    See also family separations; migrant youth and families; "particular social group"; work and schooling
childhood-in-place, 43
child labor. *See* work and schooling
Child Labor Amendment to US Constitution, 24t, 44n5
child protection and safety. *See* care and protection for youth
Children's Bureau (USDL), 24t, 25, 36
Children's Geographies (journal), 5, 6
Christians, 21, 28, 73
    See also religion
citizenship, 8, 27, 30, 32, 35, 43, 44n4, 67
    See also democratic participation
Civil Liberties Union (New York), 111
civil rights, 139n4
civil rights movement, 137, 171
class
    overviews, 43
    agricultural workers and, 36–37, 37f
    European lower, 67, 94, 101n1
    extracurricular/sports and, 149–50
    juvenile delinquency and, 112
    opt-out movement and, 87–89
    See also economic power
Clemmer, Donald, 122n5
climate change and environmental resistance (*Juliana v. United States*)
    overviews, 14, 107, 160–61, 164–65, 173–74
    apocalypses and, 162–62, 172–73
    lived experience and, 169–73
    Overstory and, 168–69
    responsibility and, 162–68
    unsettled lawscapes and, 162–64
    youthful bodies/temporal justice and, 162, 168–73
"Close to Home" initiative (New York City), 116
Coffin, Thomas, 166
Cold War, 88
Colombia, 52, 160
Colvin, Claudette, 148
Common Core Standards, 87–88
the commons, 173–74
community-based programs, 116–17
community cooperation, 96
Congreso de Jornaleros (Congress of Day Laborers), 127, 128–29, 132, 135–39
Congress of Racial Equality, 139n4
Connecticut, 24t, 25
Convention Relating to the Status of Refugees (1951), 47, 48, 61n6
Conway, Kellyanne, 74
Cook, Daniel Thomas, 79
Cook County Juvenile court, 112

Cool Places (G. Valentine), 6, 9
corrections corporations, 64
  See also prison industrial complex
cotton field workers, 37f
cotton mill workers, 29f, 35, 39
counter-narrative (counter-story), 148–49
credible fear interview, 69, 76, 77, 82n12
credible messengers, 105, 110, 116–20, 122, 122n3
criminalization
  abolitionism, prison, and, 72–73
  "child" category and, 13
  family separations and, 75–79
  global capitalism and, 77–78
  lived experience and, 129–32
  of migrants and families, 65, 75–79
  of parents, 79
  of people of color, 78–79, 106, 109, 114, 116
  of queer youth of color, 106
  race and, 78, 105, 135–38
  resistance and, 109
  targeted, 64
  See also BreakOUT! (queer and trans resistance); delinquency; juvenile justice system; prisons and imprisonment; race and policing in schools; "superpredator" narrative
"crimmigration," 64–65
critical race theory (CRT), 144–48, 155
cultural barriers, 136–37
  See also assimilation; deculturalizing institutions
Cuomo, Andrew, 87–88
Customs and Border Protection Agency (CBP), 65, 68, 77, 82n7, 83n16

deculturalizing institutions, 151–54
  See also integration
De León, Jason, 67
"deliberative power of urgency," 171
delinquency, 112–13, 116, 122n1
  See also criminalization
democratic participation, 8–9
  See also citizenship; resistance and resilience
Denton, Nancy A., 156n2
Department of Homeland Security Office of Civil Rights and Civil Liberties, 73
deportation practices, 61n3, 69, 74, 76, 79, 80, 81, 82n2, 128, 137
desegregation plan, voluntary (St. Louis, 1983–2024)
  overviews, 106–7, 142–44, 147–48, 154–55
  critical race theory and, 144–48
  funding and, 145, 146–47, 156n3
  historical context, 144–48, 151
  lived experience and, 143–44, 150, 151, 152–54

race and, 149–50
  research team, 149, 156n4
  resistance and, 13–14, 149–51, 155
  resistance to assimilation and, 151–54
desistance, 118, 123n10
"detainee" versus "undocumented immigrant," 82n1
detention centers, 64, 69, 71, 72, 81, 82n5, 111
detention of migrants, 7, 12, 28, 71–78, 75f, 80, 81, 82nn1–2
Dignity in Schools Campaign (DSC), 120, 121
DiIulio, John, 113
Dilley Pro Bono Project, 66
discipline, "child" and, 22
  See also race and policing in schools
discourse, policy impact of, 72–81, 75f
domestic service, 39
Dred Scott decision, 156n1
Drennon, Christine, 90
drug cartel, 49
DSC (Dignity in Schools Campaign), 120, 121
Du Bois, W. E. B., 91–92, 154, 155
Dumas, Michael, 155

Eaves, Latoya E., 131
economic power
  overviews, 9
  asylum law and, 77–78
  climate change policy and, 166–67
  family detention centers and, 82n5
  incarcerated people of color and, 123n7
  mass incarceration and, 114
  not-for-profit organizations and, 119
  opt-out movement and, 89–95, 99, 100–101
  short-termism of, 161
  temporal justice and, 162
  transgender Southerners and, 131
  work and schooling and, 23, 27, 43
  See also capitalism; class; employment; housing; opt-out movement and segregation (New York)
education. *See* race and policing in schools; schooling and schools; work and schooling
Ellis, Eddie, 120
Ellison, Treva, 131
employment
  formerly incarcerated and, 110, 117, 119
  forty-hour week, 24t
  segregation and, 23–24, 142
  trans people of color and, 131, 133
  See also agricultural workers; work and schooling
Energy Policy and, 165–66
"energy system," 166
enslaved people, 80

Escobar, Martha, 78
Every Student Succeeds Act (2015), 98
exceptionalism of children. *See* family separations
extractive capitalism, 107
extracurricular activities and sports, 149–50, 151–53

Fair Labor Standards Acts (1938, 1949), 23, 24t, 34
fair pay, 24t
families
    Congreso and, 136
    "particular social group" and, 49, 59
    prison experience and, 137
    standardized testing and, 19
    work and schooling and, 18, 21–23, 38
    See also family separations; migrant youth and families
"Families together AND free" Rally, 73–74, 75f
family separations
    overviews, 12, 18–19, 63–66
    activist discourse and, 70–81, 71f, 75f
    "asylum seeker" category and, 76
    class action lawsuit, 82n8
    criminalization and, 75–79
    defined, 82n2
    detentions and, 73–78, 75f
    exceptions, 65–66
    lived experiences and, 67–70
    statistics, 65–66
    zero-tolerance policy and, 64–70, 82n13
    See also "detainee" versus "undocumented immigrant"; detention of migrants; migrant youth and families
"Father," 19
Faulk, Nate, 127
federal government control
    gang violence and, 61n14
    gerontocracy and, 10, 161, 163, 167–68, 175n1
    housing market and, 95–96
    Juliana and, 164–65, 167
    standardized testing and, 101, 102n2
    St. Louis Public School district and, 146–47
    work and schooling and, 27, 33–34, 42
    See also laws and policies
feminist geopolitics, 2
formerly incarcerated people, 110, 117–18, 121–22
fossil fuel industry, 160, 164, 165, 166
Foucault, Michel, 26, 42
Freedom for Immigrants glossary, 82n1
freedom of movement, 72
Freedom Summer, 137, 139n4
Free Southern Theatre, 137
From Vice to ICE Toolkit (2016), 132, 135–38

future
    overviews, 9
    age and, 10–11
    climate change and, 163, 164, 166–67, 171
    family separations and, 81
    gerontocracy and, 167–68
    ideal, 43
    migration law and, 60
    resistance and, 14
    white nationalism and, 80
    work and schooling and, 43
    See also climate change and environmental resistance *(Juliana v. United States)*; temporality

Gaines v. Canada (1938), 156n1
gang recruitment/membership/violence, 55, 57–58, 60, 61n6, 61n11, 61n14
Garcia, Melissa, 156n4
Gault Decision, 113
gay Black men, 130
GED program, BreakOUT!, 127
gender identities
    overviews, 10, 43
    agricultural workers and, 36–37, 37f
    education and, 111
    lived experience and, 30
    school shootings and, 9
    See also BreakOUT! (queer and trans resistance); women
gender-neutral pronouns, 10
generalized grievances, 167
generational positionality, 161
    See also intergenerational time; temporality
Gen Z, 10
geographical imaginary, 64
    See also space
geographies of youth, 2–3, 4
    See also "child" and "childhood"; place; space; youth, categorized and managed
gerontocracy. *See* intergenerational time; laws and policies
Get Yr Rights youth network, 127
Ghosh, Amitav, 174
"Gifted and Talented" schools, 94
Gilmore, Ruth Wilson, 3, 72, 119, 126
Ginwright, Shawn, 8–9, 148
grassroots organizations, 105–6
    See also resistance and resilience
Great Migration, 38–39
Great Recession, 9
Green, Kai M., 131
Growing Up Global (Katz), 7, 8, 11
guardians, 122n6
Guidelines (UN), 50–51
gun violence, 9–10

Hand, William, 29, 31–32, 40, 44n4
healing justice, 127, 139n2
healthcare, 131, 132
heteronormativity, 129
Hine, Lewis, 37f, 38
Hispanics, 9, 110–11
Holloway, Sarah L., 5, 22, 30
homophobia, 130
House of Refuge (juvenile facility), 112
housing
　desegregation plan, voluntary, 8, 132, 142
　See also desegregation plan, voluntary (St. Louis, 1983–2024); opt-out movement and segregation (New York)
humanitarians, 75–76
human rights organizations, 65
Hunter, Robert, 35–36
Hurricane Katrina, 136
hypersegregation, 13, 107, 142, 156n2

ICE (Immigration and Customs Enforcement), 69, 82n2, 136
"ideal child," 21–22
identities. See citizenship; gender identities; identities, intersecting; inclusion and exclusion; "particular social group"; race; stereotypes; youth, categorized and managed
identities, intersecting, 1, 4, 5, 6, 7, 11, 12, 13, 20, 106, 121
　See also intersectional resistance; youth, categorized and managed
identity development, 131, 153, 155
"illegal immigrant," 64, 67
Illinois, 27
immigration. See family separations; migrant youth and families; "particular social group"
immigration activist, 70–73
Immigration and Customs Enforcement (ICE), 69, 82n2, 135–36
Immigration and Nationality Act (INA), 49
"immutable characteristic." See "particular social group"
imprisonment
　people of color and, 120, 123n8
　poverty and, 123n8
inclusion and exclusion
　BreakOUT! and, 134
　Congreso, 136
　family separation and, 66–67, 70
　formerly incarcerated people and, 117
　law and policy and, 13
　migrants and, 82n1
　racial capitalism and, 100
　space and, 3
industrialization
　agricultural, 35–36, 38f
　climate change and, 167
　race and, 39
　work and schooling and, 22–23, 24t, 25–26, 33, 34, 35–36, 39, 92
　See also capitalism; fossil fuel industry; prison industrial complex
innocence narratives, 78
integration, 142, 145
intentional relationship-building, 136–37
interest-convergence dilemma (CRT), 148, 155
intergenerational time, 170
international law, 65, 67, 160–61
intersectional resistance, 106, 121–22, 128–29
　See also BreakOUT! (queer and trans resistance)

James, Taj, 4, 8–9
Japanese internment, 80, 81
Jim Crow laws, 110, 114
Johnson, E Patrick, 130
Juliana v. United States. See climate change and environmental resistance (Juliana v. United States)
justice/injustice, 12
　See also juvenile justice system; resistance and resilience; social justice
Just Leadership, 121–22
juvenile justice system
　age and, 13, 113, 117, 120, 121, 127
　disciplinary referrals and, 129
　LGBTQ+ and, 126–27, 132
　lived experience and, 137
　race and, 13, 112, 126
　rehabilitation versus punishment and, 112–13, 123n6
　statistics, 110–11
　See also BreakOUT! (queer and trans resistance); laws and policies; prisons and imprisonment; race and policing in schools
Juvenile Offender Law (NY, 1978), 113, 123n7

Karnes City Family Residential Center, 82n5
Katz, Cindi, 7–8, 11
Keating-Owen Act (1916), 24t
"keep families together," 73–74
Kelley, Florence, 30, 33–34
Knights of Labor, 24t
Kysar, Douglas A., 172

Labaree, David, 27, 32
labor unions, 24t
La Familia Michoacana (Mexican drug cartel), 49
landscapes of power, 2
　See also economic power; federal government control

188 / Index

language barrier, 139
Latinx, 80, 131–32, 135–36, 137
laws and policies
    overviews, 1–2, 8, 11–13
    atmosphere of, 163–64
    climate change and, 161–64
    housing market and, 95–96
    lifelong consequences and, 10–11
    resistance to prison and, 121
    social change and, 30–31
    social construction of, 66–70
    space and, 7
    space in schools and, 2, 12
    standardized testing and, 88, 102
    temporal injustice and, 171–72
    US settler colonial, 174
    See also criminalization; federal government control; migrant youth and families; policing and enforcement; race; resistance and resilience; US Supreme Court; work and schooling
LGBTQ+, 10
    See also BreakOUT! (queer and trans resistance)
Liddell, Minnie, 145
Liddell v. City of St. Louis Board of Education, 145, 156n1
Little Rock Nine, 148
lived experience
    overviews, 1, 2
    Boomers and, 10
    BreakOut! and, 127
    children's, 4
    climate change and, 164, 169–73
    credible messengers and, 117–18
    desegregation plan and, 106–7, 109–10, 116, 143–44, 149–54
    family separations and, 67–70
    intersecting identities and, 7
    Juliana and, 169–71
    legal sanctioning and, 12
    LGBTQ and race and, 135–38
    past, 10
    place and, 161–62
    prisons and, 121, 122n4, 129, 137, 180
    queer and trans of color and, 127, 129–38
    race and policing in schools and, 114–16, 120–21, 122n4
    resistance and, 13, 70–73, 105, 106–7
    school shootings and, 9
    See also counter-narrative (counter-story); story circles; storytelling (narrative)
local control ("home rule")
    housing market and, 95–97, 98–99, 101
    race and, 97
    racial ideology and, 94
    school funding and, 89–90, 91–95, 96, 99
    school segregation and, 100–101
    See also opt-out movement and segregation (New York)
Long Island (NY), 96

Lope-Humphreys, Mayra, 118–19
Louisiana, 128
    See also BreakOUT! (queer and trans resistance)
Lovejoy, Owen, 27, 28, 34
Loyd, Jenna M., 72, 78

Mack, Julian, 112
Mahari, Bryson, 156n4
Malkki, Liisa H., 75
Manhattan, Lower East Side, 30–31
Mann, Horace, 27, 28, 41
Mara Salvatrucha (MS-13, transnational criminal organization), 52
Martin, Trayvon, 4
Maruna, Shadd, 119
Massachusetts, 24t, 25, 28, 44n5
Massey, Douglas S., 156n2
mass incarceration, 105, 114, 117, 120
Matter of A-B- (BIA 2018 and 2019), 57–58
Matter of Acosta (BIA 1985), 47, 49–50, 55–56, 59–60
Matter of A-M-E- & J-G-U- (BIA 2007), 51–52, 54
Matter of A-R-C-G- (2014), 58–59
Matter of C-A- (USCIS, 2007), 50–51, 52
Matter of E-A-G- (BA), 54
Matter of L-E-A- (219), 49, 58, 59
Matter of M-E-V-G- (BIA 2014), 51–52, 54–57, 59
Matter of S-E-G (BIA), 51–54
Matter of W-G-R (BIA), 54–55, 59
McDowell, J.R., 30, 36, 42
McKelway, A. J., 35
McKittrick, Katherine, 3, 131
Meiners, Erica, 64, 78–79
mentors, 117, 122n3
    See also credible messengers
Meredith (Judge), 145
Midwest, 27
migrant youth and families
    overviews, 6, 7, 8, 12–13, 18–19
    arrest rates (Louisiana), 128
    BreakOut! and, 127
    child labor and, 23, 31, 35, 38
    European, 67, 94, 101n1
    intersectional issues and, 128–29
    "legal" versus "illegal," 64, 67
    "migrant" versus "immigrant," 82n1
    Northern states work and schooling and, 35
    persecution of, 47–60, 60n3, 61nn5–6
    resistance and, 11, 70–73, 71f, 106
    statistics, 82n6
    undocumented, 106, 127, 132, 136
    See also BreakOUT! (queer and trans resistance); Congreso de Jornaleros (Congress of Day Laborers); deportation practices; "detainee" versus "undocumented immigrant"; detention of migrants; family

separations; *From Vice to ICE Toolkit* (2016); "particular social group"
Mills, Sarah, 9
minimum wage, 24t
mining, 35
"Minority Women's Plank," 128
Mississippi, 36, 38f, 40, 42, 139n4
Missouri, 116, 142–43, 146–47, 156n1
    See also desegregation plan, voluntary (St. Louis, 1983–2024)
Mitchelson, Matt, 72, 78
Montgomery (AL), 148
moral arguments, 27–28
    See also care and protection for youth
Ms. L. v. ICE (2018), 65, 71, 82n8

NAACP (National Association for the Advancement of Colored People), 96–97, 145, 146
nation, ideal, 43
National Center for Education Statistics, 111
National Child Labor Committee (NCLC), 25, 28, 36–38, 40
National Industrial Recovery Act (1933), 24t
nationality. *See* citizenship
National Labor Relations Act, 24t
National Trades' Union Convention (1836), 24t
National Women's Conference (1977), 128
"A Nation at Risk" report (Reagan administration), 88
Native Americans, 80
Native queer or trans person, 131–32
naturalization, 76
Nazario, Ismael, 121
Nazis, 80
NCLC (National Child Labor Committee), 25, 28, 36–38, 40
Nelson, Willie, 73
neoliberalism, 166, 168, 172
Netherlands, 160
Nevins, Joseph, 77–78
New England, 28
New England Association of Farmers, Mechanics, and Other Working Men, 24t
New Orleans, 128, 131, 136, 139n4
    See also BreakOUT! (queer and trans resistance)
New Orleans Police Department (NOPD), 127, 134, 135
"new regionalism," 99
New York, 30, 44n5, 96, 113, 116, 120, 121, 122n4, 123n7
    See also opt-out movement and segregation
New York 2140 (Robinson), 173–74
New York City (NYC), 44n6, 111, 114, 116–17, 127
    See also Bosket, Willie
New York Civil Liberties Union, 111

New York State Council of School Superintendents, 98
New York State Education Department, 88, 97–98
Nielsen, Kirstjen, 82n8
Nixon, Rob, 162
nongovernmental organizations, 123n11
"nomosphere," 161–62
"No One is Illegal" versus "No One is Criminal," 78
the North, 35, 39, 41–43, 91–92, 94
    See also regional patterns; *individual states*
North Carolina, 38f
Northeast, 27
not-for-profit sector, 119

Obama administration, 74, 88
O'Connor, Carla, 144
Office of Juvenile Justice Detention, 7, 12, 72–78, 80, 81, 82n1
    See also detention centers
Ohio, 27
"okay, Boomer," 10
Oklahoma, 37f
Olson, Elizabeth, 171
O'Neal, John, 137
opt-out movement and segregation (New York)
    overviews, 12, 19, 87–89
    economic power and, 19, 89–96, 99
    local control/housing market and, 95–97, 98–99, 101
    origins of segregation, 91–97, 100–101
    people of color and, 89, 94, 95, 101
    race and, 88–89
    race/class and, 87–88, 89
    school quality and, 97–99, 101
Oregon, 42
Oregon Federal District Court, 164–65, 166
Orfield, Myron, 99
"other," 4
    See also inclusion and exclusion
Our Children's Trust, 160, 163, 164, 171, 174
    See also climate change and environmental resistance (*Juliana v. United States*)
The Overstory (Powers), 168–69

parens patriae, 122n6
parents' rights, 28, 31–32, 41–42, 69, 79
    See also families; family separations
Parks, Rosa, 148
"particular social group"
    overviews, 18, 19, 47–48, 60
    Acosta standard and, 49–50
    defined and redefined, 47–48, 51–54, 61n10
    future law and, 60
    gang membership and, 54–56

"particular social group" (*continued*)
  as "immutable characteristic," 50, 51, 53, 55, 56, 60, 61nn10–11
  "on account of" protected ground and, 48–49
  "particular" and, 51–54, 56
  persecution of migrating youth and, 47–60, 60n3, 61nn5–6
  "social visibility" requirement (distinction test), 50–51, 52, 55, 56–57, 59
  victims of gang violence and, 57–58
  "youth" and, 55
  See also Acosta standard; *entries beginning Matter of...*; family separations
Paul, Zori, 156n4
peer educators/leaders, 117
  See also credible messengers
Pennsylvania, 24t, 25
people of color. *See* race; "superpredator" narrative
"people of color" versus "Black people," 127–28, 132–33, 134–35
petrolawscape, 161, 162, 165–68
Philippopoulos-Mihalopoulos, Andreas, 162, 171
"pipeline to prison," 114, 123n8
  See also school-to-prison pipeline
place
  Black identity and, 131
  opt-out movement and, 88–89
  See also states
policing and enforcement
  federal government control and, 112
  LGBTQ+ and, 129
  lived experience and, 129
  race and, 43n1, 112
  violence and, 143
  youth categories and, 2
  See also BreakOUT! (queer and trans resistance); ICE (Immigration and Customs Enforcement); race and policing in schools
Pollock, Mica, 149
power, 1–2, 3
  "illegal immigrant" and, 64
  intersecting identities and, 11
  management of youth and, 12
  youth categories and, 12, 19, 22
  See also economic power; federal government control; laws and policies; opt-out movement and segregation (New York); resistance and resilience
Powers, Richard, 168–69
prison industrial complex, 72, 119, 120
  See also corrections corporations
prisonization, 111, 122n5
prison-like institutions, 109, 111, 114, 122n1
  See also detention centers
prisons and imprisonment
  abolitionist frameworks and, 72–73, 76, 81
  Bosket and, 123n7
  child-saving logics and, 78–79
  costs of, 123n7
  lived experience and, 121, 122n4, 129, 137, 180
  Louisiana and, 128
  race statistics, 111
  resistance and, 122n4
  See also credible messengers; mass incarceration; prison-like institutions; school-to-prison pipeline
profiling, 127
progressives, 27, 39
  See also New York City (NYC)
property values. *See* opt-out movement and segregation (New York)
public opinion, 120, 121
Public Trust Doctrine, 173, 174

"quare," 130
queer and trans of color, 106, 130, 131, 132, 135–36
  See also BreakOUT! (queer and trans resistance)
Qvortrup, Jens, 2

race
  age and, 13, 22
  agricultural workers and, 36–37, 37f, 38, 38f
  contemporary police violence and, 43n1
  criminalization and, 78, 135
  "ideal child" and, 21–22
  identity development and, 131, 153, 155
  imprisonment and, 110–11
  LGBTQ experiences of criminalization and, 135
  local control and, 97
  opt-out movement and, 88–89
  school shootings and, 9
  From Vice to Ice and, 137
  See also criminalization; critical race theory (CRT); identities, intersecting; race and policing in schools; racial capitalism; resistance and resilience; schooling and schools; segregation; work and schooling
race and policing in schools
  overviews, 121–22
  classroom as prison-like and, 114
  credible messengers and, 105, 110, 116–19, 122, 122n3
  desegregation plan and, 149–51
  lived experience and, 114–16, 120–21, 122n4
  racism and, 110–12
  rehabilitation and, 112–13, 123n6
  resistance/resilience and, 114–15, 119–21, 122n2, 122n4
  statistics, 110–11, 114, 115–17, 119, 120

"superpredator" narrative and, 105, 109–10, 113–14
See also discipline, "child" and; juvenile justice system; prisons and imprisonment; school-to-prison pipeline; suspension/expulsion from school
racial capitalism, 91–95, 100–101, 131
racial covenants, 95, 96
racism/racial ideology, 94, 110–12, 114
See also critical race theory (CRT)
Ransby, Barbara, 122
Reagan administration, 89
Reconstruction, 91–92, 93–94
redlining, 95
Refugee Act of 1980, 47, 48, 56
regional patterns
work and schooling and, 25–43, 26m, 27, 30, 34–35, 41–42, 43
See also specific regions
religion, 25, 47, 48, 52, 161, 177
See also Christians
Remain in Mexico program, 77
res communis (Roman legal doctrine), 173–74
resistance and resilience
overviews, 2, 8–10, 13–14, 105–8
to assimilation, 151–54
climate change and, 14, 160–61
desegregation plan and, 13–14, 149–54, 155
future and, 14
historical backdrop, 148
immigration activists and, 11, 70–73, 71f
intersecting identities and, 13
lived experiences and, 13, 70–73, 105, 106–7, 110
nineteenth century, 122n6
not-for-profit sector and, 119
prisons and, 72–73, 76, 81, 122n4
race and policing in schools and, 114–15, 119–21, 122n2, 122n4
school-to-prison pipeline and, 13
white, to *Brown v. Board of Education* (1954), 145
See also agency; BreakOUT! (queer and trans resistance); climate change and environmental resistance *(Juliana v. United States)*; democratic participation; desegregation plan, voluntary (St. Louis, 1983–2024); opt-out movement and segregation (New York)
Rhode Island, 35
Richardson, Matt, 131
rights, 6, 30, 42, 81, 137, 139n4, 171, 174
See also climate change and environmental resistance *(Juliana v. United States)*; parents' rights; voter rights/registration/mobilization
Rikers Island, 121–22
Rios, Victor, 130
Rittenhouse, Kyle, 4
Roberts v. The City of Boston (1850), 94
Robinson, Cedric, 93

Robinson, Kim Stanley, 173–74
Rogers, Thomas, 98
Roman doctrine, 173–74
Roosevelt, Franklin, 24t

"safe third country" transit ban, 77, 83n16
safety, 132
Sallee, Shelley, 39, 40
schooling and schools
academic tracking, 150
BreakOUT! and, 132, 137
carceral classroom and, 114–16
extracurricular activities and sports, 149–50, 151–53
funding and, 8
"Gifted and Talented," 94
local housing market and, 98–99
mobilization and, 10
multiracial, 94
race and, 14, 106–7, 149–51
race/policing and, 109, 111
residential community and, 101
St. Louis and, 142
suspensions/expulsions from, 114, 115, 117, 120, 129–30 (See also race and policing in schools)
urban, 111
See also desegregation plan, voluntary (St. Louis, 1983–2024); laws and policies; opt-out movement and segregation (New York); race and policing in schools; school-to-prison pipeline; work and schooling
school shootings, 6, 9
school-to-prison pipeline, 13, 105, 109, 114, 115, 120, 121, 122n2, 129
sea level rise, 168, 169, 170, 173
Seattle (WA), 155
Seddon, Alfred, 40
segregation, 44n6, 155
See also desegregation plan, voluntary (St. Louis, 1983–2024); opt-out movement and segregation (New York); race
"separate but equal," 39
"separated Black school-mixed school paradox," 154, 155
Sessions, Jefferson, 57–58, 65
settler colonialism, 81
sex workers, 135–36
Shelly v. Kramer (1948), 156n1
"short-termism," neoliberal, 172
Simon, Tiffany, 156n4
Skelton, Tracy, 1–2, 5, 6, 7, 9, 11
Smith, Darren P., 9
Snorton, C. Riley, 131
social constructionist approach, 5, 64, 66–70, 76, 93
social justice, 3, 119
social media, 9
social mobility, 27

"social visibility" requirement (distinction test), 50–51, 52, 55, 56–57, 59
SONG (Southerners on New Ground), 131
the South
  Black sense of place and, 131
  gay Black men and, 130–31
  gender, race and sexuality, 131
  labor policies and legislation and, 24t
  school segregation and, 91–92, 94
  work and schooling and, 25, 28, 35, 36–37, 37f, 38–39, 38f, 39–43
  See also BreakOUT! (queer and trans resistance); race; regional patterns; *individual states*
South Carolina, 38f, 44n4
South Texas Family Residential Center (Dilly, Texas), 66, 70–73, 71f, 77
space
  climate change and, 161–62
  home and neighborhoods, 8
  hypersegregation and, 156n2
  inclusion and exclusion and, 3
  justice and, 171
  laws and policies and, 2, 12
  legal systems and, 7
  mass incarceration and, 120
  oppression and, 4
  "pipeline to prison" schools and, 114
Spivak, Melanie, 97
sports and extracurricular activities, 149–50, 151–52
standardized testing movement. *See* opt-out movement and segregation (New York)
states
  climate change responsibility and, 167
  Common Core Standards and, 89
  juvenile offender laws and, 113–14
  names of prison-like institutions and, 122n1
  opt-out movement and, 100
  parens patriae and, 122n6
  school attendance requirements, 32m
  standardized testing and, 101
  work and schooling and, 23, 25, 26m, 27–28, 30–31, 40
  See also local control ("home rule"); the North; regional patterns; the South; *individual states*
states' rights, 32–33
Stephenson, Wen, 167
step teams, 152–53
stereotypes, 90–91
  See also "superpredator" narrative
St. Louis, 141–43
  See also desegregation plan, voluntary (St. Louis, 1983–2024)
St. Louis Public School District, 146
story circles, 137–39
  See also counter-narrative (counter-story)
storytelling (narrative), 162–63, 172–73, 174
  See also lived experience; *New York 2140* (Robinson); *The Overstory* (Powers)

strip searches, 115
structural change, 121–22
structures and institutions, 7–8
Student Nonviolent Coordinating Committee, 139n4
students of color, 13, 149
suburban development, 95–97
"superpredator" narrative, 105, 109–10, 113–14
suspension/expulsion from school, 114, 115, 117, 120, 129–30
  See also race and policing in schools
Syracuse (NY), 120

Taking Children: A History of American Terro (Briggs), 80
"targeted criminalization," 64
teacher evaluations, 88
Teaford, Jon, 96
Teater, Mayra, 118–19
"teenager," 5
temporality, 3–4, 161, 162, 166–73, 178
  See also future
Tennessee, 38f
testing, school, 129
  See also opt-out movement and segregation (New York)
Texas, 36, 38f, 39–40, 66, 70–73, 71f, 75f, 129
Thiem, C. H., 7–8
Tilles, Roger, 98
Todd, Chuck, 74
trans Black women. *See* BreakOUT! (queer and trans resistance)
transgender studies, 131
trans Latinx, 137
transnational criminal organizations, 52, 54, 60
trans of color. *See* BreakOUT! (queer and trans resistance)
trans* studies, 132, 139n3
tribunal of the future, 161, 168, 169
Trump administration, 63, 65, 74, 76–77, 79–80, 81

unauthorized entry, 63, 65, 82n7
"undocumented immigrant" versus "detainee," 82n1
UNHCR, 49, 61nn5–6
UNICEF and UNESCO definitions of "child," 5–6
"unitary status," 146
United Nations, 50–51
  See also UNHCR
United Nations Convention Relating to the Status of Refugees (1951), 65
United States. *See* federal government control; the North; the South; *individual states*
United States national identity, 67
USCIS (United States Citizenship and Immigration Services), 52, 77
US Congress, 24t
US Constitution, 173, 174
US Constitutional amendments, 24t, 34

US Dept. of Education, 111
US Dept. of Justice, 65
US Dept. of Labor, 24t, 25, 36
US House of Representatives, 24t
US Human Rights Network, 120
US Marshals Service (USMS), 65
US Ninth Circuit Court of Appeals, 164–65
US presidential campaign 2020, 121
US settler colonial law, 174
US Supreme Court
  delinquency proceedings and, 113
  segregation and, 94
  work and schooling and, 24t, 32–33, 34
  See also Brown v. Board of Education (1954); climate change and environmental resistance (Juliana v. United States); Dred Scott decision

Valentine, Gill, 4, 5, 6–7, 9, 11, 22, 30, 129
van Blerk, Lorraine, 6, 9
"Vice to ICE," 135–36
violence
  among girls/boys, 130
  asylum law and, 77
  BreakOut! and, 132
  against differently categorized migrants, 80
  gun, 7, 10
  persecution of migrating youth, 47–60, 60n3, 61nn5–6
  school shootings, 6, 9
  slow, 168–73
  transgender Southerners and, 131
Voluntary Interdistrict Coordinating Council, 145, 147–48
voter rights/registration/mobilization, 119, 120, 139n4

Wacquant, Loïc, 114
Walsh-Healy Public Contracts Act (1936), 24t
Washington Cotton Mills (VA), 29f
Washington state, 155
Wayndanch School District, 96–97
Weaver, R. Henry, 172
Wells, Amy, 144
Wells, Karen, 22, 26, 42
Westchester (NY), 98
Western, Bruce, 111, 114
West Virginia, 34, 41f
white children, 36–37, 39
white county school districts (St. Louis), 145
White House Office of Faith-Based and Community Initiatives (G. W. Bush), 113
white nationalist ideology, 80

white supremacy, 25–26
white teachers, 152, 154–55
Wilkinson, J., 58
Wilson, Darren, 143
women, 19, 128, 131
work and schooling
  overviews, 17–18, 21–25, 24t, 43, 44n6
  age and, 21, 22, 24t, 25, 25–26f, 27–28, 30, 32, 32m, 34, 36–37
  exemptions and, 31
  geography and, 23
  historical geography of, 25–32, 26m, 29f, 32m, 37f, 38f, 43
  industrialization and, 25
  injurious work and, 36–37
  intersecting identities and, 12
  labor laws and policies over time, 24t, 30–31
  perceived benefits of, 29
  race and, 22, 26–27, 26f, 37–41, 41f, 44n6
  reformers and, 31
  regional crazy quilt of, 30–31, 33–43
  regional patterns, 25–43, 26f, 27
  states and, 23, 25, 26f, 26m, 27–28, 30–31, 34–35, 40
  See also agricultural workers; industrialization; race and policing in schools; schooling and schools; school shootings

Yosso, Solórzano, 148–49
youth, categorized and managed, 5, 17–20
  See also age; "child" and "childhood" and other categories; identities, intersecting; migrant youth and families; power; race; resistance and resilience
youth, geographies of, 2–3, 4
  See also "child" and "childhood"; youth, categorized and managed
Youth Assistance Program (YAP), 117–18, 122n4
youth of color
  See also migrant youth and families; "people of color" versus "Black people"; race; race and policing in schools

Zelizer, Viviana, 23
zero-tolerance family separation policy, 13, 18, 64–70, 82n13
zero-tolerance school policing, 109–10, 114, 116, 130
zoning, restrictive, 96